WHO'S WHO IN
SCOTTISH HISTORY

WHO'S WHO IN SCOTTISH HISTORY

GORDON DONALDSON
AND
ROBERT S. MORPETH

Welsh academic press

First paperback edition published in Wales by Welsh Academic Press 1996

Welsh Academic Press is an imprint of
Ashley Drake Publishing Ltd
ISBN 186057 0054

Original hardback edition published 1973 by Basil Blackwell & Mott Ltd.

A CIP catalogue record for this book is available from the British Library.

Printed and bound in Wales by WBC Book Manufacturers, Pen-y-bont ar Ogwr.

PREFACE

This volume is a Who's Who in Scottish History, and not a Biographical Dictionary of famous Scots. Consequently, the many Scots who attained fame in other countries are not included, unless they made some direct contribution to the life of their native land. On the other hand, one or two persons who were not of Scottish birth but who played an important part in Scottish history find a place in the volume.

The biographies of some well-known characters may be thought meagre, but we considered it more important to draw attention to some of the less-known, but significant, figures, especially in the cultural field, and this could be done only by abbreviating the notices of some famous men and women about whom information can be readily obtained elsewhere.

The arrangement is based on chronology, however, rather than following mechanically a scheme based on dates of either birth or death, we have tried to place each character at the point in history where they played their chief part. Within this general plan, there is a certain amount of grouping, especially from the sixteenth century onwards, of politicians, ecclesiastics, writers, artists and so forth. The Index will guide the reader not only to the persons who receive separate notices, but also to the many others who are mentioned more or less incidentally.

Pressure of space has made it impossible to include more than one or two persons who have died in the twentieth century. While many others were famous in their day and are still generally remembered, it is too soon to determine whether their renown will be permanent or to place them firmly in their historical context.

We have to express our warm thanks to Dr. John Bannerman for furnishing biographies and appreciations of some Gaelic poets, to Dr. R. D. S. Jack for giving assessments of some poets who wrote in Scots, and to Dr. Duncan Thomson for the article on George Jamesone.

INTRODUCTION

Throughout the first thousand years of Scottish history there is hardly a single figure of whom it is possible to construct anything resembling a biography. In these early centuries, when there are no records and few contemporary narratives, the historian has to lean heavily on evidence from archaeology and place-names: but such material, however it may illuminate the general picture, hardly ever contributes to the biographies of individuals. Not only is the literary evidence sparse over-all, but what does exist may be positively misleading. The few men about whom a fair amount of authentic information has quite fortuitously survived, stand out with an apparent importance, but it is impossible to place them in a real historical perspective or relate their significance to that of their contemporaries.

The consequence of the chance survival of material is illustrated right at the outset, when literary evidence for Scottish history first appears. Of the many Roman commanders who operated in Scotland, far and away the best known is Cnaeus Julius Agricola (37–93), because he had the good fortune to have as a son-in-law the historian Tacitus, who wrote a *Life* of his father-in-law. It now seems clear that Agricola, who became governor of Britain in 77 or 78, was not even the first Roman general to cross the present Border, and a pre-Agricolan penetration into south-western Scotland may have been the work of Petilius Cerialis, who had been governor from 71 to 74. Neither the chronology nor the topography of the campaigns of Agricola is wholly clear from the pages of Tacitus, but certain facts do stand out. He appears first to have repeated the exploits of a predecessor by invading Scotland from Carlisle and perhaps marching along the north coast of the Solway. Then, in 80–81, he made a two-fold thrust by routes converging on the Firth of Forth, and built a chain of forts between it and the Firth of Clyde, to hold that position while he spent a year or more conducting operations elsewhere. In 83, resuming his movement northwards, he established a camp at Inchtuthill near Perth and advanced up Strathmore. Next year he was confronted by what Tacitus calls

'a confederacy of all the states' of the native Caledonians, num-
bering 30,000 men, at a place called Mons Graupius, the situation
of which may have been anywhere between the Brechin area and
Banffshire. The natives were defeated, but Agricola did not follow
up his victory and in the following year (85) he was recalled. He
had meantime sent his fleet to round the north coast of Scotland
and prove that Britain was an island. Tacitus relates that the leader
of the Caledonian army was Calgacus, into whose mouth he puts a
conventional 'speech before battle', including the immortal criticism
of the Romans, 'They make a desert and call it peace'. Calgacus
is the first inhabitant of Scotland known to history, and his name
may be associated with the Irish *calgach* and mean 'swordsman'.

Most of the other Roman commanders are little more than
names—Lollius Urbicus, for example, who in the reign of Anto-
ninus Pius built the Antonine Wall between the Forth and the
Clyde, which was held, though not without intermissions, from
about 142 to 185. The generals who are better known are noted
not for what they did in Scotland but for their careers elsewhere.
Thus, Septimius Severus, who had become Emperor in 193, came
to Britain in his old age to press attacks against the Caledonians
between 208 and 211, when he died at York. Of his work in
Scotland we would know little but for archaeology and aerial photo-
graphy, which suggest that he largely repeated Agricola's exploits
and may have followed the eastern coastal plain right round to the
shores of Moray Firth. His successors abandoned his conquests, but
probably much of southern Scotland remained for a century within
the *Pax Romana*, through a system of treaties with native tribes,
and even after that Roman influence seems to have lingered on
among partially Romanized native peoples until after 400.

In the period after the Roman withdrawal, the important fact
in Scottish history is the introduction of Christianity. The first
missionary to Scotland whose name is known is Ninian, who is
believed to have flourished about 400, but the earliest information
about him which survives is of a date more than three hundred
years later. The Venerable Bede, in his *Ecclesiastical History*,
which was completed in 731, relates a belief that the Picts on the
southern side of 'the mountains'—presumably the mountain mass of
central Scotland—had 'embraced the true faith by the preaching of
Ninias, a most reverend bishop and holy man of the British nation,
who had been instructed at Rome regularly in the faith and
mysteries of the truth'. He goes on to say that Ninian's episcopal
seat, at a church which was dedicated to St. Martin and where

Ninian was buried, was called *Candida Casa* (the White House) and was in Bede's own day within the kingdom of the Angles of Northumbria. Bede had motives for propaganda, for he wrote at a period when the Angles, representing Roman orthodoxy against the deviations of the Celtic Church, were influential among the Picts and had established a bishopric at Whithorn, which was identified with *Candida Casa*. It therefore suited him to stress the influence of Rome among the Picts at an early date and the prestige which Whithorn deserved to enjoy among the peoples of the north. Even so, Bede tells us little, and most of the details on which a 'Life' of Ninian could be based—including a visit by him to St. Martin of Tours (d. 397)—come from even later sources. Once more, archaeology comes to the rescue to the extent of demonstrating that there was Christianity in south-western Scotland by the fifth century, and it is not improbable that, in the last phase of Roman influence in Britain, a Christian missionary laboured among the partially Romanized tribes of that area. The dearth of authentic information about Ninian opened the way to much discussion and controversy about the extent of his work, but recent opinion on the whole discounts the extravagant claims made for a mission extending over all the more populous parts of the Pictish kingdom.

Bede preserves the name of another bishop who had a prominent place in the older Scottish histories but who is, so far as Scotland is concerned, a mere 'ghost'. In the year 431–2, Pope Celestine I sent Palladius 'to the Scots that believe in Christ, to be their first bishop'. The 'Scots' were at this time still in Ireland, and it is there, if anywhere, that we can find traces of the work of Palladius, whom some would identify with Patrick. However, although his connection with Scotland is worse than dubious, the church of Fordoun in the Mearns was dedicated to Palladius and he was locally known as 'Paldy', which, with the silent 'l' so common in Scots, is close enough to 'Paddy'. Medieval Scottish writers, who believed that their forefathers had been converted to Christianity early in the third century, were mystified by the appearance of this 'first bishop of the Scots' in 432, and endeavoured to reconcile fiction and fact by advancing the theory that for its first two centuries the Scottish Church had been presbyterian.

Ninian and Palladius and many another stand in sharp contrast to Columba (521–97), the first figure in Scottish history who can be biographed with some completeness and with whom, it has been said, Scottish history therefore begins. For the earlier part of his life, which he spent in Ireland, many facts are to be found in a

Gaelic *Life* and other sources. He was born in Donegal, of royal descent on both sides, and was entrusted to the care of a priest, as a foster-father, from whom he received the beginnings of his religious education before studying at the monastic schools at Moville and Clonard. In Ireland he founded several monasteries, including those at Derry (546), Durrow (553) and Kells, but his career was interrupted by a feud with the Irish king, Diarmit. Diarmit had executed a member of Columba's kin and had forbidden Columba to retain a copy which he had surreptitiously made of a Psalter he had borrowed: the king's decision on the law of copyright was based on a homely parallel—'to every cow her calf and to every book its copy'. Columba, although his Latin name means 'the dove', was a man of irascible temperament, and he raised an army which defeated Diarmit at the battle of Culdreimhne (561). For this he was excommunicated, and his confessor, it is said, laid down as a penance that he must convert the souls of as many men as had been killed in the battle and that he must leave Ireland, never to look on it again. In 563 he moved to Scotland to establish a monastery at Iona, but, despite the tale of his irrevocable expulsion from Ireland, he visited that country again from time to time and took part in its affairs. In Scotland his work was both political and ecclesiastical. Since about 500 there had been a little Irish settlement in modern Argyll, founded by Fergus, son of Erc, to whose family Columba was related, but this kingdom of Dalriada was under heavy pressure from the Picts. Not only did Columba strengthen the faith of his compatriots, the Scots, but his journeyings in Pictland and an interview with King Brude, son of Maelchon, in a stronghold near Inverness, were designed partly to neutralize his kinsfolk's enemies. It was Columba, too, who in 574 persuaded the Scots to choose as their King the able warrior Aidan, who restored their kingdom in the face of the Picts, although after Columba's death he met with disaster at the hands of the Angles, under their great King, Ethelfrith, at Degsastane (603).

Columba's great good fortune lay in having as a biographer, or rather hagiographer, Adamnan (*c.* 625–704), who was one of his own successors, as ninth Abbot of Iona from 679. Adamnan's book on Columba's miracles, presented with a wealth of circumstantial detail, makes the saint the most vivid, flesh-and-blood figure to appear in Scotland for many centuries. Thanks to Adamnan, Columba captivated the imagination of later generations, and there was a further reason for his prestige in that Iona became the head-quarters of the church of the Scots and has ever since been regarded as a place of peculiar sanctity. Yet it is not at all clear that Columba was really so outstanding in contrast to contemporaries who were not as fortunate as he in finding biographers.

The best remembered of Columba's contemporaries is Kentigern (c. 520–?612), about whom there is ample picturesque detail in much later 'Lives'. His mother, it is said, was Theneu, daughter of the king of Lothian, who, after losing her virginity, was set afloat in a boat in the Firth of Forth and drifted to Culross, where she bore her son, who was brought up by St. Serf. Kentigern's work appears to have been chiefly among the Britons of Wales and Cumbria (which included Strathclyde in Scotland), and the story goes that at a meeting with Columba the two exchanged pastoral staffs. None of this, or of his many miracles, is authenticated, and the one fragment of early evidence which may relate to him is an entry in the *Annales Cambriae* of the death of 'Conthigernus' about 612. But Kentigern lived in legend as the founder of the see of Glasgow (with a diocese extending into north-west England), and he became the patron saint of that city. His alternative name, Mungo, means 'dear friend'.

In the same period there was Moluag, whose death is noted about 592 and whose partly legendary career bears some resemblance to Columba's. A native of Ireland, Moluag decided to establish a religious centre in the western isles, and competed successfully with Columba (to the latter's immense chagrin) for possession of the island of Lismore, which was much better situated strategically than Iona. Moluag is associated also with Rosemarkie in Ross and Mortlach in Aberdeenshire, and all three of his foundations were subsequently seats of bishoprics. His pastoral staff was preserved by hereditary keepers in Lismore, and is still in existence.

The influence of Iona, or at any rate of what is commonly called the Columban Church, extended far beyond the bounds of present-day Scotland. King Oswald of Northumbria, who, during the reign of Edwin, had spent part of his exile among the Scots, in 635 invited Aidan (d. 651), a monk of Iona, to become Abbot of Lindisfarne and Bishop of the Angles. Aidan's successor, Finan (d. 661) extended this 'Columban' mission into Mercia and Essex. Colman, who in turn succeeded Finan at Lindisfarne, encountered a Romanizing party who pressed for the adoption of a form of tonsure and a date of Easter different from those customary among the Scots. The decision went against Colman when King Oswiu held the Synod of Whitby (663 or 664), and he had to retire from Northumbria. The Northumbrian kingdom was at this time dominant politically up to the Firth of Forth and influential even in Pictland, with the result that shortly after 700 the Pictish King, Nechtan, decided to adopt the Roman usages. The reverse for the Columban tradition extended even into the land of the Scots, and Adamnan, Columba's biographer, was himself converted to the Roman point of view, though Iona did not capitulate until after his death. St. Cuthbert (?635–687), although his work straddled the present Border, does not represent continuing Scottish influence in England, for he was a native of south-eastern Scotland, which then formed part of Northumbria. His birth is assigned to Channelkirk and his youth, as a shepherd boy, to Oxton. He became a monk in Old Melrose (founded by Aidan) in 651 and ten years later succeeded Boisil as prior. He was invited to be Bishop of Hexham in 684 and was appointed to Lindisfarne in 685. There were a large number of dedications to him right across southern Scotland, but hardly any north of the Forth, and he is best known as the patron of Durham, with which south-eastern Scotland had a peculiarly close association for generations.

None of the kings who reigned in Scotland in this period had the good fortune to find a biographer, and in consequence they are shadowy figures indeed, though a surprising number of them find places in the *D.N.B.* There are names in plenty, for genealogies and lists of kings abound for the kingdoms of Dalriada, Pictland and Strathclyde, but if a king can be associated with a victory or a defeat that is usually all we know about him. Although the later Scottish kings were to trace their antecedents among the kings of Dalriada, and even to invent a list of rulers which began not with the historical Fergus about A.D. 500 but with an imaginary 'Fergus I' in 330 B.C., it was the Picts who occupied far the larger part of the country, and their kings, little though we know about them, must have been important figures. Brude, son of Bile (d. 693), began his reign about 671. He was evidently a great warrior, who is said to have 'destroyed' the Orkneys (which his predecessor, the Brude of Columba's days, had dominated) in 682, and it was presumably he who besieged the fortresses of the Scots at Dundurn (at the east end of Loch Earn) and Dunadd (in mid-Argyll) in 683. He is best known for his triumph over the Angles, for which we have the authority of Bede. When Egfrith, King of Northumbria, marched north of the Tay, Brude lured him into difficult terrain and then turned on him to defeat and kill him at Nechtansmere (Dunnichen, near Forfar) on 20 May 685.

Another great warrior King of the Picts was Angus, son of

Fergus, whose reign is dated from 731 and who died in 761. He is said to have captured Dunadd in 736 and to have 'overthrown Dalriada' in 741. He fought against both Britons and Angles, but in 756 joined Eadbert, King of Northumbria, in an attack on the Britons' stronghold of Dumbarton. It is usually to this King Angus (or 'Hungus') that there is assigned the battle against the Angles in which the Picts were assured of victory by the intervention of St. Andrew, whose white cross appeared to them in the blue sky. There is no doubt that King Angus was successful against the Angles, for Bede's continuator describes him as 'a slaughtering tyrant' who 'carried on his reign's beginning with bloody crime even to the end'. However, the details of the St. Andrew legend are hard to reconcile with any known facts. The battle is said to have taken place in the course of an expedition in 'Merc', which may be doubtfully associated with the Merse, or Berwickshire; the name of the Anglian king is given as Athelstan, but no Athelstan is known to have ruled in the north before the famous Athelstan (925–39), who indeed came into conflict with the peoples of Scotland, but only long after the Pictish monarchy was extinct; and the association of the battle with Athelstaneford, in East Lothian, has no ascertainable foundation in antiquity. The legend further relates that Angus, after his victory, met St. Regulus, who had brought relics of St. Andrew from the east, at Kinrimont in Fife, and that he there founded a church at the place which came to be known as St. Andrews. There was a second Angus, son of Fergus, King of the Picts, who died in 834, and one source assigns to him the foundation of the church of St. Andrews. The stories, whatever their origin, are attempts to explain the beginnings in Scotland of the cult of St. Andrew, and in some ways the eighth century fits better than the ninth. It is not difficult to see an intelligible sequence of events: Nechtan, King of the Picts, had certainly taken Northumbrian advice and had put his kingdom under the patronage of St. Peter (c. 711), and a successor may very well have followed up the policy of imitating Northumbria by receiving from the Northumbrian monastery of Hexham relics of St. Andrew, St. Peter's brother, and beginning the cult of that saint in his dominions. Besides, we first hear of an Abbot of Kinrimont in 747.

The termination of the Pictish monarchy and its supersession by the dynasty of the Scots of Dalriada came with Kenneth, son of Alpin (d. 858), who became King of the Scots in 841 and of the Picts in 843, though his acceptance throughout the whole of Pictland may well have taken some time. It appears that, at a point when

xiii

the Picts were suffering heavy defeats at the hands of Norse invaders, Kenneth had received reinforcements from Ireland which enabled him to invade Pictland. However, he may have had a claim to the Pictish throne through his mother, and conquest may have been a less important element than a dynastic union in bringing Scots and Picts together in one kingdom, called Alba. Kenneth is said to have invaded England (that is, Lothian), six times, and to have burned Dunbar and Melrose, but he inherited the liabilities of the Pictish kingdom and was not successful in keeping the Norse out of his realm. If it is not going too far in interpreting scanty evidence, it may be suggested that Kenneth was statesman enough to bring relics of Columba from Iona (which was proving untenable owing to Norse attacks) to Dunkeld, in order to make it a new ecclesiastical centre in the heart of his united kingdom. Kenneth's succession to the Pictish throne was not in itself conclusive for acceptance of the Dalriadic dynasty, because the Picts' matrilinear system of succession had been apt to open the throne to foreign princes, but that system seems now to have come to an end. Besides, it was the Scots who proved to be the dominant element in the united kingdom, for Irish influence swept into Pictland and the language of the Scots extinguished the Pictish tongue.

The remainder of the ninth century and the whole of the tenth yield hardly anything of interest to the biographer. The succession of the kings of Alba is known, and a succession of head bishops of the kingdom at St. Andrews seems to begin about 900, but kings and bishops alike are little more than names, and the history of the period is a dreary chronicle of battles against the Norse and attempts to expand to the south. Constantine II, son of Kenneth, was killed in battle against the Norse at Forgan in 877. Constantine III (900–42) had to deal with Norse attacks from almost all sides and also came into conflict with Athelstan, King of England. Against him he made an alliance with Danes and Britons, but the confederacy was defeated at Brunanburh (937). Malcolm I (942–54) is said to have obtained from Edmund, King of England, the former British territory of Cumbria on condition that he would hold it against the Norse, but this can have been only a temporary arrangement. Kenneth II (971–95) is said to have gained Lothian from the English King Edgar.

One of the complexities which prevailed in the tenth century and extended into the eleventh was a system of succession to the throne in which a son never immediately followed his father and a king commonly established himself after slaying his predecessor.

For example, Kenneth II succeeded after the violent death of his second cousin, Culen, and was then himself killed by Constantine III, son of Culen. Kenneth III, nephew of Kenneth II, killed Constantine III, and was in his turn killed by Malcolm II, son of Kenneth II. Malcolm II tried to secure his position by liquidating Boidhe, who was a son of either Kenneth II or Kenneth III, but this did not prevent Malcolm II's grandson, Duncan I, from being killed by Macbeth. Attempts have been made to rationalize these sanguinary ongoings by talk about 'collateral succession' or by reference to a law or convention that the rightful heir was the eldest, or ablest, male of the royal kin, but, whatever law or right may have existed, it is hard to see the actual events as anything else than a 'free for all'. In these irregularities Scotland was not, of course, unique, for few countries had as yet adopted strict primogeniture. Even in England it cannot be said to have prevailed until the thirteenth century, if indeed it prevailed then, for the events of the Wars of the Roses, in the fifteenth century, recall the bloodstained annals of the Scotland of four or five centuries earlier.

Something like authentic biographies can first be constructed in the eleventh century, when narrative evidence becomes a little more copious, and after extant charters first became available, about 1100, we are on much surer ground. Yet even after that the scarcity of material persists for another three or four centuries, because Scottish archives met with many misfortunes. A considerable proportion of the official record which had accumulated in the twelfth and thirteenth centuries was carried off to London by Edward I, and in England most of this material subsequently disappeared, though a few items which survived have been returned to Scotland in recent times. The accumulation of the next three and a half centuries was similarly removed on the Cromwellian conquest of Scotland in 1651. Records relating to private rights were returned in 1657, and after the Restoration in 1660 it was arranged to return the remainder, but one of the two ships on which the records had been loaded was lost on her voyage north. Enemy action had also been responsible for the destruction of certain records when the Earl of Hertford burned Edinburgh in 1544. But the Scots themselves were not free from blame. Periodical disturbances and the destruction of property in brawls and raids can hardly have been conducive to the security of private records, and ecclesiastical records are assumed to have suffered destruction and dispersal in the upheaval of the Reformation–though early deeds relating to church properties have in fact survived in much larger numbers than charters to laymen. There was also the result of accidental fire: some important records were lost in a fire in Edinburgh in 1700, and by an almost incredible stroke of ill-luck the early records of the General Assembly happened to be in the House of Lords when the old Houses of Parliament were burned down in 1834. Besides, the national records which had survived other misfortunes were for a long time stored under very unsatisfactory conditions and without proper supervision, so that they suffered from damp and vermin and some were removed by officials and others. It was only with the opening of the present Register House, in 1787, that the records began to be properly cared for and made available under suitable conditions.

Consequently, adequate historical information, especially about the lives of individuals, does not become copious until the sixteenth century, and down to that point the man who was fortunate enough to find a biographer in his own day or who wrote memoirs which have chanced to survive is still at a great advantage over others who were not so lucky. Only from that period onwards can we be confident that no truly significant figure lurks unknown because of a lack of adequate information about him.

Malcolm II, King of Scots (*c.* 954–1034), son of Kenneth II, who was king from 971 to 995, may have been designated as his father's heir, but for ten years the throne was contested by other members of the royal house. As soon as Malcolm was established, he continued the policy of his predecessors by aggression in the south, and, although he was repulsed from Durham in 1006, he was victorious over the men of Northumbria at Carham in 1016 or 1018 and thereby made good Scottish control over the area between the Firth of Forth and the River Tweed. About the same time, on the death of the last native king of Strathclyde or Cumbria, Malcolm's son Duncan succeeded him, so that the Scottish frontier in effect extended to the Solway and beyond it. Although Malcolm had to submit to Cnut when that king invaded Scotland in 1031, his hold over his southern territories was apparently recognized. In the north, Malcolm established good relations with Earl Sigurd of Orkney, who married one of his daughters, and he was therefore grandfather of Earl Thorfinn, who succeeded Sigurd in 1014. Malcolm's eldest daughter, Bethoc, married Crinan, Abbot of Dunkeld, and was the mother of Duncan I, and a third daughter may have been the mother of king Macbeth. Duncan died on 25 November 1034.

Macbeth, King of Scots (*c.* 1005–1057), was the son of Finlay, mormaer of Moray, apparently by a daughter of Malcolm II. He married Gruoch, widow of Gillacomgain, mormaer of Moray, and grand-daughter of a previous king. It is thus evident that Macbeth had a double pretext for asserting a claim to the throne against the heir by primogeniture. Malcolm II was succeeded by his grandson, Duncan I (*c.* 1010–40), the son of Crinan, Abbot of Dunkeld, and Bethoc, Malcolm's eldest daughter. Duncan, who had thus gained the throne by primogeniture, married a cousin of Siward, Earl of Northumbria, about 1030, and may have favoured southern ways. At any rate, his position became insecure. In 1040, after incurring heavy losses in an unsuccessful siege of Durham, he was twice defeated by his cousin, Thorfinn, Earl of Orkney, and was then killed by Macbeth at Pitgaveny near Elgin (14 August 1040). It may be that the kingdom was then partitioned between Macbeth and Thorfinn. Macbeth was challenged in 1045 by Crinan, father of Duncan I, but defeated him, and Crinan fell in the fight. In 1054 Malcolm, the eldest son of Duncan, came up with Earl Siward of Northumbria and possibly gained the Lothians. But in the main

Macbeth's reign was peaceful, and it may be assumed that he was acceptable to his Celtic subjects. He and his wife gave endowments to the Church, and in 1050 he went on pilgrimage to Rome (possibly with his ally Thorfinn). Despite his championship of native traditions, he received Normans who were driven from the court of Edward the Confessor in 1052 by an Anglo-Saxon reaction. Macbeth was defeated and killed by Malcolm, son of Duncan, at Lumphanan in Mar, on 15 August 1057. He left no issue, but his stepson, Lulach ('the Simple'), who inherited Queen Gruoch's claim to the throne, was installed at Scone and held the throne until he was overthrown and killed by Malcolm at Essie in Strathbogie on 17 March 1058. Lulach's son, Malsnectai, mormaer of Moray and benefactor of the abbey of Deer, was forced by Malcolm to enter a monastery, where he died in 1085; his grandson (by a daughter) was Angus, mormaer of Moray, who was defeated and killed by David I in 1130.

J. Dover Wilson (ed.), *Macbeth*, 1947.
Stuart R. J. Erskine, *MacBeth*, 1930.

Thorfinn, Earl of Orkney (1009–1064 or 1065), was the eldest of the three sons of Earl Sigurd by a daughter of Malcolm II, and spent his childhood at his grandfather's court. On reaching manhood he claimed a third of the earldom and ultimately made good his possession of all of it, though he was displaced for a time by his nephew Rognvald. Being, like Duncan I, a grandson of Malcolm II, he may well have believed that he had a claim to the Scottish throne. At any rate, he defeated Duncan in two battles, and the hypothesis that he then made a pact with Macbeth to partition the Scottish kingdom between them is the most probable explanation of the statement that Thorfinn held 'nine earldoms in Scotland', as well as 'all the Hebrides and a large realm in Ireland'. Although Thorfinn's father had accepted Christianity under compulsion from his overlord, the King of Norway, he had remained very much a pagan, and when he was killed at the battle of Clontarf, in Ireland, in 1014, he was fighting under his magic raven banner which brought death to him who bore it but victory to him before whom it was borne. Even in Thorfinn's early days something of the Viking tradition was not extinct, and Thorfinn spread terror when he harried widely on the coasts of Britain. Later, however, he was a peaceful ruler. About 1050 he went on pilgrimage to Rome— possibly in company with his ally Macbeth—and obtained absolution from the Pope for his misdeeds. His 'capital' was on the Brough of Birsay, a tidal island on the west mainland of Orkney, where the remains can still be seen of his hall, or palace, and of the church—'Christ's Kirk'—which he built as the seat of a bishop for his earldom. Thorfinn's wife was named Ingibjorg, and he had two sons, Paul and Erlend, who were in the Norwegian army under Harald Hardrada which was defeated at Stamford Bridge in 1066. It has been said that his widow subsequently married Malcolm III, but chronology makes this impossible and Malcolm's first wife Ingibjorg must have been a daughter of Thorfinn. The marriage, which must have taken place before Thorfinn's death, suggests that Thorfinn came to terms with Malcolm when he superseded Macbeth.

The Orkneyinga Saga, ed. Joseph Anderson, 1873.

Malcolm III, called 'Canmore' (that is, great head or chief), King of Scots (*c.* 1031–1093), eldest son of Duncan I, had to take refuge in England when his father was overthrown by Macbeth in 1040, and he spent at least fourteen years at the English court. In 1054, when his kinsman, Earl Siward of Northumbria, won a victory over Macbeth, Malcolm may have gained control of southern Scotland, but he did not become King of Scots until he had defeated and killed Macbeth on 15 August 1057 and had encompassed the death of Lulach, Macbeth's stepson, on 17 March 1058. His first wife was Ingibjorg, daughter of Thorfinn, Earl of Orkney, by whom he had three sons—King Duncan II, Malcolm (possibly killed in 1094) and Donald (d. 1085)—and after her death (or possibly divorce on grounds of consanguinity) he married the English Princess Margaret, probably in 1069. Malcolm's own upbringing must have predisposed him to favour English ways, and his second wife was a powerful source of English influence in Scotland.

Yet, despite Malcolm's debt to England, his relations with that country were far from peaceful. His first invasion of England had taken place in 1061, and after he married Margaret he was able to pose as the ally of his wife's brother, Edgar the Atheling, against the usurping Normans. A second invasion of England, in 1070, was followed by an attack on Scotland, in 1072, by William the Conqueror, to whom Malcolm had to submit to the extent of giving hostages and becoming his 'man'. A third invasion, in 1079, brought similar retaliation by Robert, William's son, in 1080. In 1091 Malcolm invaded England a fourth time, but came to terms with King William Rufus later in the year. In 1092, however, Rufus seized Carlisle, which had been within Malcolm's dominions, and when Malcolm went to Gloucester in 1093 Rufus refused to see him. This led Malcolm to make a fifth invasion of England, during which he was killed at Alnwick (13 November 1093).

Malcolm's persistent harrying of the north of England looks like the negation of statesmanship, for different tactics would have been required to commend him, or his *protégé* the Atheling, to the English as an alternative ruler to the Normans. However, besides being a benefactor of the Scottish Church, Malcolm evidently enjoyed good relations with the clergy of Durham, and was present at the laying of the foundation stone of the cathedral there two months before his death. By Margaret he had six sons—Edward, mortally wounded at Alnwick when his father was killed; Edmund, who seems to have collaborated with his uncle, Donald Bane, in his seizure of the throne after Malcolm's death, but who died a monk in England; Ethelred, who succeeded to the family abbacy of Dunkeld; Edgar, Alexander I and David, who became kings of Scots. Malcolm also had two daughters—Matilda (1080–1118), who in 1100 married Henry I of England, by whom she had a son, William, lost at sea in 1120, and a daughter, the Empress Maud, who was mother of Henry II; and Mary, who married the Count of Boulogne and was the mother of the wife of King Stephen.

Margaret, wife of Malcolm III (*c.* 1046–1093), was a daughter of Edward 'the Exile', a son of Edmund Ironside and a grandson of Ethelred II. When Cnut became King of England after Edmund's death, Edward was banished and found his way to Hungary, where he married a German princess and had three children—Margaret, Christina and Edgar the Atheling. Edward and his family returned to England at the invitation of his uncle, Edward the Confessor, in 1057, but the Exile died almost at once and the children were educated under the pious influence of the Confessor. The rejection of Edgar the Atheling's claim to succeed Harold as King of England in 1066, and the Norman Conquest, led to a renewed exile for the representatives of the old English royal family, and in or about 1069 they came to Scotland, where Margaret married Malcolm III.

Far more is known of Margaret than of her husband, for she was canonized in 1249 and, like that earlier saint, Columba, was fortunate in a laudatory biographer. He was Turgot, her confessor, an Englishman who fled to Norway after the Norman Conquest but returned to England to study at Jarrow and became Prior of Durham in 1087. Turgot presents a touching picture of a saintly Queen, whose fervour, it has been remarked, may have owed some-

4

thing to her upbringing in Hungary, a country only recently converted to Christianity. She was revered by her husband, who could not read her devotional books but had them adorned with precious stones, she was anxious to introduce more refined fashions into the Scottish court, and she was able to persuade the Scottish clergy that their 'barbarous rite' in celebrating mass, and other deviations from Roman usage, were wrong. Reading between the lines, one discerns a somewhat severe lady, who checked mirth at court and dominated her husband, none of whose children by her was given a Scottish name. One can guess, besides, that Malcolm's forceful presence at her conversations with the Scottish clergy may have had much to do with their capitulation. She has been described as 'one of those strong, interfering, pious and persistent women of whom England has successfully bred a considerable number'.[1] She corresponded with Lanfranc, Archbishop of Canterbury, and brought Benedictine monks to Dunfermline, but she also patronized some of the existing Scottish religious houses and seems to have made no changes in ecclesiastical organization. She died on 16 November 1093, on hearing of her husband's death.

Agatha Henderson-Howat, *Royal Pearl*, 1948.

Donald III, King of Scots (*c*. 1033–*c*. 1100), known as Donald Bane (Ban = fair), the younger son of Duncan I, was an exile during Macbeth's reign but found a refuge not, like his elder brother Malcolm, in England, but in the Isles, and has been described as an 'incorrigible old Celt'.[2] On Malcolm's death on 13 November 1093 Donald seized the throne and drove out the English whom Malcolm had introduced. In May 1094 he was ousted by his nephew, Duncan II, but on 12 November, after Duncan had been killed, Donald recovered the throne, possibly in association with Edmund, the second son of Malcolm and Margaret. Donald may well have been acceptable to a predominantly Celtic people, and when he was overthrown, in October 1097, it was by an English army sent up to supersede him by Edgar, another son of the English Margaret. Donald was subsequently captured by Edgar, who had him blinded. He was the last king of Scots to be buried in Iona. He had one daughter, whose descendant, John Comyn of Badenoch, was a competitor for the throne in 1291.

Duncan II, King of Scots (*c*. 1060–1094), the eldest son of Malcolm

1. Eric Linklater, *The Lion and the Unicorn* (1935), p. 36.
2. R. L. G. Ritchie, *The Normans in Scotland*, p. 64.

III, was handed over to William the Conqueror as a hostage in 1072, but in 1087, after the Conqueror's death, he was released, and knighted, by William II (Rufus). In May 1094 Duncan came north with an English army, ousted his uncle, Donald Bane, and established himself as King. In an attempt to appease his Celtic subjects he agreed to dismiss his English followers, but this was fatal to his position, and on 12 November he was killed, presumably at Donald's instance, by the mormaer of the Mearns. During his brief reign Duncan issued the earliest Scottish charter which has survived, granting to the monks of Durham certain lands in East Lothian, including the ancient ecclesiastical site of Tyninghame. Duncan married his kinswoman Octreda, daughter of Earl Gospatrick of Northumbria, and left a son, William Fitz Duncan (d. 1151), who married Alice de Rumilly, a niece of the Norman Earl of Chester. William seems not to have asserted his claims as the senior descendant of Malcolm III, and his son by Alice was William, 'the Boy of Egremont', who was drowned near Bolton about 1156. But William Fitz Duncan had a second son, possibly illegitimate, Donald MacWilliam, and he and his sons presented a serious challenge to William 'the Lion'.

Edgar, King of Scots (c. 1074–1107), fourth son of Malcolm III by Queen Margaret, was driven to England on his father's death, but evidently came north and supported his half-brother, Duncan II, during his brief reign. About 1095 King William Rufus acknowledged Edgar as rightful King of Scots, and Edgar clearly agreed to hold the kingdom as William's vassal. In October 1097, with English help, he overthrew Donald Bane. While he was accepted in the southern parts of his kingdom, there is some doubt about his position elsewhere, and it seems that he was unable to resist Magnus Barelegs, King of Norway, when the latter overran the Western Isles and reaffirmed Norwegian sovereignty there. Edgar gave endowments to the churches of Durham, Coldingham, Dunfermline and St. Andrews. He possessed an elephant (possibly brought back by someone who had been on the First Crusade) and he made over this embarrassing gift to an Irish king. Edgar died unmarried on 8 January 1107.

Magnus, Saint, Earl of Orkney (d. ?1116), was a son of Erlend, who was joint Earl of Orkney with his brother Paul, and about 1107 Magnus was granted half of the earldom, in partnership with his cousin Haakon, Paul's son. Haakon seems to have been a man of violence, Magnus a man of peace, who, when he had been taken by Magnus Barelegs on his expedition to the Western Isles *c.* 1198, had revealed himself as a pacifist who would not fight against men with whom he had no quarrel. Besides, although Magnus was prevailed on to enter into marriage, the union is said to have remained a nominal one, like Edward the Confessor's. As Magnus proved to be a just ruler, the hot-tempered Haakon became jealous of his popularity and friction arose. It was arranged that the two earls should meet to settle their differences on the island of Egilsay, each bringing two ships. Magnus turned up with the appointed complement, but Haakon arrived with eight and made it plain that he sought the life of Magnus. The latter offered to go on pilgrimage, to accept imprisonment, or even to be blinded and mutilated. Haakon himself was inclined to accept the third option, but his followers would not agree, and Magnus was killed. He was buried at Christ's Church in Birsay, founded by Earl Thorfinn, and stories soon arose of miracles which proved his sanctity. His sister had a son Kali, who took the name of Rognvald and who determined to build a great minster in his uncle's honour. This he did, in the cathedral of St. Magnus at Kirkwall (begun in 1137), to which the remains of Magnus were transferred and in which Rognvald himself was buried when he died in 1158. Thanks to the lively account of Rognvald's life in the *Orkneyinga Saga*, his personality emerges far more clearly than that of anyone else who lived in Scotland at that time.

Catherine S. Spence, *Earl Rognvald and his forebears*, 1896.

Alexander I, King of Scots (*c.* 1077–1124), the fifth son of Malcolm III and Margaret, succeeded his brother Edgar on 8 January 1107. Designated 'the Fierce', but also described as 'a lettered and godly man', Alexander clearly inherited some of his mother's solicitude for the Church and he had close ties with England, where he had probably spent the years 1093–97. As 'Earl Alexander' he was the only layman privileged to be present when the tomb of St. Cuthbert at Durham was opened in 1104, and very soon after his accession he selected Turgot, Prior of Durham, as Bishop of St. Andrews. He gave endowments to Durham, Dunfermline and St. Andrews and founded houses of Augustinian canons at Scone (*c.* 1120) and Inchcolm (*c.* 1123). Among his gifts to Scone was an island in Loch Tay, which is erroneously supposed to have been an independent priory. Alexander accepted as a bride Sybilla (d. 1122), a natural daughter of Henry I of England of whom it has been said that she had neither good looks nor courtly manners to commend her. Yet, despite his friendship with Henry I (who was at once his brother-in-law and his father-in-law) Alexander would not permit the Bishops of St. Andrews to acknowledge English supremacy. Turgot was, at Alexander's request and on the command of Henry I, consecrated by the Archbishop of York (1109) under a reservation of the rights of both churches, but subsequently there was friction with the King, and Turgot received permission to retire to Durham, where he died (1115). Alexander then applied to Canterbury, and Eadmer, a Canterbury monk, was appointed to St. Andrews in 1120, but when he made in clear that 'not for the whole of Scotland would he deny that he was a monk of Canterbury', Alexander reflected that he had gained nothing by seeking a bishop from Canterbury, and Eadmer departed in 1121, unconsecrated. The King's next choice was Robert, Prior of the new foundation at Scone, and the question of his consecration was still unsettled when the King died. Alexander's rule extended only over the lands north of the Forth, for his brother, as 'Earl David', ruled the south. The Scottish pretensions to territory south of the Tweed were not made good, and the English were able to build Norham Castle as a frontier post in 1121. Nothing is known of a rising of his northern subjects which Alexander is said to have suppressed with ferocity. He died at Stirling, probably on 23 April 1124, and was buried at Dunfermline, leaving no legitimate issue but one illegitimate son.

David I, King of Scots (c. 1084–1153), the youngest son of Malcolm III and Margaret, spent his youth in England, so that he was, in the patronizing words of an English chronicler, 'polished from his boyhood by his intercourse and friendship with us'. His sister was the wife of Henry I, and by styling himself 'brother of the Queen of the English' he showed his attachment to England under its Norman dynasty. His own marriage (1114) to Maud, daughter and heiress of Waltheof, Earl of Huntingdon, and widow of Simon de Senlis (or St. Liz), brought him the earldom of Northampton and the honour of Huntingdon and made him the greatest baron in England. During the reign of his brother, Alexander I, David ruled southern Scotland with the title of 'Earl', and founded the abbeys of Selkirk (later moved to Kelso) c. 1113 and Jedburgh in 1118. David's generosity to the Church continued after he became King, with the foundation of many more abbeys, especially of the Augustinian and Cistercian orders, the reconstitution of old bishoprics and the creation of new ones. For this he was later reproached as a 'sair sanct for the croun', but he was no altruistic visionary. Apart from the contribution made by ecclesiastical institutions to the cohesion and stability of the realm, some of his monks, with their interests in agriculture, sheep-farming, coal-working and salt-making, aided the economy. David carried further the policy of reorganizing civil, as well as ecclesiastical, institutions on Anglo-Norman lines. With an influx to Scotland of Normans, English and Flemings, feudal tenure was extended, the sheriffdom and the justiciary were developed, castles were erected as centres of royal and baronial authority and burghs were organized around the castles. David's innovations did not go unchallenged, but with southern help he was able to suppress Celtic resistance. After a rising in Moray, the mormaer of that province, Angus, a descendant of King Lulach, was killed (1130) and in 1134 another leading rebel, Malcolm MacHeth, probably an illegitimate son of Alexander I, was imprisoned. David's intervention in England against King Stephen, which led to his defeat at the battle of the Standard (1138), was ostensibly on behalf of his niece Matilda, who contested the English throne with Stephen, but David clearly had territorial ambitions: for a time he ruled as far south as the Tees and in 1149 he secured from the future Henry II an undertaking that Scotland would retain Northumberland, Cumberland and Westmorland. Like Alexander I, David resisted English demands for the subjection of the Scottish Church, and he had his brother's nominee for the bishopric of St. Andrews, Robert, consecrated by the Archbishop of York without any profession of obedience. By his Queen, who died in 1130, David had three or four children, but the only one to reach adult years was Henry (c. 1114–1152), Earl of Northumbria and Northampton, who married Ada, daughter of William, Earl of Warenne, and had three sons—Malcolm IV, William I and David, Earl of Huntingdon—and three daughters. On Henry's death in 1152, David designated his grandson, Malcolm, as his successor. He died at Carlisle on 24 May 1153.

R. L. G. Ritchie, *The Normans in Scotland*, 1954.

Malcolm IV, King of Scots (1141–1165), called 'The Maiden', was the eldest son of Henry, son of David I, by Ada, daughter of the Earl of Warenne. He had as his tutor his uncle Waltheof, Abbot of Melrose. When Malcolm's father died in July 1152, David instructed Duncan, Earl of Fife, to conduct the boy round the kingdom to demonstrate his position as heir. Next year Malcolm became King, at the age of twelve. Although the government of the country was mainly in the hands of Anglo-Normans, the traditional rite of in-

9

auguration on the Stone of Scone was carried out. The accession of a minor was an opportunity for rebellion on the part of those who were disposed to challenge the dynasty and criticize its innovations, and in Malcolm's first year, besides trouble with some native landholders in the Stirling area, there was a rising in the west and north. One party to it was Somerled, a Hebridean chieftain of mixed Norse and Celtic ancestry and the son-in-law of Olaf, King of Man and the Isles. Associated with him were the sons, by a sister or a daughter of Somerled, of Malcolm MacHeth (probably an illegitimate son of Alexander I), who represented the separatism of Moray. The MacHeth interest was pacified by 1157, at the cost of investing MacHeth in the earldom of Ross, while Somerled, who had conquered the Isles and obtained recognition of his sovereignty from the King of Norway, came to terms with Malcolm in 1160.

Malcolm was summoned to the English court in 1157 and was compelled by Henry II to surrender the northern counties which the latter, in the days of his adversity in 1149, had guaranteed to the Scots. He received the honour of Huntingdon, which made him a vassal of the English King for that possession at least. In 1159 he was called to join Henry in his campaign against Toulouse, and during it was knighted by Henry. In 1163 he did homage to Henry and gave his brother David, as well as other Scots of high birth, as hostages. Malcolm's acceptance of the role of vassal seems to have caused discontent, and on his return from Toulouse in 1161 he had to face a rebellion, which he defeated. The group of 'native earls' said to have been involved is ill-defined, but one member of the group was Fergus, Lord of Galloway, who represented local separatism. Fergus is remembered as the founder of the abbey of Tongland and possibly also the abbey of Soulseat and the priory of Whithorn, and after his defeat by Malcolm in three campaigns he retired to the abbey of Holyrood, where he died in 1161.

Some three years later there was another rebellion by Somerled. He concentrated in the Firth of Clyde a force of 160 ships, with men from Ireland as well as Argyll and the western isles, but when he landed to march on Glasgow he was defeated and killed at Renfrew (1164).

To eliminate once and for all the supposed dependence of the Scottish Church on York, Malcolm sought metropolitan status for St. Andrews, but was unsuccessful. His one notable religious foundation was the Cistercian abbey of Coupar Angus (1162), but he continued in other ways his grandfather's patronage of the Church

10

and in 1159 issued the 'Great Charter of Kelso', the initial of which contains portraits of David and Malcolm.

Malcolm had evidently been infirm for some time before his death at Jedburgh on 9 December 1165. He was buried at Dunfermline. He was unmarried, and the notion that he had an illegitimate son arises from a solitary reference in which 'filii' is presumably a scribal error for 'patris'.

G. W. S. Barrow, *The Acts of Malcolm IV*, 1960.

William I, King of Scots (1143–1214), is conventionally known as 'the Lion', but there is no real evidence that he adopted the lion rampant as his heraldic device. He was the second son of Earl Henry, son of David I. On his father's death, David assigned to William the earldom of Northumberland, but Henry II of England annexed it in 1156. William succeeded his elder brother, Malcolm IV, on 9 December 1165. He was in Normandy with Henry II in 1166 and spent Easter 1170 at Henry's court at Windsor. In 1174, however, he joined with Henry's son in his rebellion against his father, and invaded England. Captured at Alnwick, he was taken to France, and by the Treaty of Falaise (8 December 1174) he acknowledged Henry as feudal superior of his kingdom and surrendered some Scottish castles. Relations with Henry later improved, for in 1185 William received the earldom of Huntingdon and next year he married Henry's nominee, Ermengarde de Beaumont. When Richard I succeeded Henry and wanted to raise money for the Third Crusade, he surrendered his feudal superiority over Scotland for 10,000 merks, by the Quitclaim of Canterbury (5 December 1189). Relations with King John (1199–1216) were less happy. In 1209 John advanced to Norham and insisted that the Scots should not attack his castle of Tweedmouth, which threatened Berwick; William agreed to pay 15,000 merks for the sake of peace and to hand over his daughters for marriage to John's sons.

After being worsted by Henry in 1174, William had been inclined to make the most of Henry's guilt for the murder of Archbishop Becket (1170), and when he founded the great abbey of Arbroath in 1178 he dedicated it to St. Thomas of Canterbury. But William was no friend to ecclesiastical independence in his own realm, for he intruded his chaplain, Hugh, into the bishopric of St. Andrews in 1178 and maintained him there in defiance of the chapter and the Pope, in a dispute which went on for years. In 1183, after William had received the Golden Rose as a mark of papal favour, Hugh was accepted at Rome, but later he was excommunicated again. It was

11

in William's reign that the Pope finally declared the Scottish church independent of any archbishop (1192).

There was a rebellion in Galloway after William's capture in 1174, when the natives drove out the French and English who had settled in castles and burghs, and William later had considerable trouble in the northern parts of his realm. In 1179 he was in action in Ross against Donald MacWilliam, grandson of Duncan II, and in 1187 Donald was killed in battle in Moray. In 1211 and 1212 there was again rebellion in Ross, but at the end of it Gothred, Donald's brother, was betrayed by his own men and executed. In 1196 and 1197 William was active against Harald Maddadson, Earl of Orkney, and seems to have established his sovereignty over Caithness, though the Earl continued to hold part of it as his vassal.

Queen Ermengarde, who founded Balmerino Abbey in 1229, died in 1234. By her William had one son, Alexander II, and three daughters—Margaret, Isabella and Marjory, none of whom married English princes as agreed in 1209; they married respectively Hubert de Burgh, the Earl of Norfolk and the Earl of Pembroke. William also had six illegitimate children, the descendants of some of whom were competitors for the throne in 1290.

G. W. S. Barrow, *The Acts of William I*, 1970.

Adam 'the Scot', or Adam of Dryburgh (*c*. 1140–1212), a native of Berwickshire, took vows as a Premonstratensian canon in the abbey of Dryburgh and won renown as a preacher to both clerical and lay audiences. He was elected Abbot of Dryburgh in 1184, but sought a more austere life than that of a canon regular. While he was abbot, he visited Prémontré, and when in France he encountered the austere Carthusian order at Val St. Pierre, where Roger, the first abbot of Dryburgh, had become a monk. Adam was so impressed as to exclaim, 'This is none other than the house of God; this is the gate of heaven.' In 1188, after consulting St. Hugh of Lincoln, he was admitted a Carthusian in the English house of Witham in Somerset, of which Hugh had been a member before becoming a bishop in 1186. Adam's writings, some of which were first published at Paris in 1518 and some in a second edition at Antwerp in 1659, show a wide range of learning in the Bible, the fathers and classical Latin authors. They include over eighty sermons and a work on the Premonstratensian order, itself cast in the form of fourteen sermons intended for reading to the canons. His *De tripartito tabernaculo* (written in 1180), extending to some 93,000 words, is an interpretation of the tabernacle built by Moses, the tabernacle of Christ,

12

which is one of faith, and the tabernacle of the Holy Spirit, in which abide the pure in heart. The *De triplici genere contemplationis* (23,000 words) describes the qualities of God, the imperfections of man and the joys of the elect. The *Soliloquium de instructione animae*, in the form of a dialogue between reason and the soul, was written while Adam was Abbot of Dryburgh and clearly relates to the advice which might be given by an elder counsellor to a young canon. The *De quadripartito exercitio cellae* belongs to Adam's Carthusian days. Adam has frequently been confused with the first prior of Whithorn (?1150–64).

James Bulloch, *Adam of Dryburgh*, 1958.

Scott, Michael (c. 1160–c. 1235), philosopher, lives in popular fame in Scotland as a wizard, thanks largely to Sir Walter Scott's allusions to him in *The Lay of the Last Minstrel*. It is not even certain that he was a native of Scotland, for he may have been born in Durham of Scottish ancestry, and legends about him exist in the north of England as well as in Scotland. He is said to have studied astronomy, chemistry and Arabic at Oxford, then mathematics and theology at Paris and to have gone from there to Padua (famous as a school of magic). The first fact certainly known about him is that he was in Toledo by 1217 and that while he was there he translated from Arabic into Latin a work *On the Sphere*. He was in medical practice in Bologna in 1220 and from there probably went to Rome, for between 1224 and 1227 he was commended by the Pope to the archbishop of Canterbury. He was offered, but declined, the Irish archbishopric of Cashel, and he apparently held benefices in England and Scotland. It is said that his translation into Latin of Aristotle's work *On Animals* (1220) gained him the patronage of the Emperor Frederick II, but there is only slight evidence of his association with Frederick's court, and the indications are that he spent his later years not there but in England and Scotland. Far more is known of Michael's writings than of his life. He translated, in addition to the works already mentioned, Aristotle's *De Caelo* and probably other works, commentaries by Averroes and a work by Avicenna on natural history. His own original writings extended to astrology, alchemy and medicine. It is understandable that studies in astronomy and chemistry and perhaps some dabbling in the occult brought him the reputation for sorcery which caused Dante to place him in the Inferno, but one can understand, for example, how the story that he feasted his friends on dishes magically conveyed from the royal kitchens of foreign lands simply exaggerates

13

the impression made by his knowledge of the rising gastronomical standards which stemmed from Moorish cuisine. The chronology of Michael's life has been misrepresented, partly because of confusion with a Michael Scott who went on an embassy to Norway from Scotland in 1290. Melrose, where Sir Walter placed his grave, is only one of several reputed burial-places.

D. M. Dunlop, *Arabic Science in the West* (Pakistan Historical Society), 1958.

Alexander II, King of Scots (1198–1249), the only son of William 'the Lion', was born at Haddington on 24 August 1198 and succeeded his father on 4 December 1214. Although he was knighted by King John in 1212, he intervened in England in the troubled situation before and after John's death, and a clause in Magna Carta promised that justice would be done to his sisters (whom John had not married to English princes as he had promised in 1209). However, when Henry III's rule was recognized, Alexander found himself on the losing side and gained nothing for his efforts. The long-standing dispute over the frontier with England was finally settled by the Treaty of York in 1237, when Alexander surrendered the Scottish claims to the three northern counties of England in return for the honour of Tynedale and the manor of Penrith, and the Border was fixed very much where it subsequently remained.

In the early years of his reign, Alexander had to suppress disturbances in various outlying parts of the kingdom. In 1215 there was a further insurrection in Moray, as a result of which Donald Ban, son of Donald MacWilliam, and Kenneth MacHeth were slain by the Earl of Ross. In 1222 the King led an expedition which is said to have subdued Argyll. In the same year there was a particularly notorious outbreak of savagery in Caithness. Bishop Adam, a former Abbot of Melrose, who had been elected Bishop of Caithness in 1213, incurred such unpopularity by collecting his revenues that a mob attacked him and burned him alive. The King led a punitive expedition and cut off the hands and feet of eighty men who had been involved. In 1235 Alexander quelled an insurrection in Galloway, again with the help of the Earl of Ross. His successes in the west and north, and perhaps an awareness that he could not hold the west mainland without the islands, inspired him to make an attempt to gain the western isles from Norway, first by negotiation, then by military operations, and it was on the island of Kerrera that he died on 8 July 1249. He was buried at Melrose.

Alexander continued his family's generosity to the Church by founding Pluscarden Priory in 1236. He married first (19 June 1221) Joan, the daughter of King John of England, by whom he had no issue and who died on 4 March 1238, and secondly (on 15 May 1239) Marie, daughter of Enguerand III, baron de Coucy in Picardy, by whom he had an only son, Alexander III. He had an illegitimate daughter, who married Alan Durward, and their grandson was a competitor for the throne in 1291.

Gilbert, Saint, Bishop of Caithness (d. 1245), belonged to the family of the Lords of Duffus in Moray and is known as 'de Moravia'. He was archdeacon of Moray for many years before he was elected Bishop of Caithness in 1223, apparently at the command of the King, who was endeavouring to consolidate his authority in the north. Gilbert's prospects as fourth Bishop of Caithness were distinctly unpromising. The first Bishop, Andrew, had probably been prudent enough never to go near the place; the second, John, had been attacked in his castle at Scrabster, about 1200, by Harald, Earl of Orkney and Caithness, who plucked out his tongue and his eyes; the third, Adam, was burned alive in his house at Halkirk. Even although Alexander II took severe vengeance for the murder of Adam, it is creditable to Gilbert that he was able to rule in peace and die in his bed. It may, however, be significant that he selected Dornoch, at the southern extremity of his diocese, as the site for the cathedral which he started to build and for the chapter of which he drew up a constitution. He is said to have discovered the gold which does exist in Sutherland. He was one of the few inhabitants of Scotland, and perhaps the only native, to be canonized in the whole medieval period, and was the last pre-Reformation Scot to find a place in the Kalendar.

Alexander III, King of Scots (1241–1286), only son of Alexander II, was born at Roxburgh on 4 September 1241 and succeeded his father on 8 July 1249. Like all his predecessors, he was inaugurated on the Stone of Scone, and at the installation ceremony a Highlander recited his pedigree back to 'Fergus I', the mythical monarch who led the Scots from Ireland to Scotland in 330 B.C. It was an appropriate incident, for Alexander was to be the last of the descendants, in the male line, of the House of Dunkeld which had held the throne since the days before English and Norman influences prevailed in Scotland. During Alexander's minority, and even at times during his personal reign, there was strong English political influence. He was knighted by Henry III in 1251 and the following day (26 December)

15

married Margaret, Henry's daughter. He was present at the coronation of Edward I in 1274. However, Alexander resisted demands that he should do homage to the English King for his kingdom.

Alexander's reign achieved a retrospective glamour as a time of peace and prosperity, by contrast with the troubles which followed it, but in truth little enough is known about it. The outstanding event was the settlement of Scotland's western frontier, just as Alexander II's reign had seen the settlement of the southern frontier. Like his father, Alexander III first attempted peaceful negotiations for the cession of the western isles, but Haakon the Old, King of Norway, was something of an imperialist and not the man to yield up territory without a struggle. He therefore led a great fleet down the west coast and into the Firth of Clyde in 1263. The famed engagement which followed, the battle of Largs (2 October 1263) was in truth a mere skirmish in which the Norwegians successfully covered the withdrawal of ships which were in danger. But the fleet had been badly battered in storms, the season was far advanced, and Haakon retired to Kirkwall, where he died. On 2 July 1266, by the Treaty of Perth, Norway agreed to cede the western isles and Man in return for 4000 merks and an annual payment of 100 merks. Not only did this success add to Alexander's prestige, but it gave the country security and peace and, as the King was still only twenty-five, his subjects looked forward to a long period of tranquillity and prosperity.

Alexander's first wife died in 1275, and his children by her were short-lived: Margaret (born 1261) married King Erik of Norway in 1281 and died in 1283, leaving a daughter Margaret, 'the Maid of Norway'; Alexander died childless in 1284; and David died unmarried in 1281. The King married secondly (14 October 1285) Yolande, daughter of Robert IV, Comte de Dreux, but on 19 March 1286 he was killed when he was on his way from Edinburgh to Kinghorn and his horse carried him over the precipitous heights on the Fife coast.

James Fergusson, *Alexander the Third*, 1937.

Thomas the Rhymer (*c.* 1210–*c.* 1294) lives in dubious tradition as the author of many prophecies, but his existence is authenticated in extant documents. 'Thomas Rimor de Ercildoun' (that is, the modern Earlston in Berwickshire) was a witness to a charter of Peter de Haga to Melrose Abbey between 1260 and 1270. This association with the Haig family is especially striking, for one of his prophecies was 'Tide, tide, whate'er betide, There'll aye be Haigs

16

at Bemersyde'—a prophecy which was held to be fulfilled when, after the First World War, Bemersyde was presented by the nation to Field-Marshal Earl Haig. He was presumably dead in 1294, when his son inherited the lands of Ercildoune as his heir. There is no authority for giving him the surname Learmonth, for this goes no further back than the unreliable Hector Boece in the early sixteenth century. Thomas evidently wrote a 'Romance of Sir Tristram' which was quoted by a contemporary continental writer and which was edited from a surviving manuscript by Sir Walter Scott in 1804. His reputation as a prophet—who foretold, for instance, the death of Alexander III—was referred to by various writers from 1338 onwards, including John Barbour, author of *The Brus*. The romantic story of Thomas and his 'ladye gaye' who was actually the Queen of Faerie, with whom he spent seven years in Elfland, does not, at least in its existing form, go back beyond 1400.

J. A. H. Murray, *The Romance and Prophecies of Thomas of Erceldoune*. Early English Text Society, 1875.

Margaret, 'The Maid of Norway', Queen of Scots (?1283–1290), was the daughter of King Erik Magnusson of Norway by Margaret (d. 9 April 1283), daughter of Alexander III. She was acknowledged as heir to the Scottish throne on 5 February 1284, and, on her grandfather's death on 19 March 1286, six Guardians were appointed to govern Scotland during her minority. By the Treaties of Salisbury (6 November 1289) and Birgham (17 March 1290) it was agreed that she should come to Scotland when it was safe for her to do so and should marry Prince Edward, son and heir of Edward I of England. Edward sent 'a great ship' to Norway to bring the child across the North Sea in May 1290, but Erik insisted that she should travel on a Norwegian ship. She left Norway in September, but on or about the 16th of that month she died in or near Orkney, 'between the hands of Bishop Narve, and in the presence of the best men who followed her from Norway'. Margaret's body was taken to Bergen, where King Erik satisfied himself as to its identity, and she was buried beside her mother in Bergen Cathedral. But in 1300, about a year after the death of Erik, a woman came from Lübeck to Norway claiming to be Margaret. She was tried, convicted and burned at Bergen as an impostor.

As soon as Margaret's death had been rumoured, William Fraser, Bishop of St. Andrews (d. 1297), who had been one of the Guardians of the kingdom since 1286, wrote to Edward I suggesting that he should be ready to intervene in Scotland to prevent bloodshed

17

and hinting that he should countenance the claim of John Balliol to the succession. Balliol's claim arose through his descent from David, Earl of Huntingdon (*c.* 1144–1219), the third son of Prince Henry, son of David I. David founded the abbey of Lindores (*c.* 1191), but after his marriage in 1190 to Maud, daughter of Hugh, Earl of Chester, his interests lay mainly in England. Apart from two sons who died young and one who died unmarried, David had a fourth son, John, 'the Scot', who succeeded to the earldoms of Huntingdon and Chester but died without issue in 1237. It was therefore through Earl David's daughters that the royal line continued after the death of the Maid of Norway. The eldest daughter, Margaret, married Alan, Lord of Galloway, and their daughter, Devorguilla, was the mother of John Balliol. The second, Isabella, married Robert Bruce, Lord of Annandale; her son contested the thone with Balliol and his grandson became King as Robert I. The third, Ada, married Henry Hastings, and their grandson, John Hastings, claimed in 1291 that Scotland, like any feudal fief, was divisible among heiresses and should therefore be partitioned among Balliol, Bruce and himself.

Bruce, Robert, 'The Competitor' (1210–1295), the descendant of a Norman on whom the lordship of Annandale had been conferred by David I, was the son of Isabella, second daughter of David, Earl of Huntingdon. In 1255 he was one of the councillors and guardians of the young Alexander III, but his career was for many years mainly in England. He supported Henry III against Simon de Montfort and after the latter's overthrow at Evesham (1265) he became governor of Carlisle, sheriff of Cumberland and, in 1268, Chief Justice of the Court of King's Bench. His first marriage was to Isobel, daughter of Gilbert de Clare, Earl of Gloucester and Hereford, and his second to Christina, daughter of Sir William de Ireby. In 1270 he went on a crusade with Edmund, the youngest son of Henry III. In 1284 he acknowledged Margaret, 'The Maid of Norway', as heiress to the Scottish throne, but on Alexander III's death in 1286 he rose in arms to claim the throne in virtue of an alleged declaration by Alexander II (then childless) in 1238 that he, as a male, should be preferred to the daughter of his mother's elder sister. In 1290, on the death of 'The Maid of Norway', he renewed his claim and in 1291, along with his son, swore fealty to Edward I, to whose judgment the competition for the throne was remitted. After Edward appointed Balliol as King, Bruce resigned his rights to his son, Robert, who had become Earl of Carrick by his marriage (*c.* 1272) to Marjory, daughter and heiress of Neil, Earl of Carrick. Carrick, who lived until 1304, was the father of King Robert I, to whom he had resigned his earldom in 1292, and of Edward, King of Ireland, as well as of three other sons, Thomas, Alexander and Nigel, all of whom were put to death by the English.

John Balliol, King of Scots (*c.* 1250–1313), was descended from John de Bailleul, a Picard who had been a landowner in England under William Rufus and whose son, Guy, had appeared in Scotland under David I. As the son of Devorguilla, Lady of Galloway, grand-daughter of David, Earl of Huntingdon, Balliol represented the senior line in succession to the throne after the death of 'The Maid of Norway' in 1290. He had only recently succeeded to the lordship of Galloway on his mother's death, and had hardly figured in Scotland, but was rather an Anglo-Norman, with estates in France as well as in England. There were twelve other competitors for the throne, but Balliol's main rival was Robert Bruce, whose family had on the whole deeper roots in Scotland than Balliol's. Bruce was Lord of Annandale, and his son had married the heiress of Carrick, so that the Bruce holdings straddled Balliol's lordship of Galloway. When the dispute was submitted to Edward I and the competitors all agreed to accept him as their lord, Edward chose Balliol, who was set on the Stone at Scone on 30 November 1292. Little is known of King John's brief reign, though an ordinance for the erection of sheriffdoms in Skye and Lorne suggests a clear grasp of the problems of government. The dominating fact was that Balliol soon found himself in an awkward position as an English vassal. Edward not only wanted him to give military service with the English army but insisted that he should answer in English courts for, among other things, the unpaid bills of King Alexander III. Balliol himself might perhaps have submitted to any indignity, but his counsellors would not permit it, and he seems in effect to have been deprived of authority. The Scots made an alliance with England's other enemy, France, in 1295, and this brought on them retaliation by Edward, who defeated them heavily at Dunbar (27 April 1296). Balliol resigned his kingdom to Edward (10 July) and, by being stripped of his royal insignia, became known as 'Toom Tabard' (the empty cloak). He was taken to England as a prisoner but after three years was allowed to retire to his French estates, where he died.

Balliol married a daughter of the Earl of Surrey and had two sons, Edward (who contested the throne with David II) and Henry who died in 1332 without issue). His sister, Alianora, married John Comyn, Lord of Badenoch, who was one of the Guardians appointed

19

in 1286 and himself a competitor for the throne in 1290. Their son, John, 'the Red Comyn', fought for Balliol in 1296 and was associated with resistance to England as long as it was carried on in the name of the absent Balliol. However, he could not co-operate amicably with the rival family of Bruce, and in a quarrel in 1299 he seized Robert Bruce, the future king, by the throat. In 1304, like most Scots, Comyn capitulated to Edward I. In 1306, in circumstances which remain mysterious, he was stabbed by Bruce in a quarrel at Dumfries and, according to a picturesque tale, was despatched by one of Bruce's followers, Roger Kirkpatrick.

Wallace, Sir William (*c.* 1270–1305), was the second of the three sons of Sir Malcolm Wallace of Elderslie in Renfrewshire, a tenant of the Stewards of Scotland. Nothing is known of his career before he appears as a leader of resistance to the administration of Edward I. By May 1297 there were several risings, one of them in Moray under Andrew, son and heir of Sir Andrew de Moray, who was Lord of Petty in Inverness-shire, Avoch in the Black Isle and Boharm in Banffshire and had been justiciar of Scotland in 1289. Wallace emerged as a guerilla leader about this time, after killing the English sheriff of Lanark. He is next heard of in Perth, when William Ormesby, Edward's justiciar, fled before him, and thereafter he seems to have ranged widely over the centre and south of Scotland. He joined forces with Moray, and at Stirling on 11 September 1297 they defeated an army under John de Warenne, Earl of Surrey, the English governor of Scotland, and Hugh Cressingham, the hated treasurer (who was killed and whose skin is said to have been distributed among the victorious Scots as souvenirs). It is in the next few months that we know most of Wallace's doings. He recaptured Berwick and invaded the north of England, where, with Moray, he issued a letter of protection to the monks of Hexham. Again with Moray, he sent a letter to Lübeck and Hamburg, on 11 October 1297, intimating that Scotland was free and that German merchants could resume their trade. Moray died in November, probably of wounds received at Stirling. Wallace was knighted, and by March 1298 was acting officially as Guardian of the realm in the name of John Balliol. But he did not command universal support. To the magnates he no doubt seemed something of an upstart; there were those who had become convinced that collaboration with the English was the only sensible policy in the long run; and as long as he was acting in the name of Balliol he could hardly expect unconditional help from the Bruce family and the supporters of their claim to the throne. At Falkirk, on 11 July 1298, Wallace was defeated by Edward I. The battle was won by the English archers, while Wallace, owing to lack of support from the nobles, was weak in the cavalry who could have scattered the archers, but there is no evidence that his small cavalry force deliberately deserted him. After the defeat, Wallace laid down the office of Guardian and lapsed into obscurity, though he is known to have gone to France in 1298 or 1299, no doubt to ask for diplomatic or military help, and he may have gone on to Rome to seek papal support. Resistance had meantime continued under the leadership of some of the magnates, though their own quarrels hindered their efforts, and by 1304 they had all come to terms with England. It seems unlikely that Wallace would have been admitted to Edward's peace even had he sought it. In 1305 he was captured by the English, taken to London and executed (23 August).

James Fergusson, *William Wallace*, 1938.

Robert I, King of Scots (1274–1329), was the grandson of the Robert Bruce who contested the throne with John Balliol in 1291. His parents were Robert Bruce and Marjory, Countess of Carrick, and he was born, probably at Turnberry, on 11 July 1274. His father, who held the earldom of Carrick in right of his wife, resigned it to his son in 1292. When Balliol was attacked by Edward I in 1296, the young Bruce served on the English side, for his family had never recognized the right of Balliol to the throne, and he took a special oath of allegiance to Edward. However, in 1297, while his father remained on Edward's side, Robert joined Wallace's rising, but there is no evidence that he took any part in the battles of Stirling Bridge and Falkirk. After Wallace's defeat, Bruce continued to associate with those who maintained resistance, and in December 1298 he was appointed one of the Guardians of the realm. Yet in 1302, while others were continuing resistance with some effect, Bruce submitted to Edward, possibly because he feared a Balliol restoration under English auspices and thought that his lands as well as his claim to the throne might be in danger. He remained in high favour with Edward for three years, until after Scottish resistance had been completely crushed and Wallace executed.

What circumstances caused Bruce to initiate a new resistance movement are not known, but, after a quarrel with John Comyn, Balliol's nephew, at Dumfries, in which the latter was killed, he was inaugurated as King at Scone (25 March 1306) and crowned by Isabella, Countess of Buchan (27 March). On 18 June he was defeated at Methven, and fled west into the wild country between Perthshire and Argyll. A defeat at Dalrigh by John Mac-Dougal of Lorne shattered his remaining force. He sent his Queen and his daughter with a detachment of men to Kildrummy, whence they fled to Tain, only to be captured there by the English. Bruce himself made his way, by Kintyre, to Rathlin and then probably to Orkney. He disappears from history until he turns up in his native Carrick early in 1307, to start a guerilla campaign there and in Galloway. After a victory at Loudoun Hill (May 1307) and the death of Edward I (7 July), Bruce headed for the north-east, where he harried the Comyn lands in Buchan and took Aberdeen and Inverness. In 1308 or 1309 he was back in the west to defeat the MacDougals in the Pass of Brander.

In March 1309 King Robert was able to hold his first recorded Parliament, at St. Andrews, where declarations in his favour were made by clergy and nobles. The next stage in his campaign was the gradual recovery of castles in the centre and south, and this proved a slow business: Perth was taken in January 1313, Dumfries in February 1313, Roxburgh and Edinburgh not until February–March 1314. However, the operations within Scotland had been accompanied by aggression in the north of England between 1311 and 1313.

After the great victory at Bannockburn (24 June 1314), there were more raids into England, and also a campaign in Ireland, where Robert went in 1316 to support his brother, Edward, in his bid for the throne of that country. Berwick fell to the Scots in 1318 and, after a victory at Mytton, in England, in 1319, there was a truce for two years. On the renewal of the war, the Scots won another victory on enemy soil, at Byland (1322), and fighting continued intermittently until a forceful invasion of England in 1327 finally brought the English to accept terms.

Meantime diplomacy had been at work elsewhere. The impatience of the Scots at the refusal of the Pope to recognize their king had led the barons to send to John XXII a letter which is reckoned the Scottish Declaration of Independence (6 April 1320), and a mission to Avignon in 1323 persuaded the Pope to give Bruce the title of King. In 1326 the Treaty of Corbeil was made with the French. At last, by a treaty formulated at Edinburgh on 17 March 1328 and ratified by Edward III at Northampton on 4 May, Bruce gained all that he had fought for, and in the following year the Pope conceded that the Kings of Scots could be anointed as well as crowned, though the bull granting this privilege arrived only after the death of the liberator King at Cardross (7 June 1329).

In the years when there was peace within Scotland, Bruce issued some wise legislation, but it is hard to assess its significance owing to the paucity of evidence for earlier reigns and the fact that so much wise legislation was later repeated almost as a matter of routine from reign to reign. It is, however, plain that there were significant developments in the burghs, many of which received from King Robert charters giving them feu tenure, which made them responsible for only a single annual payment, fixed in perpetuity. This increased an appreciation of the corporate character of the burghs, and it is hardly surprising that contemporaneously, in 1326, burgh representatives appeared in Parliament, so far as we know for the first time.

Bruce married first, c. 1295, Isabella, daughter of Donald, Earl of Mar, by whom he had a daughter, Marjory, and secondly, in 1302, Elizabeth (d. 1327), daughter of the Earl of Ulster, who bore the future David II as well as a son who died in infancy and two daughters. In 1315, when Bruce had no son, the succession was settled, with Marjory's consent, on his brother Edward, as a man skilled in war and fitted to defend the kingdom. Edward (c. 1276–1318) had taken part in his brother's campaigns, first by overrunning Galloway in 1308, and the battle of Bannockburn (at which he commanded a division) had been the outcome of his agreement in 1313 with the governor of Stirling Castle that the castle would be surrendered if it were not relieved by Midsummer Day 1314. Edward was styled Lord of Galloway in 1309 and was created Earl of Carrick, probably in 1313. Invited to assist a nationalist movement in Ireland, he landed at Larne in May 1315 and was crowned King of Ireland on 2 May 1316, but was defeated and killed at Dundalk on 14 October 1318, leaving no lawful issue. Marjory Bruce, too, was now dead, and in 1318 the crown was settled, failing male issue of King Robert, on Robert (later Robert II), her son by Walter the Steward.

G. W. S. Barrow, *Robert Bruce, King of Scots*, 1965.

Bernard de Linton (d. 1331), Abbot of Arbroath, best known as the presumed composer of the Scottish Declaration of Independence, first appears on the political scene within eighteen months of the coronation of Robert I in 1306. Nothing is known of his earlier career, except that he was parson of Mordington, near Berwick, in 1296. He may have become Bruce's chancellor at the very beginning of his reign, and certainly held the office from 1308 until 1328.

About 1311 he was elected Abbot of Arbroath at the King's instance. Among the products of Bruce's chancery, besides his routine charters, were certain state documents and manifestoes—a letter to the King of France in 1308, a declaration of the clergy in favour of Bruce in 1310, the acts settling the succession to the throne in 1315 and 1318, the Declaration of Arbroath of 1320 and the peace terms of 1326. All are composed in prose conforming to the best traditions of the medieval rhythmical *cursus,* and it has been supposed that they may well be by the same hand, that of Bernard de Linton, to whom, as an advisor, Bruce may have owed much. In 1328, when he resigned the officer of Chancellor, Bernard was, rather oddly, appointed Bishop of the Isles, which looks like demotion, though he retained a pension from Arbroath and the King gave him £100 to pay his election expenses. Possibly it was hoped that he might serve Scotland well in a see which had its headquarters in the Isle of Man, a vulnerable outpost of the realm.

Lord Cooper, *Supra Crepidam,* 1951.

Douglas, Sir James (c. 1286–1330), 'the Good Sir James', was the son and heir of William Douglas 'the Hardy', who fought with Wallace against the English and died a prisoner in the Tower of London about 1299. James therefore found himself landless, for his castle and estates of Douglas had been conferred by Edward I on an Englishman, Robert Clifford, and he seems to have joined Robert Bruce at the very beginning of his campaign in 1306. For the remainder of his life he was an almost constant comrade-in-arms of the King, so that Barbour's *The Brus* is an epic almost as much of Douglas as of Bruce, and Douglas's biography is little else than the history of campaigns against the English. He three times recaptured his castle, on the first and second occasions destroying it in the hope of preventing its reoccupation: once, after taking the castle on Palm Sunday, when the garrison was at church, he first removed articles of value, then piled together all the provisions, poured the liquor over them and finally threw on the pile the dead bodies of his prisoners, before setting fire to the whole 'Douglas Larder'. When Bruce returned to the mainland in 1307, Douglas led an advance party to the Ayrshire coast; in 1308 he led a charge which helped to decide Bruce's action in the Pass of Brander; and he took part with Edward Bruce in his campaign in Galloway. He was responsible for the capture of Roxburgh Castle in 1314 and he was knighted by the King on the eve of Bannockburn, when he commanded a brigade. Like the King, he pressed attacks on

24

England, with the sack of Hartlepool in 1315, the capture of Berwick in 1318 and (with Thomas Randolph, Earl of Moray) the rout of the Archbishop of York and his clerically-officered host at 'the Chapter of Mytton' in 1319. He was in charge of the Borders during the King's absence in Ireland with his brother Edward. Douglas was rewarded for his service with wide estates in Galloway, Lauderdale and Jedburgh, and the 'Emerald Charter' (so called because it was sealed with the King's signet) granted him uncommonly wide jurisdiction within his territories. Randolph and he led a final invasion of England in 1327. When the succession was settled in 1318, the office of Regent, should the King die leaving a minor as his heir, was assigned to Randolph, whom failing to Douglas. After the King's death and the accession of the five-year-old David II, Randolph became Regent and Douglas set out, as Bruce had instructed him, to bear the King's heart in battle against the infidels, and he was killed in an engagement against the Moors near Granada (25 August 1330).

Randolph, Thomas, Earl of Moray (d. 1332), usually called a nephew of King Robert I, may have been the son, by Thomas Randolph the elder, of a daughter of Marjory, Countess of Carrick, Bruce's mother, by her first husband. He was with Bruce in his first campaign which ended disastrously at Methven, where he was captured. He then took part with the English and operated against Bruce in Galloway. Captured again, near Peebles, by Sir James Douglas, Randolph returned to the Scottish King's allegiance and was soon in high favour. In 1309 he was Lord of Nithsdale, in 1312 he was created Earl of Moray and in 1315 Lord of Man; he was also known as Lord of Annandale. He was responsible for the capture of Edinburgh Castle in 1314, and at Bannockburn, where he commanded the left wing, he intercepted the body of cavalry under Clifford which the English attempted to throw into Stirling Castle. He fought in Ireland in 1315, he helped to take Berwick in 1318 and he took part in the operations in England which led to the Scottish victories at Mytton (1319) and Byland (1322). He acted as a Scottish envoy to the Pope at Avignon in 1323 and persuaded the pontiff to concede to Bruce the title of King of Scots.

In terms of the Succession Acts of 1315 and 1318 Randolph was nominated guardian of the kingdom in the event of King Robert leaving a minor as his heir, and on the King's death in 1329 Randolph therefore became Regent for David II. In 1332, when leading an army to resist an English invasion on behalf of Edward Balliol, Randolph died at Musselburgh.

Randolph was succeeded as Earl of Moray by his son, Thomas, who died only three weeks later, leaving no issue, and the earldom then went to the first earl's second son, John, who was killed at the battle of Neville's Cross (1346). The earldom next devolved on Agnes, daughter of the first earl, who married Patrick, Earl of Dunbar and March, between 1320 and 1324. She is remembered for her spirited defence of the castle of Dunbar against the English under the Earl of Salisbury from 13 January to 16 June 1338 and for the contemptuous way in which she treated the efforts of the attackers.

Barbour, John (?1320–1395), author of *The Brus*, a poem which recounts the deeds of Robert I, was probably a native of Aberdeen and was archdeacon of that diocese by 1357, when he acted as a commissioner for the Bishop of Aberdeen in discussions concerning the payment of David II's ransom. In the same year he had a safe-conduct to travel to Oxford with three other scholars, and he had similar safe-conducts in 1364 and 1368. On another occasion he was licensed to pass through England to France. In 1372–3 he held financial offices in the royal household and in 1377 he evidently received a pension from the crown in respect of his literary work. *The Brus* was probably written about 1375, and Barbour could clearly draw on the recollections of older men who had been contemporaries of his hero. His verses are therefore regarded as an important historical source, though from time to time he departed from the strict facts of history to magnify the romance surrounding Bruce and in the interests of literary form and unity. His style is notable for economy and simplicity and an ability to keep the story moving. The work should be seen as a conscious attempt to give Scotland a 'Romance' in the grand manner to match those of other medieval literatures, as well as to establish the place of Bruce, and perhaps also Sir James Douglas, as classical 'Worthies' or 'Champions'. Barbour is also credited with a long poem on *The Legends of the Saints*. There are MSS. of *The Brus* in the National Library of Scotland and St. John's College, Cambridge, and the first extant printed edition is that by Lekprevik (Edinburgh) in 1571. There are many recent editions, including those by W. W. Skeat for the Early English Text Society (1870–89) and the Scottish Text Society (1894) and by W. M. Mackenzie (1909).

George Neilson, *John Barbour, Poet and Translator*, 1900.

Balliol, Edward (?1283–1364), the elder son of King John, shared his father's imprisonment in England in 1296 and then retired to the ancestral estates in France, to which he succeeded on John's death. In 1324 Edward II brought him back to England by way of threatening Robert I with a rival. After Bruce's death and the accession of the child David II, Edward Balliol joined with 'the Disinherited'—those lords who had lost their Scottish estates because they had taken the English side against Bruce—in an expedition which sailed from Holderness and landed in Fife. On 12 August 1332 they routed the Scottish army at Dupplin, near Perth, and Balliol was crowned at Scone on 24 September. However, before the year was out he was surprised at Annan, his brother Henry was killed and he had to flee across the Border, hardly clad and on an unsaddled horse (17 December). Returning to Scotland in March, he was joined by Edward III in May, captured Berwick and defeated the Scots at Halidon (19 July). In February 1334 he agreed to surrender the southern counties of Scotland to Edward of England. Despite this, and his acknowledgment of Edward as his overlord, Balliol enjoyed a considerable measure of support from Scots who had perhaps never been enthusiasts for the house of Bruce and now disliked a child-king, as well as from others who saw the hand of Providence in their successive defeats. Yet resistance was so strong that Balliol was driven from Scotland again in November 1334 and, although he returned once more in 1335, he could not, even with repeated English help, make his hold on the country effective. He retired to England in 1338, and thereafter made only one further appearance in Scotland, with an incursion into Galloway after David II's defeat at Neville's Cross in 1346. He resigned his claims to the Scottish throne to Edward III in 1356. He had no children.

Ranald Nicholson, *Edward III and the Scots*, 1965.

David II, King of Scots (1324–1371), the only surviving son of Robert I, born at Dunfermline on 5 March 1324, was married in his fifth year to Joanna, sister of Edward III of England, and succeeded his father on 7 June 1329. He was the first Scottish king to be anointed at his coronation, 24 November 1331. Thomas Randolph, Earl of Moray, was at first Guardian, but he died in 1332, to be succeeded by Donald, Earl of Mar (*c.* 1295–1332). Mar had a curious record: he had been taken into English custody as a child, in 1306, and even after Bannockburn, when he was set free, he preferred to remain in England, and was not reconciled to Robert I (who was his mother's brother) until so late as 1327 or 1328. In consequence, he was not thoroughly trusted, but his regency, like Randolph's, was short, for he was killed when Edward Balliol defeated the Scots at Dupplin (12 August 1332). Sir Andrew Moray of Bothwell (d. 1338), the posthumous son of William Wallace's companion in arms, was then chosen as Guardian, but he was taken prisoner in April 1333, and in July of the same year the Scots, under a new Guardian, Sir Archibald Douglas, were defeated at Halidon and Douglas killed. The young King and his wife were sent to France for safety in May 1334. Robert the Steward, David's uncle, and John Randolph, Earl of Moray, were now joint-Guardians, and although Randolph was taken prisoner in August 1335, Sir Andrew Moray, who had been ransomed, took the lead once more and the Scots began to have some successes. English supporters were defeated at Culblain in November 1335, Moray relieved Kildrummy Castle and recaptured his own castle of Bothwell (1336).

By 1341 it was thought safe to bring the 'stout, young and jolly King Davie' back from France (where he had spent most of his time at Château Gaillard). Edward III was now at war with France, and victorious at Crècy (26 August 1346). David, in fulfilment of the French alliance and in imitation of his father's later policy, invaded England, to be defeated and captured at Neville's Cross, near Durham (17 October 1346). He remained a prisoner for eleven years, though with at least one visit to Scotland when he tried to arrange for a ransom. He was released by the Treaty of Berwick (3 October 1357), for a ransom of 100,000 merks, payable in ten annual instalments. This heavy financial burden had appreciable effects on the fiscal policy of Scotland and even on its constitutional practice, for the co-operation of the burgesses in parliament was indispensable if the money was to be raised. Despite the visitations of the Black Death (1349–50 and 1362), it seems that the economy could have borne the burden, and the peaceful policy which David now pursued was beneficial to his people. Yet the whole ransom was never paid. David has been accused of diverting to his own pleasures the money raised to pay it, but on the other hand there is evidence of sound financial administration and of wise legislation, so it may be that some of the criticism of the King was inspired by personal and family jealousies.

David had made little headway against factious nobles between 1341 and 1346, and during his captivity Robert the Steward had been an ineffective governor. The nobles possibly resented the strong hand of David, who was said to 'govern his kingdom right stoutly'. Certainly the Steward was associated with the Earls of Douglas and March in an unsuccessful rebellion. As David had no heir either by Queen Joanna (who died in England on 14 August 1362) or by Margaret Drummond (daughter of Sir Malcolm Drummond and widow of Sir John Logie), whom he married in 1364 and divorced in 1370, and as he had no liking for his nephew and heir-designate, Robert the Steward, he entertained schemes for a remission of the ransom in return for the recognition of an English prince as his successor. The Scots would have none of it, but David's plan was not unstatesmanlike, and some of the provisions, if carried out, would have preserved the integrity of Scotland more effectively than the Treaty of Union of 1707 was to do. Besides, David's diplomacy gained England's acquiescence in the deferment of the payment of the ransom. He died in Edinburgh Castle on 22 February 1371.

Ranald Nicholson, 'David II, the historians and the chroniclers', in *Scot. Hist. Rev.*, xlv, 59–78.

Robert II, King of Scots (1316–1390), was descended from Flaald, a Breton, who was a landholder in England under Henry I and whose grandson, Walter FitzAlan, became hereditary Steward of Scotland under David I. Walter, the sixth High Steward, married Marjory, daughter of Robert I, in 1315, and their son, Robert, born on 2 March 1316, was declared heir presumptive in 1318. He succeeded as Steward on his father's death in 1326. When Robert I died in 1329, his son, David II, born in 1324, became King, and David's nephew, Robert, though eight years David's senior, had to take second place. He shared in the command at the battle of Halidon (1333) and was associated in the regency from 1338 to 1341, when he had to relinquish office on David's return from France. At Neville's Cross in 1346 the Steward was among the Scottish commanders, and drew off part of the Scottish army when, it was thought, he might have done more to try to rescue the King from his captors. Robert then became Guardian of the kingdom until David returned from his English captivity in 1357. He may well have been somewhat resentful at having to hand over authority to an uncle who was eight years younger than himself, and we hear of him involved in an unsuccessful rebellion with the Earls of Douglas and March. When David died, Robert succeeded (22 February 1371).

Elevated to kingship through a lucky chance and at the age of

29

fifty-five, Robert II had neither the personal qualities nor the prestige to command much respect, and his nineteen years' reign brought increasing infirmity and incapacity. He was described in 1385 as 'no valiant man, but one who would rather remain at home than march to the field'. He therefore took no part in the wars with England in the 1380s, which were conducted by his more militant subjects, under some stimulus from France, possibly without the King's approval or even full knowledge. As early as 1381 his eldest son, the Earl of Carrick, was associated with him in the government and in 1384 was in effect appointed to rule in his place. Then, in 1388, when Carrick himself had become a chronic invalid, the King's next son, Robert, Earl of Fife, was appointed to govern.

Robert II's matrimonial history raised some problems. He had several children by Elizabeth Mure, daughter of Adam Mure of Rowallan, before he married that lady (22 November 1347) and, as he and his wife were related within the forbidden degrees, it was debatable whether the papal dispensation for their marriage could legitimate the children already born to them. After Elizabeth's death he married Euphemia Ross (1355), by whom he had two sons about whose birth there was no possible dispute. In 1373 an Act of Succession was passed, assigning the crown to the three surviving sons of the first marriage in turn and their heirs male, whom failing the two sons of the second marriage and their heirs male. But a feud between the descendants of the two marriages persisted for generations.

Robert II died at Dundonald on 19 April 1390 and was buried at Scone. By Elizabeth Mure he had four sons—John, who succeeded as Robert III; Walter, who died about 1362; Robert, Earl of Fife and later Duke of Albany; and Alexander, Lord of Badenoch; and also five daughters. By Euphemia Ross (who died in 1387) he had two sons—David, Earl of Strathearn, and Walter, Earl of Atholl; and two daughters. He also had at least eight illegitimate sons.

Robert III, King of Scots (c. 1337–1406), was the eldest son of Robert II and Elizabeth Mure and was baptized John. He was created Earl of Carrick in 1368. Before his father's death he was already something of an invalid following a kick from a horse.

When Carrick succeeded on 19 April 1390 he assumed the name of Robert, as John was considered an unlucky name for a king: the previous holders of the name included John Balliol, who had surrendered Scotland to Edward I; John, King of England, who had surrendered his kingdom to the Pope; and John, King of France, who had been captured by the English at Poitiers. But Robert III was already about fifty-three when he became King, and the change of name did nothing to enable an ageing invalid to rule effectively. He was noted more for his gentle and kindly nature than for the energy which was required of a king in those days. During much of his reign real power lay with his next brother, Robert, Earl of Fife and Duke of Albany. Disorder grew in the realm, until it was remarked that there was no law in Scotland and the whole kingdom was a den of thieves, and one of the King's own brothers, Alexander, Lord of Badenoch, was noted for his depredations in Moray, where he burned Elgin Cathedral. In 1399, on the ground that the King could not keep order and restrain the rebellious and that 'the misgovernance of the realm and the default of the keeping of the common law should be imputed to the King and his officers', David, Duke of Rothesay, the King's heir, was appointed Lieutenant of the kingdom, but he was to act with the advice of councillors among whose names that of Albany stood first. With the death of Rothesay in 1402, Albany was without a rival. As the Duke was suspected of having brought about the death of Rothesay, the old King, in the hope of preserving his younger son, James, arranged for him to be sent to France for safety, but he was captured by the English at sea. The King himself may have felt increasing insecurity, for he withdrew to the castle of Rothesay on his ancestral island of Bute, where he died on 4 April 1406. He was buried in Paisley Abbey. By his wife Annabella Drummond, daughter of Sir John Drummond of Stobhall, whom he married in 1367 and who died in 1401, Robert III had three sons—David, Robert (who died young) and James; and four daughters. He also had two recorded illegitimate sons.

Rothesay, David, Duke of (1378–1402), the eldest son of Robert III, born on 24 October 1378, was created Duke of Rothesay on 28 April 1398. He and his uncle Robert, who was at the same time created Duke of Albany, were the first dukes in Scotland, but the suggestion has been made that there is some significance in the fact that, while Albany's title derived from Alba, the ancient name for Scotland, Rothesay's came merely from the Stewarts' family castle in Bute. On 27 January 1399 the three estates, in view of the inability of the King to keep order in the realm, appointed Rothesay to act as Lieutenant, with the advice of a council. However, although reliable contemporary evidence is inadequate, the indications are that he was not fitted to exercise authority. He was betrothed first to

31

Euphemia, sister of David, 1st Earl of Crawford, then to Elizabeth, daughter of George, Earl of March, but in February 1400 he married Marjory, daughter of Archibald, 3rd Earl of Douglas. His rejection of March's daughter caused the latter to transfer his allegiance to the English King, much to Scotland's disadvantage. Rothesay's irresponsibility was presumably the reason, or possibly pretext, for his confinement in Falkland Castle on the advice of Albany and Douglas, and he died there on 26 March 1402. There were, and there have always persisted, suspicions that he had foul play, and it was thought necessary to obtain from the council, on 16 May 1402, an official declaration that 'he departed this life through the divine Dispensation and not otherwise'.

Scott, *The Fair Maid of Perth*. (H.N.)

Albany, Robert, Duke of (1339–1420), was the third son of Robert II by Elizabeth Mure. By marrying Margaret, Countess of Menteith, about 1361, he became Earl of Menteith, and on the death of his elder brother, Walter, who had married Isabella, Countess of Fife, he succeeded to that earldom through a disposition by the countess (1371–2). For many years, therefore, he was 'Earl of Fife and Menteith', but in 1398 he was created Duke of Albany. In his father's reign he became keeper of Stirling Castle (1373) and in 1382 he was appointed to the important office of Chamberlain, which he held until he resigned it in favour of his son, the Earl of Buchan, in 1407. Robert took part in the Scoto-French expedition against England in 1385 and again invaded England in 1388. In the latter year, owing to the advancing age of his father and the infirmity of his elder brother (who became Robert III in 1390), he was made Governor of the kingdom. During most, if not all, of Robert III's reign, Albany was probably the most important man in Scotland, though he was not always nominally Governor. He was suspected of causing the death of his nephew, Robert III's heir, in 1402. When Robert III died, in 1406, his younger son, James, now heir, was a prisoner in England, and Albany ruled the kingdom as Governor—in his own name, not that of the absent king—until his death on 2 September 1420.

By his first wife, the Countess of Menteith, Albany had a son, Murdoch (*c.* 1362–1425). Murdoch was appointed justiciar north of the Forth (1389). Taken prisoner when the Scots were defeated at Homildon (1402), he remained in England, on parole, until 1415, when he was exchanged for Henry, Earl of Northumberland; and it has been remarked that Murdoch's father meanwhile made no comparable effort to obtain the release of King James. Murdoch succeeded his father as Governor in 1420, but his manifest incapacity and the consequent disorder encouraged negotiations for the return of the King. When James did come back, Albany took part in the coronation at Scone (21 May 1424), but in a Parliament held at Perth ten months later orders were issued for his arrest. Tried and condemned, though on what charges is not known, he was executed on 25 May; his eldest surviving son had been beheaded the previous day, and his second son, as well as his father-in-law, the Earl of Lennox, went to the block with the Duke.

By his second wife, Muriella Keith, Duke Robert had three sons—John, Andrew (d. 1413) and Robert (d. 1431). John (*c.* 1380–1424), received the earldom of Buchan in 1406, after it had fallen to his father by the death of his younger brother, Alexander, 'the Wolf of Badenoch', and from 1407 until his death he was Chamberlain. In 1416 he was sent to England to treat for the release of James I, but without success. In 1420 he headed a force of some 7000 Scots who went to France to join in the war against the English under Henry V. On 21 March 1421, at the battle of Baugé, the Scots under Buchan and the son of the 4th Earl of Douglas were responsible for a heavy defeat of the English and thus encouraged the French to renew resistance. Young Douglas was defeated at Crevant in 1422 and returned to Scotland to raise fresh forces. In 1424 the Earl of Douglas himself arrived in France, with, it was said, 10,000 Scottish soldiers, and the French King made him Duke of Touraine and Lieutenant-General of the French forces. Buchan was appointed Constable of France but both Douglas and he were killed at the battle of Verneuil (17 August 1424).

James I, King of Scots (1394–1437), second son of Robert III, was born at Dunfermline, probably on 25 July 1394. He became heir apparent by the death of his elder brother, the Duke of Rothesay, in 1402, and was created Earl of Carrick in 1404. In 1406, when on his way to France, he was captured by the English, and remained a prisoner for eighteen years, during which he was well educated and became an accomplished man. He had occasional contacts with Scotsmen, but the Albanys, who were in control, had little desire to bring about his release. In 1420 and 1421, when Scottish soldiers were fighting against the English in France, James was taken there with the English armies in the hope that his presence would neutralize the Scots who were on the French side. Meantime the manifest incompetence of Duke Murdoch as Governor led to a

33

desire in Scotland for the King's return. James's prospects improved when he fell in love with Joan Beaufort, first cousin of Henry V. His romance is the subject of his poem *The Kingis Quair*, which, with its many echoes of Chaucer, reflects the influence of English culture on James, and its quality is such as to place him in the first rank among Scottish poets. In December 1423 the Treaty of London provided for his release in return for a ransom (nominally the cost of his maintenance and education) of £40,000, payable in six annual instalments. On 2 February 1424 he married Joan and they were in Scotland in April.

James dealt ruthlessly with all who might challenge his authority: Duke Murdoch and two of his sons were executed; the Earl of Strathearn, representing the descendants of Robert II by his second and unquestionably legal marriage, was demoted to the earldom of Menteith and sent to England as a hostage; the Earl of March had to accept the earldom of Buchan in place of his lands on the frontier; the earldom of Mar was annexed to the crown; the 5th Earl of Douglas, although he loyally supported James against the Lord of the Isles, was for a time in prison. To counterbalance the power of the nobles, James tried, without success, to bring representatives of the lesser landholders into parliament. Resolved as he was 'to make the key keep the castle and the bracken bush the cow', James showed a real solicitude for the keeping of 'firm and sure peace throughout the realm', as his first statute phrased it, and he improved both civil and criminal justice. He also appointed an advocate for the poor, and passed acts for the security and prosperity of tenants and farmers. He showed a strong hand in the Highlands, where he arrested several chiefs, including the magnate who was Lord of the Isles and Earl of Ross. It was consonant with his desire to strengthen the crown that he should try to enrich it, by stopping the diversion of royal revenues to local magnates, by acquiring earldoms and other lands by forfeiture, by taxation, and by checking the export of bullion. The last of those objectives led to a clash with the Church, since the market for ecclesiastical promotion at Rome was a magnet for Scottish clerics and their money. James censured the older religious orders for their laxity and founded Scotland's only house of the strict Carthusian order, at Perth (1429).

James seems to have attached little importance to popularity, and can hardly have gained it except among some of his humbler subjects, who did not count politically. He made enemies among the nobles by checking their inroads on crown revenues and by threatening the security of their lands; others besides nobles resented his taxation, and the fact that it was not used for the ostensible purpose of paying his ransom may have increased discontent, especially among the families of those who were left to languish as hostages. Some of his measures seem to have arisen from vindictiveness and cupidity rather than from policy. Yet the conspiracy which led to his murder, in the Dominican friary at Perth on 21 February 1437, arose partly at least from the claims of the descendants of Robert II's second marriage, and aimed at excluding James's son and transferring the crown to Walter, Earl of Atholl, youngest son of Robert II. The leaders were Sir Robert Stewart, Atholl's grandson, and Sir Robert Graham, who was uncle of the Earl of Menteith, the senior representative (though through his mother) of the issue of Robert II's second marriage. The plot failed of its ulterior purposes, and the conspirators, including Atholl, were savagely executed. Both Atholl's sons had predeceased him, and the male descendants of Robert II's second marriage were thus extinguished.

Besides twin boys, the younger of whom succeeded as James II, James I and Joan had six daughters, most of whom married abroad. After James's death Joan married Sir James Stewart, 'the Black Knight of Lorne', and by him had three sons, of whom one became Earl of Atholl and another Earl of Buchan. She died in 1445.

E. W. M. Balfour-Melville, *James I, King of Scots*, 1936.

Wyntoun, Andrew of (c. 1355–1422), historian, was a canon regular of St. Andrews and held the office of Prior of the dependent house of St. Serf's, Lochleven, from 1395 to 1413. He appears to have been a native of Portmoak, the parish adjoining Lochleven. Wyntoun's *Orygynale Cronikil of Scotland* was compiled in the later fourteenth and early fifteenth centuries at the request of Sir John Wemyss. The work, in rhyming couplets usually of eight syllables, begins with the Creation, and non-Scottish material occupies five of the nine books. The quality of the verse is quaint, and often perfunctory rather than in any way inspired, but at its best it is eminently quotable and often provides memorable references to incidents both well-known and little-known. Wyntoun, apart from his obvious value for events in and near his own day, undoubtedly had access to older material which has since been lost, and he is regarded as a useful authority for events in earlier periods about which contemporary evidence is now lacking. Apart from his historical researches, he shows a wide acquaintance with the writings of classical authors.

The work survived in several MSS., but was not printed until so late as 1795, when David Macpherson published the Scottish parts of it. It has since been printed in the *Historians of Scotland* series and by the Scottish Text Society.

Bower, Walter (*c.* 1385–1449), historian, a native of Haddington, educated in Scotland and in Paris, was very likely a canon of the Augustinian priory of St. Andrews before he was appointed Abbot of Inchcolm (of the same order) in 1418. In 1424 he was one of the commissioners appointed to collect money for the ransom of James I and in 1433 he was given the similar task of helping to collect the dowry required on the betrothal of the King's daughter to the Dauphin of France. In his later years, probably from about 1440, he compiled his great *Scotichronicon.* He based it on the work of John of Fordun. Fordun (*c.* 1320–84), who is believed to have been a chantry priest at Aberdeen, went to great pains to collect material from which to construct the history of Scotland down to the year 1383. Bower amplified Fordun's work and continued the narrative down to the end of the reign of James I. The compilation is one of the most important sources for generations of Scottish history, especially as Fordun and Bower had access to material since lost and as they incorporated the texts of certain documents. The recognition which the work enjoyed is indicated by the number of MS. copies of it which still survive. The work has not been published *in extenso* since an edition by Walter Goodall in 1759, but the earlier part (essentially Fordun's work) was edited and translated by W. F. Skene in the *Historians of Scotland* series in 1871–2.

Laurence of Lindores (*c.* 1372–1437), theologian, presumably derived his name from his birth at Lindores, and he was not, as is sometimes said, Abbot of Lindores. He graduated B.A. at Paris in 1390, Bachelor of Theology in 1399 and Doctor of Theology about 1407. He returned to Scotland about 1408 and probably started almost at once to lecture in St. Andrews. In 1411 Henry Wardlaw (*c.* 1370–1440), who had become Bishop of St. Andrews in 1403, founded a *studium generale* in his cathedral city, and in 1413 the new institution was granted university status by Benedict XIII, the anti-Pope whom the Scots supported. Laurence remained a leading figure in that university for the rest of his life, being Dean of the Faculty of Arts at its beginning and again from 1431 to 1437, and Rector in 1422. Already in the 1390s, like other promising scholars, he had repeatedly been recommended to the Pope for appointment to benefices, but the only one he is known to have held was the parsonage of Creich, which he possessed in 1408, if not earlier, and retained until his death. Laurence was a distinguished philosopher, whose lectures on the *Physics* and the *De Anima* of Aristotle were famous on the continent, but he is best known in Scottish history not for the contribution he made to the country's first university but because from about the time of his return to Scotland he was Inquisitor of Heretical Pravity. The Great Schism, when two and sometimes three popes were competing for the allegiance of western Christendom, had weakened ecclesiastical discipline, and, besides, both in England by Wyclif and in Bohemia by Hus there were challenges to the very foundations of the theological system of the Church. The Governor Albany was noted for his orthodoxy:

> He was a constant Catholike,
> All Lollard he hated and heretike

and the need to defend the Church may have been one element in the foundation of St. Andrews University. Already about the time of Laurence's return an Englishman, John Resby, was burned at Perth as a heretic (1407). He represented Wycliffite influence; the next execution, under Laurence's inquisitorship, was that of a Bohemian, Paul Crawar, who brought to Scotland the teaching of John Hus and suffered at St. Andrews in 1433. There were three other cases known to have been tried, but two of the accused recanted and the proceedings against the third seem to have been dropped.

Duncan Shaw, 'Laurence of Lindores', in *Scott. Church Hist. Soc. Records*, xii.

James II, King of Scots (1430–1460), known as 'James of the Fiery Face' because of a conspicuous birthmark, was born on 16 October 1430 at Holyrood, which was also the place of his coronation, marriage and burial. In his minority, the government was at first in the hands of Archibald, 5th Earl of Douglas, with the title of Lieutenant of the Realm, and Bishop Cameron of Glasgow, the Chancellor, but in 1439 Douglas died and Cameron was displaced as Chancellor by Sir William Crichton. Crichton, who had evidently been a trusted servant of James I, for a time shared power with Sir Alexander Livingston, but the latter gradually became predominant, Crichton was ousted from the chancellorship in 1444 and within a few years the Livingston family had engrossed all the chief offices of state and had almost complete control of the resources of the crown.

On 3 July 1449 James married Mary of Gueldres. Of their children, James III, Alexander, Duke of Albany, and John, Earl of Mar, all played their parts in history, and Mary married Sir Thomas Boyd and then James, 1st Lord Hamilton. Another son, David, died at the age of three, and another daughter, Margaret, married William, 3rd Lord Crichton. The Queen may well have had some intelligent influence on policy, and she transmitted her piety and her love of culture to her son James III. She died in 1463 and was buried in Trinity College Church, Edinburgh, which she had founded in the previous year, but when that building was demolished in the nineteenth century her remains were removed to the royal vault at Holyrood.

Very shortly after his marriage, in the arranging of which Sir William Crichton clearly had a hand, James asserted himself by suddenly overthrowing the Livingstons and taking authority into his own hands (September 1449). His reign is best known for the struggle of the crown with the Douglases, who, besides enormous territorial possessions and military prestige, were closely connected by marriage and descent with both branches of the royal house. The 5th Earl had married Euphemia Graham, a descendant of Robert II's second marriage, and this may have brought his children under some suspicion in the eyes of the reigning line. At any rate, his sons, William (6th Earl) and David, were seized at the 'Black Dinner' in Edinburgh Castle and put to death on 24 November 1440. The next earl was their great-uncle, James 'the Gross', who was suspected of having had a hand in bringing about their deaths and who himself died in 1443. But the dead boys had a sister, the Maid of Galloway, and she married in succession her cousins the 8th and 9th Earls, so carrying to them her place in the royal line. The 8th Earl, on refusing to break a treaty he had made with the Earl of Crawford and the Earl of Ross (who was also Lord of the Isles), was stabbed to death by the King himself in 1452, and the 9th Earl then repudiated allegiance to James. But by reliance on sound advisers and by raising up new men as earls and lords, the King prepared for action. It may be significant, for example, that Sir William Crichton, who is first styled 'Lord Crichton' in 1447, was Chancellor again from 1448 to 1453. Crichton, who in 1449 founded the collegiate church of Crichton (which still stands), died in 1454, but the King seems to have followed the resolute advice he had given him. At any rate, in 1455

38

the King struck at the Douglas faction. The Earl fled, his brothers were defeated at Arkinholm, and their estates were forfeited. The Earl became a pensioner of the English King and now, by referring to 'James calling himself King of Scots', he disputed James II's right to the crown.

The struggle brought home to the King the need to conserve the territorial and financial resources of the crown, especially at a time when operations against the nobles in their castles necessitated the employment of those expensive weapons, cannon. In 1455, on the fall of the Douglases, an Act of Annexation provided that certain lands and revenues were to remain inalienably with the crown. James's success had been so conspicuous that in 1458 his Parliament congratulated him on so suppressing law-breakers that 'no masterful party' remained, and exhorted him to implement sound legislation, so that his subjects might thank God for sending them 'such a prince to be their governor and defender'.

However, James showed signs of vainglorious ambition and of a reckless acquisitiveness which might in the end have made him as unpopular as his father had become. His vainglory led him to demand from the King of Norway the arrears of the payment due for the Hebrides in terms of the Treaty of Perth in 1266, and it led him also to attempt the recovery of the castle of Roxburgh, which had been in English hands for more than a century. This expedition, combined with his interest in cannon, was his undoing, for at the siege of Roxburgh a cannon burst and killed him as he stood nearby (3 August 1460). James's widow continued the siege, with ultimate success.

G. Donaldson, *Scottish Kings*, 1967.

Douglas, James, 9th Earl of (1426–1488), succeeded on the murder of his brother, the 8th Earl, by James II, and considered that the King's deed had absolved him from allegiance to the crown. With another brother, the Earl of Ormond, he rode into Stirling, where he formally proclaimed the withdrawal of his allegiance to James Stewart, and he sent a message to Henry VI of England offering to do homage to him instead. He obtained a dispensation enabling him to marry his brother's widow, and when he was in England in 1453 as a commissioner in negotiations for a truce, he brought about the liberation of her uncle, Malise, Earl of Menteith, who had long been in England as a hostage and who, as the senior representative of the descendants of Robert II's second marriage, was a possible rival to King James. War broke out in 1455. The King was well prepared and acted swiftly against the Douglas lands and castles, and he succeeded in detaching some of Douglas's supporters. The Earl fled to England, and his brothers, who carried on the war, were defeated at Arkinholm (1 May 1455). Douglas became a pensioner of England, claiming that he had been dispossessed by 'him who calls himself King of Scots'. Douglas had always been inclined to the Yorkist side in England, whereas the Scottish government had supported Lancaster, and when the Yorkist Edward IV became King, in 1460, Douglas was in high favour with him. In 1462, along with the Lord of the Isles, he made a treaty undertaking to assist in the conquest of Scotland, in return for a promise that he would partition Scotland north of the Forth with the Lord of the Isles. Douglas, with English backing, did cross the Border, but had little success, and the Scottish government soon came to terms with Edward, thereby neutralizing his *protégés*. In 1482, when James III's brother, the Duke of Albany, was also an exile in England and was recognized by Edward IV as 'Alexander IV, King of Scots', Douglas joined in an English invasion of Scotland, but the King soon recovered his authority. In 1484 Douglas and Albany made a fresh incursion into Scotland, but on its defeat Douglas was captured and was confined in the abbey of Lindores until his death.

Kennedy, James (*c.* 1408–1465), Bishop of St. Andrews, was the son of James Kennedy of Dunure and Mary, daughter of Robert III and widow of the Earl of Angus. He went to St. Andrews University about 1426 and graduated M.A. in 1429. He then studied at Louvain, but returned to Scotland probably in 1435. He was clearly a favourite of his uncle James I, who in 1437 forced him on the chapter of Dunkeld as their Bishop, though he was only in subdeacon's orders and was barely of canonical age for the episcopate. Later in the year the Pope provided him to the bishopric, and he proved by all accounts to be an energetic diocesan. In 1439 he went on a mission to Rome and won such favour there that the Pope gave him the abbey of Scone and in 1440 provided him to the bishopric of St. Andrews. Kennedy was thus strongly on the papalist side, at a time when the papacy was threatened by the conciliar movement, which would have subordinated the Pope to a General Council and which was strongly supported in Scotland. James I himself, at least until his last year, had strenuously resisted papal encroachments, but as long as Kennedy was influential there was no revival of antipapal legislation. No doubt the Bishop, besides being a papalist by conviction, saw the value of papal support at times when the monarchy was weak.

Kennedy was always closely in touch with the court: just as he had escorted Princess Margaret to France for her marriage in 1436, so he escorted Princess Mary to Zealand for hers in 1444. During James II's personal reign, the King is said to have relied much on Kennedy's sage counsel. While it may be only a picturesque tale which relates how the Bishop, by taking up a sheaf of arrows, showed the King that although his enemies were irresistible in combination yet they could be broken one by one, that is certainly the policy which James pursued. Kennedy is credited also with a statesmanlike influence in the minority of James III, and his death while that minority continued removed an element of stability and experience from the government.

Kennedy's name lives, above all, for his work at St. Andrews University. In 1450 he founded the College of St. Salvator, for which he built a splendid church and to which he made many munificent gifts, including a bell called 'Katharine' which may lie behind the legendary figure of 'Kate Kennedy', the bishop's niece, who still figures in undergraduate festivities at St. Andrews. The Bishop is said to have spent as much on a ship, 'the Bishop's Barge', as on his chapel, and as much again on his splendid tomb, which still survives in the chapel.

There had always been an element of rivalry between the Bishops of St. Andrews and Glasgow, and it is probably significant that on 7 January 1451, almost immediately after Kennedy's foundation of St. Salvator's, a bull establishing a university at Glasgow was obtained by William Turnbull (c. 1400–54), who had become Bishop of Glasgow in 1448.

A. I. Dunlop, *Life and Times of James Kennedy*, 1950.

James III, King of Scots (1452–1488), eldest surviving son of James II, was born in May 1452. During his minority, authority was exercised for a time by his mother (until her death in 1463) and by Bishop Kennedy (until his death in 1465). There were many troubles, arising partly from the relations of Scotland with the two English parties of York and Lancaster, and the Yorkist Edward IV in 1462 made a treaty with the Lord of the Isles and the exiled Earl of Douglas by which Scotland was to be partitioned between them, as English vassals. The Scottish government gradually came round to an accommodation with Edward, so neutralizing those troublesome subjects.

41

In the later years of the minority, power lay with the Boyd family. Robert Boyd, son of Sir Thomas Boyd of Kilmarnock, had been created Lord Boyd on 18 July 1454. On the death of James II he was one of the Regents appointed to act in the minority, and he several times took part in the negotiation of truces with England. In 1466 his brother, Sir Alexander, was appointed instructor to the King in military exercises, and on 10 July Lord Boyd and Sir Alexander in effect kidnapped the King and carried him to Edinburgh Castle, of which Sir Alexander was keeper. The King, on 13 October, gave his public approval to the Boyds' action, and a few days later Parliament declared Lord Boyd sole Governor of the realm. In August 1467 Boyd was appointed Chamberlain, and he went on embassies to England and to Denmark, the latter being to conclude the treaty of marriage between James III and the Princess Margaret, by which the Norwegian crown's lands and rights in Orkney were pledged as part of her dowry. Boyd's son, Sir Thomas, who had married the King's sister, Mary, in 1467 and had been created Earl of Arran, went to Denmark to bring the princess to Scotland, where she married James on 13 July 1469. During his absence, the Boyds' enemies threatened their ascendancy, and Arran, warned by his wife before he landed at Leith, returned to Denmark. The Boyds were condemned by Parliament in November 1469. Lord Boyd was sentenced to death, but found safety in England until his death about 1481. Arran was forfeited, but lurked on the continent and in London until he died about 1473. His wife, Princess Mary, had no children by him, but she married James Hamilton of Cadzow, who had become 1st Lord Hamilton in 1445; their son was created Earl of Arran and their daughter, Mary, married the 2nd Earl of Lennox, so transmitting a place in the royal succession to that family.

James III has been traditionally reproached for his patronage of 'low-born favourites', some of whom were in truth cultivated men whose society was attractive to a King who had intellectual and artistic interests and who inherited from his mother a devotion to the Church. Besides, his reign was one which saw a great growth of Scottish prosperity, reflected in the creation of many new burghs and in the erection of many fine buildings, especially collegiate churches. James's tastes and his favourites alike fit into this context, and so many developments associated with the next reign had their beginnings in this that James III has some claim to be considered a Renaissance prince.

The traditional account of the reign goes on to relate that the

King's brothers, Alexander, created Duke of Albany in 1458, and John, created Earl of Mar in 1459, possessed qualities of virile leadership which the King lacked, but we have far too little evidence to determine whether there is any truth in this. At any rate, Albany and Mar were imprisoned on some suspicion, but, while Mar died in prison, possibly murdered (1479), Albany escaped from Edinburgh Castle to France and then made his way to England, where he was accepted as a tool by Edward IV, who designated him 'Alexander IV, King of Scots'. In 1482 he accompanied an English army which invaded Scotland. James set out to meet it, but at Lauder his nobles took the opportunity to press their demands for the dismissal of the unpopular favourites, and hanged them over the bridge. Albany was then for a time dominant, but the King soon recovered his authority. Albany returned to England and was forfeited, but in 1484 he invaded Scotland again, this time in conjunction with James, 9th Earl of Douglas, only to be routed at Lochmaben (22 July). Douglas was captured, Albany escaped to France, where he died in 1485. After a short time troubles revived, and in 1488 James had to face a coalition of nobles who defeated him at Sauchieburn (11 June). After the battle the King, in the words of the parliamentary record, 'happinit to be slane'—murdered, it appears, by a man who, posing as a priest, came to shrive the King after he had been thrown from his horse.

James was not destitute of either energy or intelligence, for he could act with decision, and he, like his father, tried to counterbalance the older peers, by creating new peers, some of whom gave him strong support to the end. Some of his troubles evidently arose from monetary difficulties in an expanding economy, but the King was accused of doing nothing to ease them by hoarding bullion in a 'black box'. Another reason for his unpopularity may have been his readiness—perhaps far-sighted—to come to terms with England and to entertain many proposals for intermarriage with the English royal families.

Queen Margaret, a woman of such noted piety that she was a candidate for canonization, died at Stirling in 1486, leaving three sons—James IV; another James, born about 1475, Duke of Ross from 1488 and Archbishop of St. Andrews from 1497 until his death in 1504; and John, Earl of Mar from 1486 until his death in 1503.

G. Donaldson, *Scottish Kings;* R. L. Mackie, *James IV, King of Scots*, chap. 1.

Angus, Archibald, 5th Earl of ('Bell-the-Cat') (*c.* 1449–1513), succeeded his father, the 4th Earl, on 12 March 1463. Owing to the general dearth of information for this period, little is known of his activities for some years after he attained his majority in 1470. It appears that his sympathies lay with Alexander, Duke of Albany, rather than with King James III. Though he was active enough in the national cause by raiding Northumberland in 1480, yet in 1482, when the King led an army towards the Border to meet Albany and the English, Angus seized the opportunity to press on James the nobles' demands for redress of grievances. At Lauder there occurred the incident which gave Angus his nickname of Bell-the-Cat. The story is that when the disgruntled nobles agreed to force the King to dismiss his favourites, the objection was raised that they were like the mice who decided that it would be in their interest to hang a bell round the cat's neck but could find none of their number to take the necessary action. 'I will bell the cat,' said Angus, and he took the lead in the actions which ended in the hanging of several of the King's favourites over Lauder Bridge. Angus collaborated with Albany in 1482–3, but little more is known of him until 1488, when he sided, perhaps reluctantly, with the opposition which led to James III's death. At first in favour with James IV, he engaged in treasonable dealings with England which led in 1491 to his disgrace and his loss of the lordship of Liddesdale, on the south-west march. Reconciliation with the King was followed by his appointment as Chancellor (1493–7) and warden of the middle marches, but in 1501–2 he was again under arrest. In 1513 he advised the King against the invasion of England, but despite his age he loyally followed him in the earlier stages of the campaign, and two of his sons, one of them his heir, were killed at Flodden. In the crisis which followed, Angus was one of the advisers of the Queen Mother and was Provost of Edinburgh. He died about the end of November 1513, not long surviving Flodden, and was succeeded by his grandson.

James IV, King of Scots (1473–1513), was born, probably at Stirling, on 17 March 1473, and so was over fifteen when his father was killed. No Regent was appointed, and Scotland had the unusual experience of twenty-five years of personal rule by an able King. He had an intelligent, inquiring mind, and showed it by his practical interest in scientific experiments, in surgery and in dentistry. Under his patronage there came into being the Royal College of Surgeons of Edinburgh (1506), King's College, Aberdeen (1495), and St. Leonard's College, St. Andrews (1512). In 1496 an act was passed

44

making it compulsory for men of substance to have their sons educated in arts and law, and in 1508 the printing press was introduced. Literature flourished, with the poets Robert Henryson, William Dunbar and Gavin Douglas. The King was interested in building too: it was in his reign that the first royal residence was erected at Holyrood, and he left his mark on Linlithgow Palace as well. He won popularity by his accessibility to all ranks of his subjects and his humanity to the poor and unfortunate.

In James's reign the Court of Session took very much its final form as something like a permanent court with professional judges, and his firm policy towards the Highlands (including the suppression of the lordship of the Isles) was accompanied by the establishment of additional sheriffs and justices in the west. James pointed a new way to enriching the crown by exploiting the concession received by James III in 1487, whereby the Pope agreed to take the King's wishes into account when filling high offices in the Scottish Church. James's younger brother, the Duke of Ross, was appointed Archbishop of St. Andrews when he was only twenty-one, and on his death, unconsecrated, seven years later, the King's illegitimate son, Alexander, was appointed to succeed him at the age of eleven. Alexander was sent to Italy to study under Erasmus, and in 1512 consented to the foundation of St. Leonard's College at St. Andrews, but he fell with his father at Flodden when he was still no more than twenty. In 1510 he had been appointed Chancellor. Both Alexander and his uncle also held various abbeys, the revenues of which indirectly enriched the crown.

In his foreign policy, James was never averse from military adventure, and a considerable proportion of his income was expended on armaments. His best-known ship, the great *Michael*, was reputed to be the largest vessel of her time, and it was said that all the woods of Fife were cut down to build her. In artillery, too, James had skilled advice, and he formed a train of cannon which impressed the English into whose hands they fell at his death. He sent men to assist his brother-in-law, the King of Denmark, against the Swedes, and probably encouraged his sea-captains to attack the Lübeckers, who were allies of the Swedes. In 1495, when Perkin Warbeck, who claimed to be a scion of the house of York, came to Scotland, James took up his cause, and next year invaded England on his behalf.

Yet James had no desire to see a European war. In 1502 he concluded with England a 'Treaty of Perpetual Peace', as part of the settlement which included his marriage to Margaret, daughter of Henry VII, on 8 August 1503. James could reconcile this new

45

obligation, to England, with Scotland's traditional alliance with France, only as long as England and France were at peace. Besides, James was an enthusiast for a crusade against the Turks, who were now threatening central Europe, and he saw himself, with his fine navy, as admiral in a united enterprise. But the Pope, Julius II, was too occupied with power-politics to give such a plan his blessing, and ultimately formed instead a Holy League directed against France. When England joined the Holy League, James formally renewed the Scottish alliance with France, and when an English army invaded France, in 1513, he could not stand aside. Thanks to his popularity, the efficiency of his government and the prosperity of his subjects, he was able to rally the nation, Highland and Lowland alike, and led across the Border over 20,000 men, probably the largest force that had ever left Scotland. But some of James's skilled gunners had gone off with his fleet to France, leaving his valuable cannon to be mishandled, and the Scottish spears proved no match for the English bill and longbow. When battle was joined, at Flodden, James's impetuousness in rushing into action at the head of his own division contributed to a disaster in which he met his death (9 September 1513).

Besides two sons and two daughters who died in infancy, James IV and Queen Margaret had a son who succeeded as James V and another son born posthumously who died before he was two. Of his five illegitimate children, two were boys—Alexander, the boy-Archbishop, son of Margaret Boyd, and James, son of Janet Kennedy. James (1499–1544) was created Earl of Moray in 1501 and, like Alexander, was well educated. In the reign of James V he was lieutenant of the north isles and warden of the east and middle marches, and in the final crisis of the reign he stood by his half-brother against the majority of the nobles. On James V's death he was a member of the council of regency.

R. L. Mackie, *King James IV of Scotland*, 1958.
A. J. Stewart, *Falcon*, 1970.

Harry the Minstrel, or 'Blind Harry' (*fl.* 1470–1492), is remembered as the author of narrative verses on *The Acts and Deeds of the illustrious and valiant champion, Sir William Wallace*. There is an account of him by John Major (1470–1550): 'Henry, who was blind from his birth, in the time of my infancy composed the whole book of William Wallace, and committed to writing in vulgar poetry, in which he was well skilled, the things that were commonly related of him. For my own part, I give only partial credit to writings of this description. By the recitation of these, however, in the presence of men of the highest rank, he procured, as he indeed deserved, food and raiment'. The poet is not, however, entirely unknown to record, for the *Accounts of the Lord High Treasurer* mention small payments to him between 1490 and 1492, and recent research indicates that he was not blind from birth, that he had a fair education and that he was of considerable social standing. The minstrel himself declared that he based his work on that of John Blair, a Benedictine monk of Dunfermline, who had been educated at Dundee and Paris and who was a contemporary of Wallace. Harry's expressed intention was to warn the Scots against England and against those Scots who favoured an English alliance—a context which fits with the middle and later years of the reign of James III. About twenty editions of the poem were published from the sixteenth century to the eighteenth, and it undoubtedly did a great deal to shape Scottish opinion, or at any rate sentiment, in an anti-English direction.

Matthew P. McDiarmid (ed.), *Hary's Wallace*, Scot. Text Soc., 1967–9.

Henryson, Robert (*c.* 1430–1500), a noted poet of whose biography hardly anything is known, can with some confidence be identified with a schoolmaster of Dunfermline. From his style of 'Maister' it can be inferred that he took the degree of Master of Arts, very likely on the continent, and as his writings show evidence of legal, as well as medical, knowledge, he may well have been the Robert Henryson, Master of Arts and Bachelor in Decreets, who joined Glasgow University, probably to lecture on law, in 1462. His baccalaureate may possibly have been from Rome. His works which have survived include *Orpheus and Eurydice, The Testament of Cresseid, Robene and Makyne* and *Morall Fabillis,* the last based on Aesop but with a strong native flavour and throwing light on social conditions of Henryson's day. Henryson is usually said to have continued the 'Chaucerian tradition', and his *Cresseid* is related to or inspired by Chaucer's *Troilus and Cressida,* but a century had not passed without bringing many changes, and there is much in Henryson's poems which reflects the quite new atmosphere which was coming in with the development of humanism in the late fifteenth century.

John MacQueen, *Robert Henryson,* 1967.

Dunbar, William (*c.* 1460–1514), described as the most 'professional' of early Scottish poets, was a native of Lothian and graduated Master of Arts, probably at St. Andrews in 1479. He was a priest, but it is doubtful if he was, as often said, a Franciscan friar. He had evidently rendered some services to the government before 1500, possibly in missions to the continent, and he was in England in 1501 in the course of the negotiations leading to an Anglo-Scottish treaty and the marriage of James IV to Margaret Tudor (which he celebrated in *The Thrissill and the Rois*). The King rewarded Dunbar, perhaps partly for his poetry and partly for other services, with a pension which rose from £10 yearly in 1500 to £80 in 1510, but Dunbar perpetually complained of being inadequately recompensed. He disappears from record after 1513, but the date of his death is unknown. In his verse, the influence of Chaucer is still evident, for example in *Twa mariit wemen and the Wedo*, but the greater sophistication and complexity of the work of Lydgate are reflected in *The Golden Targe*. He had command of a wide range of forms and metres, some derived from French and Italian sources. He was at his most entertaining, if not at the highest levels of poetic attainment, in satirical verses like *The Fenyeit Freir of Tungland* (an attack on John Damian) and *The Flyting of Dunbar and Kennedie*. His *Lament for the Makaris*, with its refrain 'Timor mortis conturbat me', movingly recalls a number of earlier poets who are not otherwise known. At his best he achieves formal neatness with mastery of style and language, and his *Of the Nativitie of Christ* is still a singularly effective Christmas carol.

J. W. Baxter, *William Dunbar*, 1952.

Douglas, Gavin (*c.* 1474–1522), poet and Bishop of Dunkeld, was the third son of the 5th Earl of Angus ('Bell-the-Cat'). He studied at the universities of St. Andrews and Paris and about 1496 was appointed to the parsonage of Hauch or Prestonkirk. By 1503 he had been promoted to the provostry of the collegiate church of St. Giles, Edinburgh. When, after the death of James IV at Flodden, Queen Margaret married Gavin's nephew, the 6th Earl of Angus, Gavin was marked out for high favour and for a political career. He was nominated to the archbishopric of St. Andrews, as well as to the office of Chancellor, but a change in the political situation and the flight of Margaret and Angus to England prevented him from gaining possession of those offices. In 1515, however, he became Bishop of Dunkeld, though he had to use force to evict a rival claimant, a brother of the Earl of Atholl. Gavin went to France with the Governor Albany in 1517, perhaps as a kind of hostage for Angus. On his return to Scotland, his continued involvement in the tortuous affairs of the time led to his presence at the 'Cleanse the Causeway' affair (1520), when the Douglases and the Hamiltons came to blows in the streets of Edinburgh and the Bishop tried to mediate. After Albany returned from France in 1521, Gavin was exiled from Scotland and received at the English court. He died in London and was buried in the chapel of the Savoy.

In his poetry, Douglas skilfully adapted his native Scots, with an admixture of foreign words when their use was indispensable, to produce some very polished verse, notably in *The Palace of Honour* (partly based on Petrarch and Boccaccio) and a translation of Virgil's *Aeneid*, written in 1512–13 but not published until 1553. The translation is accompanied by prologues to the various books which reveal the poet's appreciation of the Scottish scene. It is doubtful if *King Hart*, often attributed to Douglas, was in fact his work.

There is a memoir in Gavin Douglas, *Poetical Works* (1874); and a biographical note in David F. C. Coldwell, *Selections from Gavin Douglas*, 1964.

Damian, John (*fl.* 1504–1513), described as 'a French leech', but possibly an Italian, recorded as 'Damianus de Falcutiis', was an alchemist who impressed James IV by his promises to transmute baser metals into gold, and he was supplied by the King with money and material for his experiments. In 1504 James had him appointed Abbot of Tongland. He went on to claim that he had discovered how to fly, and took off from the ramparts of Stirling, with wings made from birds' feathers strapped to his arms. When he was fortunate enough to land in a midden and merely break his thigh, he offered the explanation that he had made the mistake of using the feathers not of eagles which sought the sky, but of hens which sought the midden. He resigned his abbacy in 1509, but a pension of 200 gold ducats out of it was reserved to him and he was still in Scotland after Flodden.

Elphinstone, William (*c.* 1431–1514), Bishop of Aberdeen and Chancellor, a grandson of the laird of Pittendreich in Sterlingshire, was born and educated at Glasgow, where he took his M.A. in 1462. He became parson of Kirkmichael before going in 1465 to study law at Paris and then at Orleans. He returned to Scotland about 1471, to be made 'official' (that is, the Bishop's judicial deputy) at Glasgow, and in 1478 he became 'official' of Lothian. He supported James III, who made him a Privy Councillor and a judge and sent him on embassies to France and England. He became James's Chancellor in February 1488, but laid down the office on the King's death in June; under James IV he was again employed on embassies to the continent and to England and was for a time keeper of the privy seal. James III nominated him to the bishopric of Ross on 3 August 1481, but he had still not been consecrated when he was translated to Aberdeen on 19 March 1483, and indeed was not consecrated until 1488 at the earliest. At Aberdeen he completed the central tower of the cathedral and planned a choir and transepts, but he is best known for his foundation of King's College, Aberdeen, which received a papal bull making it a university in 1495. It was intended that provision should be made for the teaching of theology, canon and civil law and medicine, as well as arts. Elphinstone's name is associated, though without evidence, with the 'Education Act' of 1496, making it compulsory for men of substance to send their sons to school. He was responsible for the preparation of the *Aberdeen Breviary* (1509–10), one of the first books to be printed in Scotland and designed to take the place of the Sarum Breviary hitherto used there; the King issued an order in 1507 that missals, manuals and other liturgical books with legends of Scottish saints, collected by Bishop Elphinstone, should be used in time to come, to the exclusion of books of the Sarum use. Elphinstone advised King James against the Flodden adventure, and after the disaster, it was said, he was never again seen to smile. During James's reign Elphinstone was passed over for ecclesiastical promotion, but on 5 August 1514 the Scottish council recommended him for the archbishopric of St. Andrews. However, he died at Edinburgh on 25 October 1514, in his eighty-fourth year.

Leslie J. Macfarlane, 'William Elphinstone', in *Aberdeen University Review*, xxxix, 1–18, 1961.

Chapman (or Chepman), Walter (*c.* 1473–*c.* 1538), was a pioneer of printing in Scotland. He first appears on record in 1494, as a clerk in the office of the King's secretary, but he was a merchant who traded in timber, wool, cloth and other articles and made enough money to buy the estate of Priestfield or Prestonfield (1509) as well as other property. Many references show that he was closely associated with the court and high in the royal favour. It was Chapman who supplied the money for the establishment in the Cowgate, Edinburgh, of the first Scottish printing press, in 1507, and Andrew

Myllar brought to the enterprise the knowledge of the craft which he had learned in France. The King gave the partners a licence to print and the right to prevent the importation of books from other countries, and their monopoly was reaffirmed in 1509. In 1508 the first productions, some verses of Henryson and Dunbar, appeared, and the greatest work of the press which has survived is the *Aberdeen Breviary* (1510). In 1513 Chapman founded a chaplainry of St. John the Evangelist in 'the Chapman aisle' in the church of St. Giles, Edinburgh. In 1514–15 he was dean of gild of Edinburgh and in 1526 James V presented him with a tavern in the burgh. He was buried in 'the Chapman aisle'.

Barton, Robert (*c.* 1470–1540), merchant, naval commander and administrator, was one of the first laymen of middle-class rank to become prominent in Scottish affairs. Son of John Barton, a Leith seaman who in 1473 commanded the *Yellow Caravel*, one of James III's ships, Robert was himself engaged in mercantile activity by 1492. For many years after 1494 he and his brothers, John and Andrew, were intermittently engaged in privateering, partly in terms of letters of marque which had been granted to them to avenge the loss suffered by their father at the hands of the Portuguese about 1470, and they gained great repute as daring seamen who did much mischief to ships of many countries. But the brothers engaged in peaceful commerce as well—in so far as peace and war could be distinguished at sea—and Robert began a career of service to James IV, from whom he received trading privileges and for whom he carried out many commissions, especially in the purchase of materials and even ships for the royal fleet. Also in James IV's reign Robert began the practice of lending money to nobles, lairds and burgesses and sometimes acquiring their land when they failed to repay, so that in the course of time he became the owner of extensive estates, centred largely on Over Barnton, of which he had a crown charter in 1508.

As a naval commander Robert first appeared in 1502, in an expedition to help King Hans of Denmark, and he served also in expeditions to the Western Isles in 1504 and 1505. In 1511 Andrew Barton was so destructive of English shipping that Henry VIII retaliated by sending Sir Edward Howard against him, and in the engagement which followed Andrew was fatally wounded and lost both his ships to the enemy. This episode was one factor which led to a worsening of Anglo-Scottish relations and in the end to Flodden. In 1512 Robert was serving in the French navy and attacking

English ships, and when in Scotland for a time in 1513 he may have helped to sway the King towards war. His brother John was with the Scottish fleet which set out for France before Flodden, but Robert himself had apparently returned to France earlier. In 1514 he was on a mission to France to invite the Duke of Albany to come to Scotland, and when Albany became Governor of the realm Robert supported him.

Albany appointed Robert to the offices of Comptroller of the Kingdom and Custumar of Edinburgh (1516), and Robert began an energetic administration. He held the office of Comptroller until 1525 and again from 1529 until 1531, and he held the other great financial office, that of Treasurer, from 1529 to 1530. He was thus in office through many changes of government, and seems to have been able to work with everyone except the Earl of Angus. It was Angus's uncle who, quite unjustifiably, held it a fault in Albany that he had appointed 'a very pirate and sea reiver' to the office of Comptroller. The period was not conducive to sound finance, and when Barton demitted office as Treasurer he was £6,779 out of pocket. His prospects of repayment were not good, but he was to some extent compensated by continued royal favour, which brought certain material advantages.

W. Stanford Reid, *Skipper from Leith*, 1962.

Wood, Sir Andrew, of Largo (*c.* 1460–1540), naval commander, is believed to have been born in Largo, and he lived much in Leith, from which he traded to the continent with his ships the *Flower* and the *Yellow Caravel*. In an age when there was no royal navy and when there was little if any distinction between trading vessels and warships, Wood served James III, who granted him the lands of Largo in 1483 and knighted him a few years later. Wood was loyal to James to the end of his reign. But once James IV was established on the throne Wood served him with equal loyalty. As commander of the *Yellow Caravel* he defeated an English fleet in the Firth of Forth in 1489 and later he captured the English admiral Stephen Bull with his three ships, after a running fight from St. Abb's Head to the mouth of the Tay. Wood was employed by the King on his expeditions in 1495 and 1504 to the western isles, where ships had an important part to play. When the King built his famous ship, the great *Michael*, Wood was her commander, but she never saw action. In the minority of James V, Sir Andrew acted as an envoy to the continent, and he was still alive in 1538. It is said that when he was living in retirement in Largo in his old age he had a canal cut from his home to the church, so that he could go there by water.

James V, King of Scots (1512–1542), son of James IV and Margaret Tudor, was born at Linlithgow on 10 April 1512 and became King on his father's death, at the age of seventeen months. During his minority the country suffered through the conflicting interests of Scottish magnates, the vagaries of the Queen Mother, and the effects of the frequent changes in the relations between England and France, so that there were only the briefest spells of stable government. The King's experiences in his youth affected his whole character and outlook. He was the product not only of political instability but of a broken home, for although Queen Margaret married Archibald Douglas, 6th Earl of Angus, as her second husband, she was soon seeking a divorce. Any influence Margaret may have had on the King would have been to instil a hatred of Angus, who, moreover, attained a dominating position in the kingdom when James was fourteen and incurred the boy's implacable hostility by keeping him a captive for two years. The mere fact that Angus represented the English interest may well have done much to turn James against it. The boy's education cannot have been as neglected as is sometimes said, for he had as his tutor Gavin Dunbar (d. 1547),[1] who became Archbishop of Glasgow in 1524 and Chancellor in 1528; on the other hand, the boy can have had little moral guidance, and Angus was accused of deliberately encouraging his stepson in a precocious career of vice.

James's policy during his personal reign (1528–42) was largely determined by the impoverished state of the crown and the acquisitiveness to which this led: 'This King inclineth daily more and more to covetousness,' it was once remarked. Both in his dealings with the Church and in his foreign policy James was therefore dominated by the desire for money. At a time when the Lutheran Reformation had begun to affect Scotland, and when Henry VIII's proceedings led him on to repudiate the papal supremacy, James's attitude was orthodoxy—at a price. By playing on the fears of the Pope, he was permitted to levy two heavy taxes on the Church, one on the pretext of the defence of the realm, the other on the pretext of the endowment of the Court of Session as a College of Justice (1532), and he also had a free hand to distribute the wealthiest Scottish abbeys among his illegitimate infants. James's foreign policy was directed

---

1. To be distinguished from his namesake (d. 1532) who was Bishop of Aberdeen.

53

towards obtaining a well-endowed bride. In a period when the great powers of Europe were engaged in successive wars, and when there was the question of a possible crusade against Henry VIII, Scotland played a part out of all proportion to her wealth and resources, and James found himself wooed by each sovereign in turn. After negotiations for marriages to kinswomen of the Emperor Charles V, to Catharine de' Medici and to Henry VIII's daughter, Mary, he ultimately married two French brides—the Princess Madeleine, daughter of France I (1 January 1537), who survived her arrival in Scotland for only six weeks, and then Mary of Guise-Lorraine (June 1538), and each of them brought him a very substantial dowry. James hoarded much of the wealth he acquired, but he spent lavishly on buildings, and fine work of his reign is to be seen at Falkland and Stirling.

In his internal policy, James was severe against those who broke the law or challenged his authority. The Borders had been more than usually disturbed during the troubled minority, and in the course of the King's personal reign nearly all the Border magnates were under arrest at one time or another. The Borderer who lives in legend and ballad is 'Johnnie Armstrong', who may have been either John Armstrong of Gilknockie, whose hasty execution at Carlanrigg, on the road to Langholm, is assigned to 1529, or 'John Armstrong *alias* Black Jok' (a brother of Thomas Armstrong of Mangerton), who was sentenced to death on 1 April 1530. The story goes that Armstrong and thirty-six followers appeared before James arrayed in such finery that the King exclaimed, 'What wants yon knave that a king should have?' and ordered all of them to be hanged. Armstrong, it is said, asked in vain for pardon, and then lamented,

> 'I have asked grace at a graceless face,
> There is nane for my men and me.'

He went on, 'Had I known, Sir, that you would have taken my life this day, I should have lived upon the Borders in despite both of you and King Harry.' James V took energetic action in the north and west of his kingdom as well, and showed unusual enterprise in cruising round the northern and western isles in 1540, arresting various chiefs *en route*.

But James's justifiable severity passed too easily into vindictiveness, and in some instances his cupidity for the property of wealthy men stimulated him to action against them on various pretexts. He favoured middle-class men, some of them able administrators, rather than the nobles. The counterpart of James's attitude to the nobles, whom latterly he seems to have alienated almost completely, is his reputation as The Poor Man's King, popular with his humble subjects, among whom he wandered in disguise. It was, after all, mainly those who had property who had reason to fear 'so sore a dread king and so ill-beloved of his subjects'. His measures against law-breakers may have gained him some popularity, and there was certainly legislation in favour of the lower ranks of the people, though most of it can be paralleled in other reigns.

James's French marriages signified that he had fallen under the influence of the French and Roman Catholic faction. Henry VIII, anxious that Scotland should not be used as a base against him, endeavoured to entice him away from the French alliance. There were many in Scotland who agreed with Henry, and the later years of the reign saw the emergence of two clearly marked parties, the divisions between whom go a long way to explain the disaster with which the reign ended. In 1542 Henry VIII and his Scottish supporters prevailed on James to agree to a meeting at York. The Scottish clergy, fearful of the possible consequences, made lavish offers and succeeded in making James break his appointment. Henry, in his fury, launched an invasion of Scotland, and James had to raise an army to counter it. Many joined the host 'against their hearts', others did not join it at all, and the nobles in particular now felt that they had more reason than ever to avoid risking a repetition of Flodden. It was an army financed by the clergy and commanded by the last of the King's favourites, Oliver Sinclair, that was routed at Solway Moss (24 November 1542). James dragged himself wearily to his Queen at Linlithgow, then to Falkland, quite evidently with no will to live, and he died on 14 December 1542.

By Mary of Guise James had two sons, whose deaths in infancy in 1541 may have contributed to his breakdown, and a daughter, Mary, born six days before his death. His illegitimate sons were: James (I), Commendator of Kelso and Melrose (d. 1557); James (II), Commendator of St. Andrews Priory and later Earl of Moray; James (III), who died young; Robert (I), Commendator of Holyrood and later Earl of Orkney; Robert (II), Commendator of Whithorn (d. 1580); John, Commendator of Coldingham (d. 1563); and Adam, Commendator of the Charterhouse of Perth (d. 1575).

G. Donaldson, *Scotland: James V to James VII*, 1965.
Caroline Bingham, *James V*, 1971.

Albany, John Stewart, Duke of (*c.* 1484–1536), was the son of Alexander, Duke of Albany, brother of James III, by his second wife, Anne de la Tour. As Duke Alexander's first marriage to Catharine, daughter of the Earl of Caithness, was regarded as invalid, the death of James IV in 1513 made Albany heir to the Scottish throne after the infant James V and his younger brother, who died in 1515. Immediately after Flodden the Scots urged Albany to 'come home' and lead them once more against the English, but he did not arrive in Scotland until May 1515 and then (as France had meantime come to terms with England) he brought advice to keep the peace. He was proclaimed Governor by Parliament on 15 July 1515, and on 13 November 1516 Parliament formally acknowledged him as his father's only legitimate son and therefore heir presumptive. He went to France in June 1517 and concluded the Treaty of Rouen, providing for mutual assistance between France and Scotland and for the marriage of James V to a daughter of Francis I, but France at this point renewed her peace with England, refused to implement the treaty and detained Albany in France until November 1521. Then, with a further change in French policy, he was released to stimulate the Scots into invading England. He led two expeditions (between which he again visited France to bring men, munitions and money), but found that the Scots were now far from enthusiastic about risking a repetition of Flodden. He left Scotland finally in May 1524. Thereafter, besides commanding a French army in Italy, Albany continued to act as a Scottish agent on the continent and had considerable influence on James V's diplomacy. Thus, he favoured a match between James and Catharine de' Medici, who was his niece, though he was forced in the end to negotiate her marriage to the future Henry II of France; and he had a hand in the negotiations which led the Pope to authorize James to levy heavy subsidies from the Scottish Church. Albany married in 1505 his first cousin, Anne de la Tour, who died in 1524 without issue. He died on 2 July 1536.

M. W. Stuart, *The Scot who was a Frenchman*, 1940.

Beaton, James (*c.* 1480–1539), son of John Beaton of Balfour in Fife, graduated at St. Andrews in 1493 and first appears as a dignitary in the Scottish Church as chantor of Caithness (1497–9) and provost of the collegiate church of Bothwell (1502–3). In 1504 he was appointed to the abbey of Dunfermline, obviously at the instance of the King, to whom he was a valued servant. From 1505 to 1509 he was Treasurer of the Kingdom. In 1508 he was appointed to the bishopric of Galloway, but before he was consecrated for that see he was elected to the archbishopric of Glasgow and was consecrated in 1509. He now resigned Dunfermline, so that it could go to the King's illegitimate son, Alexander, who also became Chancellor of the Kingdom, but was killed at Flodden in 1513. Immediately thereafter, Archbishop Beaton crowned the infant James V and became Chancellor. Being a supporter of the French alliance, he found himself with a competitor for the chancellorship in the person of Gavin Douglas, put forward by the Queen-Mother, Margaret Tudor, and her brother, Henry VIII, but the pro-French party prevailed and Beaton was much in favour when Scotland was governed by John, Duke of Albany. He received the revenues of the abbeys of Kilwinning in 1516 and Arbroath in 1518. When Albany went to France in 1517, Beaton was one of the Regents appointed to act in his absence, but unity could not be preserved among them, and Beaton, as a supporter of the Earl of Arran against the Earl of Angus, was involved in the affray in Edinburgh between their followers, known as 'Cleanse the Causeway' (1520), when, according to a familiar tale, the Archbishop's conscience was heard to 'clatter' as he struck his breast and revealed that he had a suit of armour under his clerical garb. It was while Albany was once more responsible for the government of Scotland that Beaton was promoted from Glasgow to St. Andrews (1522). On Albany's final departure and the seizure of power by the anti-French faction, Beaton was for a time in prison, but he retained the office of Chancellor until 1526. There can be little doubt that he deserves credit for preserving a stable element in Scottish administration throughout most of the long minority of James V. James began to rule in person in 1528, but Beaton seems never to have enjoyed the full confidence of the King, who preferred his own former tutor, Gavin Dunbar, Archbishop of Glasgow. In the comparative retirement of his later years, Beaton took an interest in the development of St. Andrews University and was responsible for the initiation of what finally became St. Mary's College.

Herkless and Hannay, *Archbishops of St. Andrews*, iii, 1910.

Angus, Archibald Douglas, 6th Earl of (*c.* 1489–1557), son of the Master of Angus, who was killed at Flodden, was the grandson of the 5th Earl ('Bell-the Cat'), whom he succeeded in 1514. He married (6 August 1514) Margaret Tudor, widow of James IV, and they endeavoured, with the support of Henry VIII, to rule the country, but in terms of James IV's will Margaret's rights as tutrix to her son had expired with her re-marriage, and in 1515, when John, Duke of Albany, became Governor, they were driven into England. Angus was soon reconciled to Albany, and when the latter went to France in 1517 Angus was a member of the commission of regency. He showed so little capacity for statesmanship that he was described by his uncle Gavin as 'a young witless fool', and instead of co-operating with the other Regents, including the Earl of Arran, he caused trouble in the south-east, one incident in which was the 'Cleanse the Causeway' affair in Edinburgh in 1520, when Angus and the Douglases drove the Hamiltons (followers of Arran) from the town. He soon had to withdraw to France. When Albany finally retired from Scotland, and James was 'erected' as King by Arran and Margaret, Angus was named as one of the Queen's counsellors, but he and his wife had been estranged since 1517 and there was no hope of their acting together. After a period in which the realm was 'marvellously divided', Angus obtained control of the King's person at the end of 1525 and dominated Scotland for two and a half years. On the King's escape (May 1528), Angus had to flee to England, where he remained for fifteen years, while James pursued his kin with relentless severity. After James's death, Angus came back in January 1543 and acted as an English agent, subsidized by Henry VIII, until the end of 1544. Then, perhaps because the Scottish government succeeded in outbidding Henry, Angus took the national side, and led the Scots to victory at Ancrum (27 February 1545). He commanded the Scottish van at Pinkie (10 September 1547), but distrust between him and the Governor, Arran (son of Angus's old rival of the 1520s), may have contributed to a disastrous defeat. By Margaret Tudor Angus had a daughter Margaret (1515–78), who married the 4th Earl of Lennox and became mother of Lord Darnley.

Hamilton, Patrick (1504–1528), Lutheran preacher, was the son of Sir Patrick Hamilton of Kincavel, natural brother of Lord Hamilton, and Catharine Stewart, daughter of Alexander, Duke of Albany, brother of James III. As a boy he was made Commendator of the abbey of Fearn. He went to France, graduated at Paris in 1520 and then studied at Louvain. On the continent he absorbed Lutheran doctrines. He returned to Scotland in 1523 and advocated reformed theology at St. Andrews until he had to flee in 1527, this time to Germany, where he met Luther, Melanchthon and other reformers. He published a set of Latin theses, long known as 'Patrick's Places', containing a digest of reformed theology. When he came back to

Scotland once more, Hamilton was tried for heresy, convicted, and burned at St. Andrews on 29 February 1528. Both his teaching and his martyrdom made a considerable impression, and the result was to stimulate the spread of reforming doctrines.

Peter Lorimer, *Patrick Hamilton*, 1857.

Major (or Mair), John (1470–1550), historian and philosopher, born at Gleghornie near North Berwick, studied for a time at Cambridge and in 1493 went on to Paris, where he graduated M.A. in 1496. In 1518 he returned to Scotland to become professor of theology at Glasgow and in 1522 removed to St. Andrews. From 1525 to 1533 he was again in Paris, but thereafter settled at St. Andrews, where he was Provost of St. Salvator's College. Major's best-known work in later times has been his *Historia Majoris Britanniae* (which can be read either as 'The History of Greater Britain' or 'Major's History of Britain'), completed shortly before he left Paris in 1518 and printed there in 1521. He treats of both English and Scottish history, and was to some extent a pamphleteer of the cause of Anglo-Scottish friendship. His approach as an historian was more critical or at any rate less credulous than that of his predecessors. In so far as his political philosophy emerges, it is to the effect that authority derived from the people and was not vested in kings. Major was also aware of the need for reform in the Church, and in his *Disputationes de Potestate Papae et Concilii* (Disputations about the Power of the Pope and the Council) he expressed his opposition to the immersion of clerics in civil affairs. Some of his works did little more than reflect the continuing preoccupation of the universities with antiquated philosophy: in 1519 he published a Commentary on the first and second books of the Sentences of Peter Lombard and in 1521 an Introduction to Aristotle's Dialectics. His latest work of note was *In Quatuor Evangelia Expositiones luculentae* (1529)—a commentary on the four gospels.

A. J. G. Mackay, 'Life' prefixed to *A History of Greater Britain*. Scot. Hist. Soc., 1892.

Boece, Hector (*c.* 1465–1536), born at Dundee, of the family who were lairds of Panbride, was educated first at Dundee grammar school and then at the Universities of St. Andrews and Paris. He became a professor of philosophy at the College of Montacute or Montaigu (1492–8) and made the acquaintance of Erasmus. After Bishop Elphinstone had founded King's College, Aberdeen, he invited Boece to become its Principal, and during his tenure of that office he had some able colleagues—Alexander Galloway (d. 1552), parson of Kinkell and Rector of the College, who is said to have written a description of the Western Isles but is better known for his interest in the adornment of churches with sacrament houses and similar furnishings; his own brother, Arthur Boece, who was tutor in canon law; and John Adamson, a learned Dominican who did much to maintain and revive the scholarly traditions of the order to which he belonged. Boece's *Lives of the Bishops of Aberdeen* was published at Paris in 1522. In undertaking a History of Scotland he may have been stimulated by the example of John Major, who had been his fellow-student at Paris and whose *History of Greater Britain* was published in 1521, but whereas Major had been critical Boece was credulous in the extreme, so that reference has been made to 'that book of marvels which Boece called a History of Scotland', and its author has been characterized as 'the father of lies'. There is certainly much in his accounts of the early centuries of Scottish history which is so far from being substantiated that it is hard to see any source for it except the author's invention. The work, in Latin, was published at Paris in 1527, and it was translated into Scots, at the command of James V, by John Bellenden. Boece received a crown pension of £50 Scots from 1527 to 1534 and was then presented to the parsonage of Fyvie.

Aberdeen University, *Quatercentenary of the Death of Hector Boece*, 1937.

Lindsay, Robert, of Pitscottie (*c.* 1532–1580), is well remembered as the first vernacular prose historian of Scotland, but very little indeed is known of his life. The estate of which he was laird lay in the parish of Ceres, Fife, near Cupar, and he was presumably a cadet of the noble family of Lindsay, possibly a younger son of William Lindsay of Pyotstoun, who was a son of Patrick, 4th Lord Lindsay of the Byres. He is mentioned in records in 1553, 1560 and 1562, and a Robert Lindsay of Pitscottie who died about 1592 may have been his son. His *Historie and Cronicles of Scotland*, covering the period from 1436 to 1575, is noted for the author's credulity and his liking for the picturesque, so that the work is eminently quotable as a source for dramatic, though sometimes not otherwise authenticated, incidents. His work was professedly a continuation of Boece's *History*, and he therefore began with 'the eighteenth book', which is a translation of Boece for the period 1436 to 1460. The account of the period 1460 to 1542 is a compilation from other writers, some of them not extant, and from narratives Pitscottie had heard from his elders, but still showing errors and confusion. Then, from 1542, he writes as a contemporary, and this is the most valuable part of the work. He came of a strongly Protestant family, and his observations, many of them in brief, diary-like entries, reflect his standpoint. The work was not printed until 1728, and it was edited by A. J. G. Mackay for the Scottish Text Society in 1899.

MacGregor, James (d. 1551), churchman and litterateur, was a son of Dougal MacGregor and was born near Fortingal in Perthshire. Father and son were witnesses to a charter in 1511, the latter already a priest and a notary. James became vicar of Fortingal and was Dean of Argyll (or Lismore) from 1514 until his death. He was buried in the church of Kenmore, near Fortingal. He is chiefly remembered for the MS. collection of Gaelic verse known as *The Book of the Dean of Lismore*, which was compiled by him, with the help of his brother Duncan, between 1512 and 1526. Little is known of Duncan except that he was an accomplished scribe and, as his own verse in the compilation shows, a poet trained in the classical mode.

The verse in the *Book of the Dean* falls into three main groups— poems by Scottish authors, poems by Irish authors, and Ossianic ballads, mainly ascribed to heroes of the Fenian cycle and common to both Scotland and Ireland. In a Scottish context the greatest claim on our interest lies with the first group, which is the earliest anthology of Scottish Gaelic poetry that we possess. The poems, ranging in date of composition from *c.* 1310 to *c.* 1520, are, without exception, composed in the syllabic metres of the classical bards. Yet their authors were not all professional poets: Giolla-Colaim Mac-an-ollaimh, represented by three poems, was a court poet of the Lord of the Isles, while Fionnlagh Ruadh was bard to John, chief of Clan Gregor, who died in 1519; on the other hand, the poem which begins the *Book of the Dean* and urged its compilation was composed by Finlay, chief of Clan Macnab (d. 1525). Two women are represented, one the wife of MacNeill of Gigha and the other Isabella, Countess of Argyll, probably the wife of the first Earl. The subject matter is in the main conventional, and includes eulogies, laments, clan poetry, and satires, but there is also a long and interesting composition on 'thigging' (begging by forcible extortion) and another urging the destruction of wolves.

Neil Ross (ed.), *Heroic Poetry from the Book of the Dean of Lismore*, Scottish Gaelic Texts Soc., 1939.

F

Lindsay, Sir David (?1486–1555), Lyon King of Arms and poet, was the son of David Lindsay of the Mount, about three miles from Cupar, Fife. It is assumed that he studied at St. Andrews University, and he was already about the court in some capacity in James IV's reign. In James V's minority he was one of the King's ushers and, though not, at least formally, a tutor to the King, he was a royal 'familiar', who later addressed the King thus:

> Quhen thou was young I bore thee in my arme
> Full tenderlie till thou begouth to gang;
> And in my bed oft happit thee full warme,
> With lute in hand, sine sweitly to thee sang.

Lindsay was out of favour while James was in the hands of his mother and of Angus (1524–8), but during the King's personal rule he became a man of some consequence. By 1530 he was a herald and from that point he was employed in a series of embassies to the Emperor and the Kings of France and England. He was with the King when he went to France to marry Madeleine, on that Queen's death he composed an elegy, and when Mary of Guise arrived in Scotland Lindsay prepared a masque to welcome her. Already in 1535 he had been styled 'Lyon Herald', and by 1542 he was certainly Lyon King of Arms and a knight. He was employed in further embassies in Queen Mary's minority, and in 1546 was associated in some way in the events at St. Andrews after the murder of Cardinal Beaton (on which he wrote *The Tragedy of the Cardinall*).

Most of Lindsay's poems are to some extent tracts for the times, inspired by a love of Scotland and a desire for the country's welfare. *The Dreme* (1528) and *The Complaynt of Schir David Lindsay* (*c.* 1529) are appeals to King James to exercise his office worthily. *The Testament of the Papyngo* (1530) and *Kitteis Confessioun* (before 1542) are satires against the Church. In his greatest work, *The Satire of the Three Estates* (first version not later than 1540, later versions 1552 and 1554), Lindsay castigates the evils in Church, State and society alike in a work of great dramatic power which has been revived with impressive effect in recent years. All the abuses which Lindsay brings out so vividly can be substantiated by other evidence. There can be little doubt that, although the *Satire* was performed before representatives of 'the Establishment', and to their amusement, it must have contributed to the unrest which brought about the Reformation. *The History of Squyer Meldrum*

(1550) is in a different vein from most of Lindsay's works, for it is written in memory of an old friend. In the *Dialogue betuix Experience and ane Courteour* (?1552) and *The Monarche* (1553) we have the satirist again. Although he was such a courtier. Lindsay was in the best sense 'popular', for his heroes seem to be the oppressed lower orders, personified in John the Commonweil, who appears in both *The Dreme* and *The Three Estates*. He shows more originality than any other Scottish poet up to his time, but on the other hand, especially in his longer works, his craftsmanship lacks technical perfection.

W. Murison, *Sir David Lindsay*, 1938.

Mary, Queen of Scots (1542–1587), daughter of James V and Mary of Guise, was born at Linlithgow on 8 December 1542 and became Queen on her father's death six days later. During a temporary ascendancy of a pro-English and reforming party in 1543 she was betrothed to Henry VIII's son, Edward, aged six, but before the end of the year the pro-French and Roman Catholic faction triumphed and the agreement was repudiated. Henry, in retaliation, ordered the devastating invasions of 1544 and 1545 which are known as 'The Rough Wooing'. After a further invasion, and the defeat of the Scots at Pinkie (10 September 1547), Mary was sent for a brief space to the security of the island priory of Inchmahome. The Scots could not expel the English from south-east Scotland by their own resources, and France agreed to give them help, on condition that Mary was sent to France (1548).

In April 1558 she married Francis, the Dauphin, aged fourteen, and secretly agreed that, should she die without issue, her kingdom would fall to the French crown. Her husband succeeded as Francis II in July 1559, but he died on 6 December 1560 and the control of French affairs was taken over by his mother, Catharine de' Medici, who was no friend to Mary. Meanwhile, in Scotland, a revolution had taken place which amounted to the rejection of the French alliance and the papal supremacy, but Mary decided that her best prospects now lay in her native kingdom. On the accession of Elizabeth of England in November 1558, Mary had become heir presumptive to the English crown as grand-daughter of Margaret Tudor: not only so, but Roman Catholics, who did not acknowledge the legality of Henry VIII's marriage to Anne Boleyn, Elizabeth's. mother, thought Mary's claim to England stronger than Elizabeth's.

After landing at Leith (19 August 1561) Mary, on the advice of James Stewart, Earl of Moray, and William Maitland of Lethington, conceded to the reformed Church recognition and modest endowment, while she retained her Mass in her own chapel and prosecuted priests who said Mass elsewhere. Such a moderate, or perhaps equivocal, policy, might commend her to both Roman Catholics and Protestants in Scotland, England and the Continent. While her advisers sought a firm understanding with Elizabeth, there were also negotiations for her marriage to the son of Philip II of Spain and other continental princes. Finally, out of affection rather than policy, she married on 29 July 1567 her first cousin, Lord Darnley, who stood next to her in the English succession.

Mary lost much support by her marriage: the ceremony was a Roman Catholic one, although Darnley was not himself a practising Roman Catholic; Elizabeth professed to be furious, so that those who favoured an understanding with her found their policy thwarted; and Darnley's family had many private enemies among the nobility. Moray and others raised a rebellion, which Mary energetically suppressed, but she was soon estranged from her husband and she relied much on non-aristocratic courtiers, including David Riccio, a musician who had come to Scotland in the train of the ambassador of Savoy and had become Mary's French secretary. Disaffected lords disliked Riccio's influence, Protestants suspected him as a papal agent, and Darnley professed to think the Italian overfamiliar with the Queen. A band of Protestant lords, along with Darnley, murdered Riccio at Holyrood on 9 March 1566, in or near the presence of the Queen, who was six months pregnant. Mary survived the ordeal, and detached Darnley from his allies. Prince James was born on 19 June.

In the later months of 1566 Mary's renewed disgust with her husband was accompanied by her growing favour for James Hepburn, Earl of Bothwell. Soon there was talk of a divorce from Darnley or of more violent means of dissolving the marriage. Mary was certainly aware of schemes for her husband's elimination, but on the whole it seems unlikely that she had foreknowledge of the actual plot which led to his murder at Kirk o' Field on 10 February 1567. The truth about the murder continues to elude historians, but the Casket Letters, on which much reliance was placed to prove Mary's guilt, are not, in the absence of the originals, reputable evidence; the copies probably represent concoctions made by manipulating genuine letters and making some interpolations. Bothwell, however, was a party to Darnley's murder—or so at least all contemporaries believed. Yet he was acquitted after a show of trial, he then abducted Mary, possibly with her consent (24 April) and obtained a divorce from his wife (7 May). On 15 May Mary married him, to the scandal of even her warmest supporters. She had formerly taken the reformed Church under her protection (19 April) and the marriage was a Protestant one. Faced with a confederacy of nobles at Carberry, Mary surrendered (15 June), to be imprisoned in Lochleven Castle and compelled to abdicate in favour of her son (24 July). Escaping on 2 May 1568, Mary obtained much support, but was defeated at Langside (13 May). Four days later she crossed the Solway and asked for Elizabeth's protection.

At the end of 1568 conferences took place at York and Westminster at which representatives of Mary and her opponents had a hearing before commissioners of Elizabeth, with a view to determining whether or not Mary should be restored. No decision was formally announced but Mary was detained in England for the rest of her life. In Scotland, her cause was maintained against the supporters of King James until 1573. In England she became a focus for plots by English Roman Catholics and foreign agents, all of them frustrated (though sometimes initially encouraged) by the agents of the English government. Elizabeth was frequently urged to have Mary executed, but always hesitated until public revulsion at Mary's complicity in Babington's plot for the assassination of the English Queen forced her hand. Beheaded at Fotheringhay (8 February 1587), Mary was buried at Peterborough, whence her body was removed to Westminster Abbey in 1612.

David Hay Fleming, *Mary, Queen of Scots*, 1898.
Antonia Fraser, *Mary, Queen of Scots*, 1969.
Gordon Donaldson, *Mary, Queen of Scots*, 1973.
M. H. Armstrong-Davison, *The Casket Letters*, 1965.

Arran, James Hamilton, 2nd. Earl of (*c.* 1516–1575), Governor of Scotland, was the son of the 1st Earl, whom he succeeded in 1529. As his grandmother had been a daughter of James II, he became heir presumptive to the crown on the death of John, Duke of Albany, in 1536. He had given some signs of leanings towards the Reformation, and on the death of James V Cardinal Beaton attempted to exclude him from the office of Governor, to which many thought his place in the succession entitled him. Beaton's scheme failed, Arran was acknowledged as Governor until Mary should reach her 'perfect age' of twelve years, and for a few months he followed a policy of friendship with England and encouragement of the reformers. However, his position was open to challenge by the Church, for he was the child of a marriage following a divorce which some thought of dubious legality, and this fact, combined with his constitutional irresolution, caused him to capitulate to Beaton and the more conservative faction and to renounce the treaty with England whereby Mary was to be married to Prince Edward.

Arran remained Governor, and used his position to enrich his family, but he had little freedom of action, for his heir was in effect a hostage, at first with Beaton until the latter's murder in 1546 and from 1548 at the French court. When Mary was sent to France in 1548, French influence in Scotland increased, but Arran's acquiescence was purchased by his elevation to the dukedom of Châtelherault (1549). In April 1554, when Mary was still only eleven, he was prevailed on to resign the regency in favour of Mary of Guise, the Queen Mother.

When the revolt against French domination and Roman Catholicism broke out, in 1559, the Duke could not commit himself until his son escaped from France, but thereafter he became the figurehead of the provisional government which the insurgents established. He had no place in the administration set up by Queen Mary when she returned to Scotland in 1561. He opposed Mary's marriage in 1565 to Darnley, the heir of the Hamiltons' rival house, that of Lennox, and he took part with the Earl of Moray in the futile rebellion which was raised in protest.

Châtelherault was then an exile in France and England until early in 1569, by which time Mary had been deposed and Moray had become Regent for James VI. As Châtelherault was opposed both to Mary's deposition and to Moray's assumption of the regency, he became titular head of the 'Queen's Party', and his property suffered in the course of the war with the 'King's Party'. He came to terms with James VI's government in 1573.

He married a daughter of the 3rd Earl of Morton. His eldest son, James, styled Earl of Arran, was often thought of as a prospective husband for Mary and in 1560 was a suitor for the hand of Elizabeth, but he became insane in 1562 and was confined until his death (1609); the second, John (c. 1538–1604), Commendator of Arbroath, ultimately succeeded to the family titles and in 1599 was created Marquis of Hamilton; the third, David, died unmarried; the fourth, Claud, Commendator of Paisley, was ancestor of the Dukes of Abercorn.

Beaton, David (?1494–1546), Archbishop of St. Andrews and Cardinal, after education at the University of Paris, appears as Chancellor of Glasgow Cathedral in 1519 and he was appointed Commendator of Arbroath in 1524 on the resignation of his uncle, James, who had just exchanged the archbishopric of Glasgow for that of St. Andrews. He began his service to the state at an early age, for he was ambassador to France in 1519, Keeper of the Privy Seal in 1528 and ambassador to France once more in 1533. By 1538 he was so high in the royal favour that he was sent to France to conduct the King's second wife, Mary of Guise, to Scotland. The French government, seeing him as a pillar of the pro-French faction in Scotland against the wiles of Henry VIII, made him Bishop of Mirepoix at the end of 1537; in the same year the Scottish government had him appointed coadjutor and successor to his uncle, the Archbishop of St. Andrews, who died in 1539; and the Pope recognised this papal champion by making him a Cardinal in 1538. Subsequently he became a legate *a latere*.

After the death of James V, an attempt by Beaton to seize power was frustrated by the pro-English party, and he was for a time in prison, but by the middle of 1543 he was again at large to revive his party, crown Queen Mary and entice the Governor Arran away from the English side. He became Chancellor in this year. For the remainder of his life his task was mainly to preserve an *entente* between Arran and the Queen Mother, to maintain the French connection and at the same time avoid falling under French domination. His anti-English policy, leading as it did to devastating invasions in 1544 and 1545, brought him considerable unpopularity, and the fact that he demonstrated his zeal for orthodoxy by prosecuting heretics made enemies for him as well. It can be said that his policy was somewhat negative, for, unlike his successor, John Hamilton, he did nothing positively to strengthen the Church or purge it from abuses.

Beaton's name is always associated with that of his best-remembered victim, George Wishart (*c.* 1513–46). Wishart was a native of Angus and was probably both a pupil and a teacher at the grammar school of Montrose. The area was one which received an early taste of the Reformation coming across the North Sea from the Lutheran countries, and Wishart was charged with heresy because he had taught the New Testament in Greek. In 1538 he left Scotland and probably spent some time in Germany and Switzerland before settling at Corpus Christi College, Cambridge. In 1543 he returned to Scotland in the train of the English envoys who came to urge Henry's scheme for marrying Queen Mary to Prince Edward. Wishart's preaching, which attracted much attention at Montrose, Dundee, Ayr and elsewhere, is therefore to be seen in a political context, but the impression conveyed by John Knox, who became his disciple, suggests that he was possessed of spiritual insights and mildness of manner which it is hard to reconcile with international intrigues. Henry, who saw Beaton as the great enemy of England, was encouraging plots for his assassination, and it cannot be determined whether or not the reformer is to be identified with the 'Scottish man called Wishart' who was involved in them. At any rate, it was as a heretic, not as a criminal plotter, that Wishart was arested and handed over to Beaton, to be burned at St. Andrews on 1 March 1546.

The desire to avenge Wishart was one element in the conspiracy which led to Beaton's murder in his castle of St. Andrews on 29 May 1546, but the Cardinal had private feuds with Fife lairds which may have had as much to do with his death as either religion or Henry's schemes. Among his assassins were John Leslie, brother of the Earl of Rothes, Norman Leslie, the Earl's son, James and William Kirkcaldy of Grange and Sir John Melville of Raith.

John Herkless and R. K. Hannay, *The Archbishops of St. Andrews*, vol. iv, 1913.

Mary of Guise-Lorraine (1515–1560), Queen of James V and mother of Mary, Queen of Scots, was a daughter of Claude, Duc de Guise She was married first to the Duc de Longueville, who died in June 1537 and by whom she had a son. She was contracted to James V in January 1538, married by proxy on 18 May, landed at Crail on 10 June and married the King a few days later. In the contest for power after James's death, Mary, whose maternal rights over her infant daughter could not be ignored, opposed the Earl of Arran when, as Governor, he adopted a policy favourable to England and the Reformation. She aligned herself with Cardinal Beaton, who succeeded before the end of 1543 in making Arran reverse his policy. In 1544 there was a move to substitute Mary for Arran as Governor, and already at this stage she showed marked political ability in creating a party by taking into account the interests of various individuals. The attempt to supersede Arran failed, and there was a kind of reconciliation at the end of 1544, followed by a year and a half during which Beaton was really the guiding hand which kept Mary and Arran in double harness.

When, after 1548, it became necessary to reconcile the Scots to the upbringing of their Queen in France, Mary again showed her political skill. In 1550 she went to France, taking with her a number of Scottish notables so that they could be subjected to French influence and exposed to French financial inducements. Early in 1554 Arran was constrained to resign the governorship in her favour, and she was free to carry out a French policy in Scotland. Her position was in many ways difficult. Money had to be found for military operations against England, and the resultant taxation was highly unpopular. She tried with some success to ease the situation by persuading the Pope to grant subsidies from the Church. To allay opposition, she was lenient to the reformers, and she showed some appreciation of their case by instructing Archbishop John Hamilton to summon the third of his reforming councils.

However, with the death of Mary Tudor (wife of Philip of Spain) in November 1558 and the Treaty of Cateau-Cambrésis in March-April 1559, the threat to France from Spain was removed, and France could concentrate on an anti-English and anti-Protestant policy. From the spring of 1559, therefore, Mary 'appeared altogether altered' and turned fiercely on the Scottish reformers, who rose in arms against her. In the ensuing military operations she was at one stage driven back to Dunbar, but her professional French forces (amounting ultimately to probably 4,000 men) could hold the field against the insurgents' untrained levies, and she soon recovered Edinburgh and turned Leith into an almost impregnable fortress. Although the rebels 'suspended' her from the regency on 21 October 1559, their cause seemed very uncertain of success until English help was obtained, first by sea, then by land. France was now troubled by internal strife and could send no reinforcements, so negotiations were set on foot. The way to a settlement was eased by the death of Mary in Edinburgh Castle on 11 June 1560. It is impossible to withhold admiration from a woman who could presumably have lived in comfort in France but chose to remain in Scotland out of a sense of duty to her country, her Church and her daughter's rights.

E. M. H. McKerlie, *Mary of Guise-Lorraine*, 1931.

Knox, John (?1512–1572), Reformer, was born at Haddington and probably educated at the grammar school there and the university of St. Andrews, but next to nothing is known of his life for thirty years and more, except that he became a priest. In 1546 he attached himself to the Protestant preacher George Wishart, who was put to death shortly afterwards. When Wishart's persecutor, Cardinal Beaton, was murdered, and St. Andrews Castle held by the murderers, Knox joined them (1547), but, when the castle fell to a French expedition, he was shipped to servitude in the French galleys.

On his release, in terms of a peace treaty (1549), he made his way to the Protestant England of Edward VI. He attained some note as a preacher at Berwick, Newcastle and London and as a spokesman of the left wing of the Protestant party. When he was offered the bishopric of Rochester he declined it, out of a prudent regard for his own safety: he foresaw that Edward's reign would not last and would be followed by a papalist reaction. Therefore, unlike several of Edward's bishops, he was able to escape when Mary Tudor succeeded.

He spent some time in Frankfurt, where he had a quarrel with more moderate English reformers, and then settled as minister to a congregation of English exiles at Geneva, where he learned to admire the theology and discipline of John Calvin. He visited Scotland in 1555–6, and clearly contributed to the shaping of the movement which was soon to issue in rebellion against France and Rome. After Elizabeth succeeded Mary Tudor, he applied for permission to enter England, with which he had so many ties, but this was refused him, for he had tactlessly denounced female rulers in his *First Blast of the Trumpet against the Monstrous Regiment of Women*. In May 1559 he returned to Scotland, to preach a sermon at Perth which stimulated the looting of religious houses, though on reflection he coolly attributed the violence to 'the rascal multitude' rather than to 'the brethren'. The revolt thus initiated was successful, with English help, in the following year, and the Protestant party was in control.

When Queen Mary returned in 1561, Knox was deeply distrustful, and in a number of interviews (of which, however, we have only his own accounts) he rated the Queen for her religion, her plans to marry a Roman Catholic, and behaviour which he considered indecorous. He applauded the murder of Riccio, and when the murderers failed to gain power he left Edinburgh for Ayrshire and then spent some months in England, returning only after Mary's overthrow and in time to preach at the coronation of James VI. He was, inevitably, in high favour with the government carried on by James VI's Regents, but he was driven from Edinburgh when the castle there was held by the adherents of Mary and took refuge in St. Andrews from May 1571 to August 1572.

Although Knox was on the left wing of the Protestant party of his day, he was much more moderate than many who came after him. He told Mary, for instance, that he did not 'utterly condemn' dancing. In his views on Church government he was so far from being a Presbyterian that his farewell advice to the Church of Scotland was that it should have bishops. Often thought of as a dour and sour Scot, Knox was much anglicized in speech and outlook and was one of the most important agents in the extension of English political and cultural influence in his native country. His first wife was English, and he sent their two sons to England for their education. When he was over fifty he married, as his second wife, the sixteen-year-old daughter of Lord Ochiltree.

Knox's *History of the Reformation,* containing not only his memoirs but a large number of documents, is an indispensable source for the history of the period as well as the main evidence for his own biography. It should, however, be said that, while he had many virtues, modesty was not one of them, and he may exaggerate his own importance. Certainly had his *History* not survived he would be a much less famous figure, for other contemporary sources have far less to say about him.

Eustace Percy, *John Knox,* 1937.
Jasper Ridley, *John Knox,* 1968.
Gordon Donaldson, *The Scottish Reformation,* 1960.
W. Croft Dickinson (ed.), *John Knox's History of the Reformation* 2 vols., 1949.

Erskine, John, of Dun (*c.* 1508–1591), Reformer, was educated at King's College, Aberdeen, and grew up in a period when Lutheranism was making some headway in the Scottish east coast ports and their hinterland. He travelled and studied on the continent, and brought back with him in 1534 a French scholar to teach Greek in the grammar school of Montrose. Erskine showed that he was on the reforming side when he associated with George Wishart, a near neighbour and a connexion by marriage, who also taught in Montrose, before beginning the career which led in the end to his being put to death as a heretic in 1546. Among lairds and burgesses of Angus who embraced the Reformation, Erskine was an influential figure, for, besides being himself a laird, he was for a time Provost of Montrose, his mother was a daughter of Lord Ruthven and his first wife was a daughter of the Earl of Crawford.

Probably for a time Erskine, like many others, conformed against his convictions, but in 1555–6 he was impressed by the arguments against attending Mass which were put forward by John Knox, whom he entertained for a time at Dun. In December 1557 Erskine, along with the Earls of Argyll, Glencairn and Morton and Lord Lorne, signed the 'First Bond', pledging himself to work for the overthrow of 'Anti-Christ' and the setting up of a Protestant church,

71

but he subsequently attempted to mediate between Mary of Guise and the Reformers.

At the first General Assembly, in December 1560, Erskine was present as a representative of the burgh of Montrose, but the assembly deemed him 'apt and able to minister' and in 1562 he was inducted as superintendent of Angus and Mearns. He was five times Moderator of the General Assembly, and his 'long travails in the ministry' were referred to appreciatively. He continued to administer his diocese until his death, apparently little affected by the Presbyterian arguments that the office of superintendent or bishop (which Erskine himself equated) was unscriptural. Both in 1571 and 1584 he showed that he was a supporter of episcopacy, and he probably never departed from Lutheran attitudes to which he had originally been converted. He was universally esteemed. He soothed Queen Mary on one occasion after Knox had reduced her to tears, and, when she offered to hear reformed preachers, she said that above all others she would gladly hear the superintendent of Angus, 'for he was a mild and sweet-tempered man'.

R. Selby Wright (ed.), *Fathers of the Kirk*, 1960.

Bothwell, Adam, Bishop of Orkney (*c.* 1530–1593), was the son of Francis Bothwell, who was Provost of Edinburgh and a judge of the Court of Session, and other members of the family attained office in the law and in the Church. By marriage Adam was the uncle of John Napier of Merchiston, and among his cousins were Sir William Kirkcaldy of Grange and Sir John Bellenden of Auchnoule, the Justice-Clerk. His learning in Hebrew, theology and law is attested by his library, and there is some indication that he was interested in science as well. After holding the parsonage of Ashkirk in succession to his uncle and brother, he was provided by the Pope to the bishopric of Orkney on 2 August 1559 and consecrated shortly thereafter. The revenues were so heavily burdened by pensions to various laymen that a mere pittance was left for the Bishop. Bothwell was in his diocese during the critical months when the reformed Church was being set up in Scotland, and early in 1561 he determined, despite some local opposition, to carry through the reform of his diocese. On this visit and subsequent visits in nearly every year until 1566 he extended the reformed ministry to almost every parish in the islands. In thus conforming, and continuing his work as a bishop within the reformed Church, Bothwell takes his place with two others—Alexander Gordon of Galloway (?1516–75) and Robert Stewart of Caithness (*c.* 1517–86).

72

From January 1564 Bothwell was a Lord of Session and in 1567 he began to be involved in politics. He officiated at the marriage of Queen Mary to the Earl of Bothwell, but joined the party which rose in rebellion against that marriage, and he anointed the young King James VI when he was crowned as Mary's successor. The Bishop next took part, with Kirkcaldy of Grange, in the pursuit of the Earl of Bothwell to Shetland, and, when Kirkcaldy's ship was wrecked, the Bishop saved his life by a spectacular leap into an overcrowded boat—an incident long remembered. In 1568–9 he accompanied the Regent Moray to the conferences at York and Westminster, where the charges against Mary were examined, and he was personally responsible for the actual presentation of the accusation of murder, when Moray would still have withheld it.

The General Assembly, which had been offended by Bothwell's part in Mary's third marriage, deprived him of his functions in the Church, and in 1568 Lord Robert Stewart, Mary's half-brother, compelled him to surrender the bishopric revenues for those of the abbey of Holyrood. Although the General Assembly subsequently rehabilitated him, Adam took no further part in the administration of the diocese, but he retained the title 'Bishop of Orkney' until his death.

Gordon Donaldson, 'Bishop Adam Bothwell and the Reformation in Orkney', in *Scott. Church Hist. Soc. Records*, xiii, 85–100.

Carswell, John (*c.* 1525–1572), superintendent of Argyll and Bishop of the Isles, was a student at St. Andrews in 1541, and in 1544–5 was one of the West Highland supporters of the Earl of Lennox and the pro-English faction. He may have gone to England for a time, but when the 4th Earl of Argyll (d. 1558) and his son, the 5th Earl, emerged as champions of the reforming cause Carswell was an obvious candidate for patronage at home. At any rate, by 1551 he was treasurer of the diocese of Argyll and parson of Kilmartin (the parish in which his residence was situated), and he also held the office of chancellor of the Chapel Royal. After the success of the reformers in 1560, Carswell was appointed superintendent of Argyll, with jurisdiction over at least some of the islands as well as the mainland. He clearly gained the favour of Queen Mary, from whom he received a gift of the revenues of the bishopric of the Isles in January 1565, and on 24 March 1567 he was formally provided to that bishopric. It was obvious that an arrangement whereby the superintendents of the reformed church should be maintained from the revenues of bishoprics had much to commend it on practical grounds.

Of Carswell's energy in extending the reformed Church in his diocese there is no doubt, and his great achievement was to provide the people with a printed service-book in their own tongue. The Book of Common Order, sometimes called 'Knox's Liturgy', originally prepared for the English congregation at Geneva, was prescribed by the General Assembly for use in public worship in Scotland in 1562. Carswell had this book translated into Gaelic, and when it appeared, in 1567, it was the first book ever printed in that language. Only one perfect, and two imperfect, copies are known to survive. Besides translating the service-book as it stood in the English version, Carswell added certain prayers, including a form for blessing a boat, and he also translated a Catechism which, however, was not published until long after his death.

The Bishop-superintendent took Mary's side in the disputes between her supporters and those of her son, James VI, and this brought him under censure by the General Assembly, which in 1569 criticized him for not having asked its sanction before he accepted the bishopric at the Queen's hands. Carswell lived in popular tradition on account of his remarkable appearance and his alleged greed:

> 'Great Carswell of Carnassary,
> With legs five quarters long,
> A hump like the rump of a heron,
> With empty gizzard, greedy and strong.'

He was also remembered because the day of his burial at Ardchattan Priory, on Loch Etive, was so uncommonly stormy even for that part of the world that it became proverbial to say, 'This is like the day the bishop was buried.' Carnassary Castle, the home of Carswell's family, occupies a position commanding the land route between Oban and Lochgilphead and also the pass leading to Loch Awe.

The Book of Common Order, translated by Mr. John Carswell, ed. Thomas McLauchlan, 1873.

Hamilton, John, Archbishop of St. Andrews (1512–1571), a natural son of James, 1st Earl of Arran, became Commendator of the abbey of Paisley in his childhood (1525) and spent some time on the continent, where he was believed to incline somewhat to Lutheranism. In 1543, when his half-brother, the 2nd Earl of Arran, became Governor, John returned to Scotland, to begin the direction of

Hamilton policy which he continued until his death. It was partly his influence which swayed the Governor to come to terms with Cardinal Beaton and the French party. He was Keeper of the Privy Seal from 1543 to 1546 and Treasurer from 1545 until 1554. In 1546 he was appointed Bishop of Dunkeld, and in 1547 promoted to St. Andrews.

As Archbishop he pursued an intelligent policy, designed to go some way towards satisfying the demands for reform without altering the ecclesiastical structure, and at the same time to commend the Hamilton interest to men of diverse views. During his primacy three councils of the Scottish Church (1549, 1552, 1559) passed a whole code of legislation to curb abuses in the church system; a *Catechism* was issued in his name which made some concessions to Lutheran views and did not mention the papacy; and, as a practical measure to improve the educational standards of priests, the endowment of St. Mary's College, St. Andrews, was completed.

Hamilton's measures did not avert revolution, which came in 1559–60. His brother, now Duke of Châtelherault, became the figurehead of the reforming party, but John neither made a firm stand for Roman Catholicism nor accepted the reformed Confession of Faith. In 1563 he was imprisoned for a time for saying Mass, but in general he retained most of his revenues and some of his judicial powers—which he used, for example, to issue dispensations for matrimony. He officiated at the baptism of James VI, but Mary, for very good reasons, insisted that this 'pocky priest' should not use the rite of the spittle.

The Archbishop was suspected of being privy to the murders of both Darnley and the Regent Moray, and he was a leading figure in Mary's party after her deposition in 1567. He was captured by the King's forces when Dumbarton Castle fell to them in 1571 and was hanged at Stirling (7 April 1571).

John Herkless and R. K. Hannay, *The Archbishops of St. Andrews*, vol. v, 1915.

Kennedy, Quentin (1520–1564), Commendator of Crossraguel, was the son of Gilbert, 2nd Earl of Cassillis, and was educated at the Universities of St. Andrews and Paris. After holding the vicarage of Girvan, he was presented to the vicarage of Penpont in succession to his brother, and then, although he was not a monk, was appointed to the abbacy of Crossraguel in 1548 in succession his uncle. His own career thus illustrated some of the abuses of the unreformed Church, which he admitted in *Ane Compendious Tractive* (1558), but he was strongly opposed to the Protestant reformers. In 1559 he challenged John Willock, who was reckoned the leading Protestant preacher, to a debate, but no disputation took place and each accused the other of shirking a contest. In 1561 he wrote an 'Oration' against John Knox, but it was not published until 1812 and it is uncertain how widely it may have been known at the time. However, when Knox arrived in Ayrshire in August 1562 on a preaching tour commissioned by the General Assembly, Kennedy challenged him to a debate, which was held at Maybole for three days at the end of September. The subject was the scriptural foundation of the Mass, and the argument centred largely on the supposed parallel between the sacrificial character of the Mass and the offering of bread and wine by Melchizedek in presence of Abraham (Genesis: xiv, 18). Many thought that Kennedy came well out of both the proposed debate with Willock and the actual debate with Knox. In 1563, when there was a drive against priests who illegally celebrated Mass, Kennedy was warned of the likelihood of action against him, but apparently he was not prosecuted.

Winyet, Ninian (*c.* 1518–1592), Roman Catholic controversialist, was a native of Renfrewshire and may have been educated at Glasgow University, but there is no record of his graduation anywhere in Scotland, whereas we do know that he took degrees later in life on the continent. He was ordained priest in 1540 or 1541 and about ten years later was teaching in the grammar school of Linlithgow. He was not, as often said, provost of St. Michael's Church in that town. Winyet refused to accept the reformed Confession of Faith and was therefore deprived of his office as schoolmaster in 1561. Although freely admitting the faults and abuses in the old church system, Winyet was soon conspicuous as a resolute opponent of the Reformation in the shape it took in Scotland, and he showed remarkable acuteness in probing the weaknesses and inconsistencies in the Reformers' position. In *Certane Tractatis for Reformatioun of Doctryne and Maneris*, printed in May 1562, he set forth his views with such effect that in September he had to leave the country and make his way to Antwerp, where he printed his *Buke of Four Scoir Thre Questiouns*. To the latter he attached a letter to John Knox in which he twits him with his English accent: 'Gif ye, throw curiositie of novationis, hes foryet our auld plane Scottis quhilk your mother leirit you, in tymes cuming I shall wryte to you my mynd in Latin, for I am nocht acquyntit with your Southeroun.' This remark is characteristic of the good humour and satire which, rather than any bitterness, mark Winyet's writings. His own works, it need hardly be said, are models of the Scots prose which the Reformers' influence was soon to drive out of use for serious purposes, and he ranks with Quentin Kennedy as one of the few able defenders of the old régime. By 1565 Winyet was at the university of Paris, where he remained intermittently for several years, though he visited England to serve Mary in 1571 and was briefly in Scotland also at that time. Later he went to Douai. In 1577, after complex negotiations, the 'Scottish monastery' at Ratisbon (actually a foundation dating from the time when the 'Scots' were in truth Irish) was reconstituted as a house for Scottish exiles and Winyet was made its Abbot. He died on 21 September 1592 in his seventy-fourth year. Among his later works were *Flagellum Sectariorum* ('The Scourge of the Sectaries'), 1581, and *Velitatio in Georgium Buchananum* ('A skirmish against George Buchanan'), 1582.

J. H. Burns, *Ninian Winyet* (Catholic Truth Society of Scotland pamphlet), 1959.

Lesley, John (?1527–1596), Bishop of Ross, described by John Knox as a 'preastis gett', or priest's bastard, was in truth the son of a priest who held the office of official, or judicial deputy of the Bishop, in the diocese of Moray and who started his son on a career like his own. John graduated in Arts at Aberdeen, then, after being ordained, studied law at Toulouse, Poitiers and Paris (1549–54), becoming a Doctor in Both Laws (that is, civil and canon). Returning to Scotland, he was official of the diocese of Aberdeen by 1557, doctor of canon law at King's College and in 1559 canon of Oyne. He was sent in 1561, presumably on behalf of the more conservative faction in Scotland, to confer with Queen Mary before her return, and he came back to Scotland with her in August.

In January 1564 Lesley was appointed a Lord of Session. In February 1566 he was provided by the Pope (on royal nomination) to the abbey of Lindores, and in April Mary invested him in the temporality of the bishopric of Ross, to which he was provided, apparently by the Pope, in the following January, though he received a second provision to Ross as late as 1575, and very likely was not consecrated until that point.

He supported Mary when her troubles started in 1567 and was one of the commissioners who put her case at the conferences at York and Westminster in 1568–9, but he was clearly at this stage neither an uncritical admirer of the Queen nor an intransigent Papist, for an Englishman said that he seemed 'almost a Protestant'. He became

77

involved in trouble in England through the plots of the Italian Ridolfi on Mary's behalf, and under torture or the threat of it revealed many of the plans of the conspirators. On his release, he went to the continent, to make efforts on Mary's behalf in France and at Rome (1574-5). He became Suffragan-Bishop and Vicar-General of the diocese of Rouen in 1579 and in 1592 was appointed Bishop of Coutances. Forfeited in Scotland in 1568, he was rehabilitated in 1587 and the rehabilitation annulled in 1589. He died at St. Augustine's monastery of Gertrudenberg near Brussels, on 31 May 1596, in his seventieth year.

In London in 1569 Lesley wrote *A defence of the honour of the right high, mighty and noble princess Mary,* which is partly a defence of Mary against the criminal charges brought against her and partly an assertion of her right to the English succession, as well as a counterblast to John Knox's denunciation of the right of females to rule. This work was many times reprinted, mainly for the consumption of English Roman Catholic *émigrés*. He also wrote a *History of Scotland*, published at Rome in Latin in 1578 and in translation by the Bannatyne Club in 1830 and the Scottish Text Society in 1888-95. It contains many valuable observations but must be used with caution, not because of the author's moderate bias but because some of his statements are demonstrably false.

Moray, James Stewart, Earl of (1531-1570), 'the Good Regent', was an illegitimate son of James V by Margaret Erskine, the wife of Robert Douglas of Lochleven. He was made Commendator of St. Andrews Priory in 1538, and was probably educated with a view to a career as one of those titular ecclesiastics who played a large part in affairs of state. At any rate, he attended the University of St. Andrews, but little is known of his life until 1548, when he served with the Scottish forces fighting against the English in south-east Scotland and then accompanied his half-sister, Queen Mary, to France. He went to France again in 1550 in company with Mary of Guise, and as part of her policy of conciliating Scots who might resent her schemes he received the commendatorship of Mâcon, in France, as well as that of Pittenweem.

Lord James may already have been inclined towards the reforming cause, but of course he conformed outwardly and in 1555 incurred the censure of John Knox, who, on a visit to Scotland, denounced attendance at Mass. He was not one of the signatories of the 'First Bond', by which, in December 1557, the Earls of Argyll,

Glencairn and Morton, Lord Lorne and Erskine of Dun undertook to further the setting up of a reformed Church. On the outbreak of the revolt against Mary of Guise in May 1559, Lord James served for a brief period in the government army, but at the end of the month joined the insurgents. When the Reformers triumphed in 1560 he was thought by some to be a possible candidate for the throne, should Queen Mary not return from France, but when her husband, Francis II, died and it became clear that she would come back, Lord James was sent to prepare her for governing Scotland and to put the Reformers' views before her.

James made it evident that he would be prepared to allow the Queen the private exercise of the religion of her choice, and Mary naturally preferred the advice of such a moderate rather than risk falling under the domination of extremists. Therefore, for more than three years of Mary's personal rule, the direction of policy lay largely with Lord James (created Earl of Mar in 1562 and Earl of Moray in 1563) and Maitland of Lethington. One by one Moray's rivals were eliminated—the young Earl of Arran by his rashness and subsequent insanity, the Earl of Bothwell by his association with Arran's madcap scheme to kidnap the Queen, and the Earl of Huntly by his defeat and death at Corrichie. The Darnley marriage project threatened both Moray's personal ascendancy and his aim at an understanding between Mary and Elizabeth, and in 1565 he therefore raised a futile rebellion, easily crushed by Mary in an expedition called the Chaseabout Raid. He fled to England, where he found that Elizabeth, who had given him encouragement in advance, had no use for him after his failure.

Next, by a remarkable *volte-face*, he negotiated with Darnley and the lords who resented the influence of David Riccio: Darnley was to be invested in full kingship, giving his heirs the right to succeed failing heirs by Mary, Riccio was to be murdered, and Moray was to regain power. The murder took place, but, owing to Mary's skill in detaching Darnley from his allies, she was able to exile the murderers. However, Moray, who had re-entered Edinburgh only on the day after the murder, escaped condemnation. Before the end of 1566 Moray was aware of plots against Darnley, and his fore-knowledge of the murder of Darnley at Kirk o' Field is strongly suggested by the fact that he left Edinburgh (admittedly, to visit his wife, who was ill) on the afternoon before the crime took place. Thereafter, foreseeing that a situation might develop in which Mary would be overthrown by dubious means, he decided to go sightseeing abroad, and was thus able, after taking no part in the rebellion which resulted in Mary's deposition, to return and assume the regency.

Moray defeated Mary at Langside on her escape from Lochleven. At the end of 1568 and the beginning of 1569 he went to York and Westminster to take part in investigations of Mary's guilt, and ultimately, after producing the Casket Letters, directly accused her of murder. Elizabeth delivered no sentence but Moray returned to continue his government. As Regent he did much to maintain order and to secure the position of the reformed Church, but he made many enemies among Mary's supporters and among rival nobles, especially the Hamiltons. It was by James Hamilton of Both-wellhaugh that he was murdered at Linlithgow (23 January 1570).

Moray married Agnes Keith, daughter of the Earl Marischal, in February 1562, and had no son. His elder daughter, in 1580, married James Stewart, eldest son of Sir James Stewart of Doune, and this son-in-law of the Regent became 'the Bonnie Earl o' Moray', who, like his father-in-law, was the darling of the ultra-Protestant party and at feud with the Earl of Huntly, who was more sympathetic to Roman Catholicism. The Bonnie Earl was murdered by Huntly at Donibristle on 7 February 1592.

Maurice Lee, *James Stewart, Earl of Moray*, 1953.

Maitland, William, of Lethington (*c.* 1525–1573), politician, was a son of Sir Richard Maitland of Lethington (1496–1586), who was a Lord of Session and Keeper of the Privy Seal and was one of those lairds trained in law who provided something of a new professional class in the sixteenth century.

Although Sir Richard compiled a volume of Decisions of the Court of Session for 1550–65 and a *History of the House of Seton* (printed by the Maitland Club in 1829), he is best known for his services to Scottish poetry. He formed a collection of Scottish verse, in two MS. volumes, one a folio with 176 items and the other a quarto with 96. His own verses, which show considerable merit, were written mainly in his later years and contain the reflections of an ageing man who acutely assessed the Scottish scene and was especially critical of the nobles for their selfish neglect of the general weal. Like most East Lothian lairds, Sir Richard's sympathies were from an early date with the Reformation or at any rate with the cause of friendship with England, but he saw politics rather than religion as the dominant consideration, and he seems to have transmitted his views to his better-known sons, William and John.

William, Sir Richard's heir, was educated at St. Andrews and abroad and then entered the service of Mary of Guise at a time when she was following a policy of conciliation. He became Secretary of State on 4 December 1558, but he soon joined the Reformers, less because of any zeal for religion—he was in truth something of a sceptic and extremely cynical about the unrealistic approach of men like Knox—than because of his devotion to the cause of Anglo-Scottish amity. His diplomatic skill did much to secure the English help which brought about the victory of the Reformers in 1560. After Mary's return in 1561 he helped to shape her moderate policy and continued to work for an accommodation between her and Elizabeth. He was largely displaced from political influence after Mary's marriage to Darnley, though he remained about the court and in January 1567 married Mary Fleming, one of the Queen's Maries. He was almost certainly a party to the murder of Darnley in the following month.

In the course of the struggles which followed Mary's marriage to Bothwell and her subsequent deposition, Maitland was at first on the side of the Regent Moray, whom he accompanied to York and Westminster to present an indictment of Mary. Later, however, he was won to the Queen's side and had some success in presenting its case to Elizabeth in such a way as to discourage her from serious intervention in favour of King James. As his wife was a sister of Lord Fleming, who himself belonged to the Hamilton following through marriage, Maitland had reasons of kinship for attaching himself to Mary's party, which included many old friends to England and the Reformation as well as a number of leading aristocrats whom Maitland probably preferred to the middle classes who largely supported James. Maitland was with Sir William Kirkcaldy of Grange when Edinburgh Castle was held as Mary's last stronghold and was captured when Elizabeth at last sent up a siege train to batter' it down. His health had for some time been completely broken, but some thought that he hastened his end by poison and so escaped execution.

E. Russell, *Maitland of Lethington*, 1912.

Darnley, Henry Stewart, Lord (1545 or 1546–1567), elder son of Matthew, 4th Earl of Lennox, and Margaret Douglas (daughter of Margaret Tudor by the 6th Earl of Angus), was born in England, for Lennox was forfeited and exiled for furthering Henry VIII's designs in Scotland in 1544–5. Lady Lennox's sympathies were on the Roman Catholic side, and she tried to groom her son as a

81

Roman Catholic candidate for the succession to the English throne, but Lennox himself was a Protestant, and Darnley conformed to the Church of England under Elizabeth. A match between him and Mary, Queen of Scots, his cousin, had been in men's minds intermittently since his birth, and it would seem to have been contrary to Elizabeth's interests to permit the union of two claimants to her throne, yet she allowed Darnley to go to Scotland in February 1565. Mary took an immediate liking to him as 'the best-proportioned long man she had seen', and, after creating him Earl of Ross and Duke of Albany, married him on 29 July 1565.

Although Darnley had some accomplishments in music and penmanship, and shared Mary's love of hunting and other outdoor recreations, he was intellectually and morally worthless: one contemporary described him as 'an agreeable nincompoop', another as 'more like a woman than a man, for he was handsome, beardless and lady-faced', and yet another as being 'much addicted to Venus's chamber'. Therefore, although the government was conducted in the names of 'King Henry and Queen Mary', it was impossible to give Darnley a real share of authority. His petulant arrogance alienated the nobility, but some lords who resented the influence of Mary's secretary, Riccio, conspired with Darnley, who professed a personal jealousy of Riccio, to murder the Italian (9 March 1566). A brief reconciliation with Mary followed, and their son was born on 19 June, but by the autumn of 1566 they were completely estranged and Mary was a party to plans for a divorce and perhaps for other means of ridding herself of her husband. Darnley on his side was in touch with continental powers and possibly endeavouring to plot against his wife on the pretext that he would serve the Roman Catholic cause (to which he had recently shown a novel devotion) better than she had done. At the end of the year he fell ill at Glasgow, probably of syphilis, and Mary, after going to nurse him, brought him for his convalescence to Kirk o' Field, Edinburgh. When his residence was blown up on 10 February 1567, Darnley's body was found in the garden, where he had evidently been strangled or smothered: it has been suggested that he was responsible for storing the gunpowder under the house, with the intention of blowing up Mary, and that when he awoke to sounds of movement or a smell of burning he fled hastily in his nightshirt, only to encounter his own enemies outside.

R. H. Mahon, *The Tragedy of Kirk o' Field*, 1930.

Bothwell, James Hepburn, 4th Earl of (*c.* 1535–1578), succeeded his father in 1556. The influence of his uncle, Patrick Hepburn, Bishop of Moray, one of the most immoral of the pre-Reformation prelates, may have done something to shape his dissolute character. Yet he was not without principles. While he never wavered in his attachment to the Reformation, his consistent hostility to England was such that he declined to accept the pro-English policy of the reforming party, and, after the outbreak of the revolt of 1559–60, he remained loyal to Mary of Guise, whose cause he served by intercepting subsidies sent by Elizabeth of England to the insurgents. After the return of Queen Mary in 1561, Bothwell was out of favour while the Earl of Moray and Maitland of Lethington pursued their policy of seeking an understanding with Elizabeth, and he was accused of being involved in a scheme of the young Earl of Arran to seize the Queen. He spent the greater part of three years in prison or in exile, and was not welcomed back to Scotland until Moray had raised his rebellion after the Darnley marriage and the Queen turned to Moray's rivals for support. She again relied on Bothwell in the difficult days after the Riccio murder.

How far the favour Mary showed to Bothwell from the autumn of 1566 was due to passion remains debatable, because Bothwell was well worth cultivating for political reasons. He was perhaps the greatest magnate in southern Scotland—Sheriff of Edinburgh and Haddington, Warden of the Marches, master of the Castles of Borthwick, Crichton, Hailes, Dunbar and Hermitage and Lord High Admiral—and his loyalty was assured. On Bothwell's side, it is not to be forgotten that his ancestors had repeatedly shown what was euphemistically called 'kindness' to widowed queens, and it would have been quite in character for him to aim at Mary's hand, after first making her a widow by removing Darnley.

After the murder of Darnley, in which he certainly had a hand, Bothwell divorced his wife, Jane Gordon, sister of the Earl of Huntly, was created Duke of Orkney and married the Queen (15 May 1567). From the field of Carberry, where Mary surrendered to the insurgent lords, he fled to his dukedom, narrowly escaping capture by Kirkcaldy of Grange, and thence he made his way to Norway, where he was unlucky enough to fall into the hands of the kinsmen of a Danish lady, Anna Throndsen, whom he had earlier seduced. Therefore, after some initial bluster about being the consort of a reigning sovereign, he was imprisoned by the Dano-Norwegian government for the rest of his life. He died in the castle of Dragsholm, in the north of Zealand, and a body reputed to be his is to be seen in the nearby church of Faarevejle.

R. F. Gore-Browne, *Lord Bothwell*, 1937.
Margaret Irwin, *The Gay Galliard*, 1941. (H.N.)

Balfour, Sir James, of Pittendreich (c. 1525–1583), described by John Knox as 'blasphemous Balfour' and by a later writer as 'the most corrupt man of the age', was yet a competent lawyer who contributed to the systematization of the Scottish legal system. A son of Michael Balfour of Montquhany in Fife, he was, like other Fife lairds, an associate of the murderers of Cardinal Beaton and helped to hold the castle of St. Andrews after the Cardinal's death (1546). On its capture by the French in 1547, he was sent to the galleys with John Knox, but was released or escaped after about two years. He next appears as 'parson of Flisk' and an ecclesiastical lawyer, but this did not mean that he was in orders, though it qualified him to become one of the nominally clerical judges in the Court of Session. When Mary set up the new Commissary Court of Edinburgh to take over the Church's old jurisdiction in matrimonial cases, Balfour was chief commissary (1564) and he became a Privy Councillor in July 1565 and Clerk Register in February 1566 —one of the middle-class men on whom Mary relied after she had alienated many of the nobility.

Balfour was universally believed to have had a hand in the murder of Darnley, and he certainly had the opportunity, for his brother owned the house adjacent to Darnley's lodging. Appointed captain of Edinburgh Castle at Bothwell's instance, he refused to allow Mary and Bothwell to use it as a refuge and threw in his lot with the lords who rose in rebellion in June 1567. The Regent Moray made him Commendator of Pittenweem at the end of 1567 and President of the Court of Session in December, with a pension of £500, while the office of Clerk Register was restored to James MacGill, whom Balfour had displaced. Balfour's career had been so devious that he was distrusted by all factions, so that he was deprived of the Presidency, probably in 1570, and he acted for a time with the supporters of the exiled Mary. He came to terms temporarily with the Regent Morton, but in the later 1570s he had to withdraw to France, to return only on Morton's fall in 1580. However, one of many attempts to revise and codify Scots law was a project during Morton's regency, and Balfour took part in this, with the compilation of his *Practicks*, a digest of decisions of the Court of Session; it was not published until 1754, but is still of great value. Balfour's family was rehabilitated in 1584 and his eldest son became Lord Balfour of Burleigh in 1606.

'Biography' in *Balfour's Practicks*, vol. i. Stair Society, 1962.

Kirkcaldy, Sir William, of Grange (*c.* 1520–1573), eldest son of Sir James Kirkcaldy, who was Treasurer from 1537 to 1542, was one of the Fife lairds who took a leading part in the Reformation. Like others among them, he was involved in the murder of Cardinal Beaton in 1546 and after it he negotiated with England for help to enable the murderers to hold St. Andrews Castle. On the surrender of the castle to the French, he was captured and imprisoned for a time in Mont St. Michel, from which he escaped. Despite his religious and political background, he was able, at a time when France was deeply divided and many notable Frenchmen were Huguenots, to serve with distinction as commander of a hundred light horse in the French army. He gained a great reputation as a gallant soldier, described by Henry II of France as 'one of the most valiant men of our age' and by a Scot who knew him well as 'gentle and meek like a lamb in the house, but like a lion in the fields'.[1]

In 1559 he was back in Scotland to put his military skill at the disposal of the reforming party, and he did them good service in stubbornly contesting the ground when they were hard pressed by the French in Fife. Like many Protestants, he opposed Mary's marriage to Darnley, joined in the rebellion raised by Moray on that occasion and had to flee to England, but was later pardoned. In 1567 he joined the lords who rose against Mary and Bothwell, and it was to him that Mary surrendered at Carberry. He then took part in the pursuit of Bothwell to Shetland, he fought in the Regent Moray's army at Langside and was made captain of Edinburgh Castle by Moray. However, Kirkcaldy adhered to the original declared aims of the rebellion of 1567—the liberation of the Queen from Bothwell and the safety of Prince James—and he felt that Mary was unfairly treated when she was imprisoned and compelled to abdicate. He must have been uneasy under Moray's regency, and in 1571 he was persuaded by Maitland of Lethington, who had been committed to him as a prisoner, to declare for the exiled Mary. He strengthened the defences of Edinburgh Castle and from it commanded the town. He was responsible for the attempt to seize the Regent Lennox at Stirling which led to Lennox's death (in defiance of Grange's commands and wishes). He continued to hold the castle until the Regent Morton brought in an English force with

1. Sir James Melville, *Memoirs*, p. 101. Folio Society, 1969.

an adequate artillery train to batter it down. After its fall (29 May 1573) he was hanged (3 August).

L. A. Barbé, *Kirkcaldy of Grange*, 1897.

Melville, Sir James, of Halhill (1535–1617), courtier, was a son of Sir John Melville of Raith and Helen Napier, of the Merchiston family. His father, like many Fife lairds, joined the party which supported an English alliance and the reformed cause, and he was executed for treason in 1548. James too became a friend to England and to the Reformation, but was not a strong party man and was both critical of English attempts to dominate Scotland and unsympathetic to the more zealous Reformers. His brothers, Sir Robert, of Murdocairny, and Sir Andrew, of Garvock, attached themselves to Queen Mary's party after her deposition, they were both in Edinburgh Castle when it was held in her interest by their sister's son, Kirkcaldy of Grange, and Andrew was master of Mary's household during her captivity in England. James, too, was devoted to Mary, but appears to have seen more clearly than his brothers that her cause had no future, and he did not take an active part in the strife between her supporters and those of her son.

As a boy Sir James had gone to France in 1550 and remained there and in other parts of the continent until 1564, except for a visit to Scotland in 1559. He was for some years attached to the French court, he served in the French army and, after Mary's return to Scotland in 1561, he attached himself to the Elector Palatine and saw a good deal of Germany and Italy. On his return to Scotland in 1564 he was soon employed on an embassy to Elizabeth to discuss the proposal for Mary's marriage to Robert Dudley, Earl of Leicester. In 1566 he was sent to announce to Elizabeth the birth of Prince James. For many years he was never far from the centre of affairs, but seems to have done little to influence their course.

Melville is best remembered for his *Memoirs of his own Time,* which he put together in the 1590s and which, as they represent the recollections and gossip in old age of a man somewhat given to self-importance, should be read with some reserve. But, because of his close acquaintance with court life and his gift of vivid narrative, they are among the most frequently quoted sources for the period. It is Melville who recounts his embarrassment when Elizabeth pressed him to declare whether she or Mary was the fairer, and who described the vanity which led Elizabeth to show him how she danced 'more high and disposedly' than Mary and how well she played on the virginals—an accomplishment in which he evidently thought she had the advantage, for truth compelled him to say no more of his own sovereign's performance than that she played 'reasonably for a Queen'. It was Melville, too, who related that when Elizabeth heard the news of the birth of Prince James she burst out that the Queen of Scots was lighter of a fair son, while she was a barren stock.

There are several editions of Melville's *Memoirs*, the latest, with a biography, edited by Gordon Donaldson for the Folio Society, 1969.

James VI, King of Scots (1566–1625), the only child of Mary, Queen of Scots, and Lord Darnley, was born at Edinburgh Castle on 19 June 1566. Raised to the throne by the lords who had extorted his mother's abdication on 24 July 1567, and crowned at Stirling on 29 July, he was educated as the young hopeful of the Protestant party, under a strict régime. The design was to instil into him a thorough academic training and to indoctrinate him with a contempt for his mother and a belief in the rights of subjects against their sovereigns. The Earls of Moray, Lennox, Mar and Morton in turn held the office of Regent, until in the spring of 1578 a palace revolution brought Morton's regency to an end, and authority was vested nominally in the twelve-year-old King. However, Morton soon recovered power and exercised it until the end of 1580.

By that time James's adolescent affections had been captured by a cousin from France, Esmé Stewart, whom he created Duke of Lennox, and influences were at work in Scotland which awakened James to the possibility of coming to terms with France or Spain and the Papacy, and perhaps liberating his mother, all in defiance of the lessons of his earlier mentors. The ultra-Protestant and pro-English faction, alarmed by the drift of events, seized James in the Raid of Ruthven in August 1582 and held him captive until the following June. He probably never either forgot or forgave those who subjected him to this indignity and who deprived him of Esmé, who was dead by the time James escaped from the Ruthven faction. He then relied for over two years on James Stewart, Earl of Arran, whose régime legislated against the extreme Protestants by reaffirming episcopacy and firmly subjecting the Church to the State. Meantime the Ruthven faction were exiled in England and had the support of many English politicians. They returned in December 1585 to bring about another *coup d'état*, and a kind of coalition government was formed, the leading man in which was soon John Maitland of Thirlestane, who became Chancellor and who, it was said, 'kept the

King on two grounds sure, never to cast out with the Kirk or with England'.

At what precise date James's own will began to shape policy it is hard to say, but from the earliest point at which he expressed his views he indicated that he intended to be above faction and to bring about conciliation on the basis of a *via media* between the ultra-Protestants and the more conservative party led by a group of northern earls. His task was extremely difficult, especially as he had neither adequate finance nor armed might at his disposal. It was by shrewd and subtle diplomacy that he succeeded, by 1597, in depriving both the extreme factions of much of their force, and from that point he began to emerge as the most effective ruler Scotland had ever had. The last attempt to upset his government was the Gowrie Conspiracy in 1600. From the outset James's outlook had been much influenced by his prospects of succeeding Elizabeth, and when he finally did so in 1603 his English kingship increased his prestige and gave him a personal security in sharp contrast to the alarms and excursions of his earlier years.

Government of Scotland at long range, through carefully selected agents, proved highly successful. The loyalty of the old noble families was gained partly by the King's gift of cajolery and partly by the skilful manipulation of the unprecedented patronage which he had at his disposal through the crown's assumption of the control of ecclesiastical property. At the same time, men of middle class origin, in effect professional administrators, were raised to office. The Church was brought under control through the revival, stage by stage, of an episcopate appointed by and responsible to the crown and by firm action against the leaders of the Presbyterian party. The law was enforced as never before, even in the outlying parts of the country, and the Borders, the West Highlands and Islands and Orkney and Shetland became for the first time fully integral parts of the realm.

All James's measures were designed by a well-trained intelligence. He was one of the most learned of sovereigns, and his published works are voluminous. Although not a first-rate poet, some of his verse shows charm as well as erudition and technical skill, and his patronage of foreign poets like Du Bartas as well as of a circle of poets associated with his own court did much to encourage this branch of literature. In his prose works he set down his political ideas, as well as his antipathy to tobacco and to witchcraft. But James was no mere theorizer: he had learned the lessons of Scottish history, he was an acute observer, and he was too shrewd to fall into the errors which had brought disaster to those of his predecessors who had spurned the nobility and whose measures had passed beyond firmness to severity.

In his later years James lost some of his sureness of touch, partly because there was no longer a challenge to stimulate him, partly out of indolence and partly because the adulation of his English subjects went to his head. On a visit to Scotland in 1617—the only visit he paid after 1603—he made it clear that the Scottish Church must come into line with the Church of England in worship as well as in government, and in 1618 he forced through a General Assembly the Five Articles of Perth, which provided, among other things, for kneeling at Communion. This requirement aroused very strong opposition and revived divisions in the Church which had previously seemed on the way to being healed. But even after this James showed that he knew when to withdraw, for although his Articles remained the law they were not enforced, and no further innovations were made. In the reign of his son, Scots were to look back with regret to 'the wisdom of blessed King James'.

On 24 November 1589, at Oslo, James married Anne, daughter of Frederick II of Denmark and Norway, and by her had seven children. The eldest, Henry, born in 1594, died in 1612; Charles succeeded his father; Elizabeth married the Elector Palatine; the others died young.

D. H. Willson, *James VI and I*, 1956.
G. Donaldson, *Scotland: James V to James VII*, 1965.
Jane Oliver, *Mine is the Kingdom*, 1937. (H.N.)

Buchanan, George (1506–1582), scholar, was born at the Moss, Killearn, Stirlingshire, on the fringe of the Highlands, but of a Lowland mother, Agnes Heriot. His father died when he was a child and when he was about fourteen his uncle, James Heriot, sent him to the university of Paris, where he studied for two years, when his uncle's death made him leave France. On his return to Scotland, he served in one of the Regent Albany's abortive expeditions against England (1523) and in 1524 went to St. Andrews University, where he studied logic and philosophy under John Major and took his B.A. degree. In 1526 he returned to Paris in Major's company to complete his studies for the M.A. degree (1528) and remained in Paris for ten years, lecturing at the College of Sainte Barbe and acting as tutor to the Earl of Cassillis. When he returned again to Scotland (1537) James V soon appointed him tutor to one of his sons, but after he had written a satire against the Franciscans he was imprisoned as a heretic. He escaped to England and thence to France, where he became a professor at Bordeaux. Later he went to Portugal (1547), where he was again arrested for heresy and confined by the Inquisition. After a year and a half he was released and returned to Paris (1553).

In 1561 Buchanan came back to Scotland. With his great stock of learning and his cosmopolitan culture, he was acceptable to Queen Mary, whose marriage to the Dauphin in 1558 he had celebrated in verse and with whom he now sometimes read Livy in the evening after dinner. He received a pension of £500 from the abbey of Crossraguel and became Principal of St. Leonard's College, St. Andrews (1566). He was alienated from Mary by the murder of Darnley, for Buchanan, owing to the place of his birth, had an hereditary attachment to the Lennox family. After Mary's deposition he was Moderator of the General Assembly in 1567 and became the pamphleteer of the King's Party and the principal detractor of Mary. He helped to prepare the accusations brought against Mary in England in 1568–9, and accompanied Moray and the King's commissioners as an assessor to the conferences where those charges were considered. Buchanan was made Keeper of the Privy Seal and preceptor to the young King James, whom he held in such 'awe', we are told, that the King remarked years later that he could not approach a certain person without trembling, 'he so reminded him of his pedagogue'. It is not difficult to discern the probable effect on James of his upbringing by this aged scholar who taught the boy that his mother had been a whore.

Apart from his writings against Mary, Buchanan produced his *De Jure Regni Apud Scotos*, which, although not published until 1579, was written to justify the deposition of Mary in 1567. This work was long influential as a kind of revolutionists' handbook and was several times reprinted in the seventeenth century. His translation of the Psalms into Latin verse brought him international fame as a Latinist. One contemporary described him as 'easily the first poet of our age' and a recent critic has gone so far as to say that 'taking verse and prose together, Buchanan may be thought the finest Latin stylist of all time, for his verse is much better that Cicero's attempts at poetry, and his prose far surpasses that of Seneca.'[1] Buchanan retained his interest in education, and took part in plans for university reform in the 1570s. His last work was his Latin *History of Scotland*, printed at Edinburgh in the year of his death. There is a story that when someone who had read his manuscript asked him if

1. Douglas Young, *St. Andrews*, p. 178.

he thought it politic to print some of his views on Queen Mary, his answer was, 'Tell me if I have told the truth'. Buchanan died in Edinburgh and was buried in Greyfriars Churchyard.

P. H. Brown, *George Buchanan*, 1890.

Lennox, Matthew Stewart, 4th Earl of (1516–1571), succeeded his father, the 3rd Earl, when he was killed (4 September 1526) in a vain attempt to rescue James V from the 6th Earl of Angus. Matthew spent a considerable time in France, where another branch of his family—the Aubigny Stewarts—were established, but returned in 1543, after the death of James V. The Earl of Arran had become Governor, but Lennox's family stood next in the succession after him, and his claim was the stronger in that Arran's legitimacy was not above dispute. Lennox arrived as a pro-French rival to Arran, but when Arran renounced his pro-English policy Lennox promptly went over to the English camp, and from 1544 to 1546 acted repeatedly, though ineffectually, as an agent of Henry VIII in various expeditions to the south-west of Scotland and the Firth of Clyde. For his unpatriotic activities he was forfeited (1 October 1545) and he remained an exile in England for nearly twenty years.

Lennox married (6 July 1544) Margaret Douglas, who, as the daughter of Margaret Tudor by the Earl of Angus, stood next after Mary, Queen of Scots, in the English succession, and some thought that their son, Lord Darnley, had a better claim than Mary, because he was born and brought up in England. Lennox was allowed to return to Scotland in September 1564 and his forfeiture was rescinded in December. Darnley followed next year, and the Lennoxes were in the ascendant on Darnley's marriage to Mary, though with their anti-national record they can hardly have been popular. After Darnley's murder, Lennox returned to England (which his wife seems never to have left) and he tried rather ineffectually to intervene in the proceedings against Mary in 1568–9.

After the Regent Moray was murdered, Lennox was put forward as an English candidate for the Scottish regency (to which, as the King's grandfather, he had a reasonable claim); he was declared Lieutenant of the Kingdom in May 1571 and Regent in July. However, he was not acceptable to his family's enemies nor to those who regarded him as an English agent, and there was little hope that he would end the resistance of Mary's supporters unless he obtained powerful English help, which was not forthcoming. He was shot in a skirmish at Stirling on 4 September 1571. His second son, Charles, was his heir, and Charles, on his death in 1576, left a young daughter, Arabella.

Morton, James Douglas, 4th Earl of (*c.* 1516–1581), second son of Sir George Douglas of Pittendreich, younger brother of the 6th Earl of Angus, married Elizabeth, daughter of the 3rd Earl of Morton, and succeeded to that earldom in right of his wife in 1550. When the Angus Douglases were banished in 1528, this young member of the house evidently remained in Scotland, lurking under an assumed name and serving as a farm-manager. In the military operations of 1548 he was taken prisoner by the English and remained in captivity until 1550. In 1552 he became a Privy Councillor and in 1557 he gained control of the Angus estates in the minority of the young earl, his nephew, who did not come of age until about 1575. At the end of 1557 Morton was one of the signatories of the 'First Bond' in which a few notables declared their determination to work for the overthrow of the Roman Church.

During Mary's personal reign, and while the ascendancy of Moray lasted, Morton became Chancellor (January 1563) and retained the office until he was dismissed for his part in the murder of Riccio (February 1566) and had to flee to England. Pardoned with the rest of the Riccio murderers in December 1566, he returned to Scotland in January 1567 and had foreknowledge of the murder of Darnley, though, as he firmly asserted before his execution, he was not an actual participant. On Mary's fall, it was Morton who 'discovered' the Casket Letters, and he took part, with Moray, in the conferences held in England to assess Mary's guilt.

After Moray's death Morton became the leading man in the King's Party—indeed, even in 1567 he had been Regent-designate, should Moray decline the office—although he did not become Regent until November 1572. His policy, in the tradition of the Angus Douglases, was one of firm friendship with England, whence he at last, in 1573, received the help necessary to extinguish the resistance of the Queen's party. In ecclesiastical affairs he went some way towards reshaping the Scottish Church along English lines, but he took no effective action against Andrew Melville and the Presbyterians. He dealt ruthlessly with Mary's supporters, who were excluded from office as long as he was in power, and he took energetic action to restore order throughout the country. Though accused of rapacity, he does not seem to have been responsible for any excessive financial exactions, but he did take some care to see that provision was made for his four illegitimate sons.

Morton's fall was due as much to personal animosities as anything else, and he had made the error of taking no steps to ingratiate himself with the young King. He resigned the regency in March 1578 and spent a brief period in retirement, 'making the alleys of the garden even, his mind in the mean time occupied in crooked paths',[1] but by the summer he was again at the head of the administration. At the end of 1580 his enemies caused him to be denounced as an accessory to Darnley's murder, and he was beheaded on 2 June 1581. Elizabeth, whom he had served so well, took no effective action to save him, though his fall meant that the country came under the domination of an anti-English faction. Morton had no lawful issue, and when his wife died she had been insane for twenty-two years. The earldom passed to William Douglas of Lochleven, a member of a collateral line.

Melville, Andrew (1545–1622), the founder of Scottish Presbyterianism, was the youngest son of an Angus laird. He learned Greek at the grammar school of Montrose and, after studying at St. Andrews University, went in 1564 to the continent. After some time at Paris and Poitiers he settled in Geneva, by this time dominated by Calvin's successor, Theodore Beza, and he became a professor in the Academy. On his return to Scotland in 1574 he became Principal first of the College of Glasgow and then, in 1580, of St. Mary's College at St. Andrews. His work at Glasgow was continued by his successor, Thomas Smeton (1536–83), who had come under Melville's influence on the continent and had returned to Scotland in 1577 to become minister of Paisley.

Melville's own academic interests were in 'the tongues', and he was a great educationist, who did much for the reorganization of Scottish university education and made an enduring impression on his students. His published works are negligible, and it was clearly by personal contacts and by his great academic reputation that he became so influential in ecclesiastical politics. In the Scotland to which he returned, there was much uncertainty on the polity and endowment of the Church and on the relations between Church and State. Melville, primed by Beza, had all the answers: the office of bishop was to be abolished and presbyteries to be set up, the reformed Church was to have all the old ecclesiastical property, and Church and State were to form 'Two Kingdoms', though in such a way that, while the lay power could not interfere in the Church, ministers could 'teach the magistrate his duty'. Melville was able

1. Sir James Melville, *Memoirs*, p. 105. Folio Society, 1969.

H

to build up a strong party, mainly of younger men, who supported his views, and they soon prevailed in the General Assembly to the extent that the second Book of Discipline, expressing most of Melville's programme, was adopted in 1578. But the proposals could not be put into effect without parliamentary action, and there was soon a clash between the Assembly and the government, to which Melville's programme was not acceptable. At the height of the dispute, in 1584, Melville, threatened with imprisonment, had to flee to England, and Parliament passed the 'Black Acts', reaffirming episcopal government and the control of crown and Parliament over the Church.

Melville returned at the end of 1585, and from 1586, as Presbyterianism began to make headway until it was in the end authorized by Parliament in 1592, Melville found himself rising in the royal favour, for the King was depending on the ultra-Protestants against the Roman Catholic element. In this situation the ministers were tempted to go ever further in their claims to dictate policy, and Melville, who did not know the meaning of tact, rebuked 'God's silly vassal', as he called the King to his face, both for his personal habit of profanity and for his policy. From 1597 onwards, however, the King, who had now subdued the Roman Catholic faction, began to prevail against the ministers, and by 1604 he was able to suspend the meetings of the General Assembly. The Presbyterians, fearing the suspension might be permanent, felt impelled to make a stand and defy the King. In 1606 Melville and six others were summoned to London, ostensibly for consultation. There Melville poured scorn on the furnishings of the chapel royal and dismissed the Archbishop of Canterbury's garments as 'Romish rags'. He was detained in London for five years and was then allowed to go overseas, and he ended his career as a professor at Sedan (1611–22).

Andrew's nephew, James (1556–1614), was educated at St. Andrews University and came much under his uncle's influence on the latter's return from the continent in 1574. He was a colleague of Andrew at both Glasgow and St. Andrews. Like Andrew, he was in exile in England in 1584–5 and again from 1606, when he was not allowed nearer Scotland than Newcastle and Berwick. James Melville wrote an *Autobiography and Diary* (published by the Bannatyne Club and Wodrow Society), which, besides its value for important church affairs, gives an account of his education and of his life as minister of Anstruther from 1586. The impression one is apt to form is that James was a much gentler and more mild character than his uncle Andrew, but Archbishop Spottiswoode declared that

Andrew was 'but a blast' whereas James was 'a crafty, biding man'.

Thomas McCrie, *Andrew Melville*, 1819 and later editions.

Adamson, Patrick (?1537–1592), Archbishop of St. Andrews, otherwise known as Constance or (a more probable form) Couston, was a native of Perth and was educated at St. Andrews University. When the reformed church began to take shape in 1560, Adamson was one of those thought 'apt and able to minister', and by 1562 he was minister of Ceres, in Fife. Already he was clearly an outstanding man, and was appointed as 'commissioner' for Aberdeenshire, which meant that he carried out the functions which were elsewhere executed by bishops and superintendents. In 1564 he received permission to go abroad as tutor to the son of James MacGill of Rankeillor, a Lord of Session, and he himself pursued legal studies in Paris. On the birth of Prince James in 1566, Adamson wrote prophetic verses hailing him as Prince of Scotland, England, France and Ireland: Queen Elizabeth was furious, and, although Adamson was not within her reach, he was prosecuted by the French government. Despite this, he continued his studies at Bourges, and was still in France at the time of the massacre of St. Bartholomew's Eve in 1572.

Adamson had already been invited to return to the ministry of the Scottish Church, and he now accepted. He was minister of Paisley and commissioner in Galloway, and attracted the patronage of the Regent Morton, who nominated him to the archbishopric of St. Andrews in 1575. Adamson made it clear that he regarded his episcopal office as something for which he was not answerable to the General Assembly, and soon enunciated a high concept of episcopacy as of divine institution. He was therefore the chief antagonist of Andrew Melville, the Presbyterian leader, and the controversy between them became more acute when Melville was appointed Principal of St. Mary's College in St. Andrews, where the Archbishop was in the habit of preaching and lecturing. During the period of Presbyterian ascendancy (1581–3), Adamson was in danger of excommunication, but as soon as King James escaped from the hands of the ultra-Protestant faction he was in favour and was sent on an embassy to England in November 1583, partly for political purposes and partly to seek the support of the English authorities for the episcopal party and policy in Scotland. In the latter part of his mission he had little success, for he received a rather cool reception from Archbishop Whitgift and could not counteract the influence of the Puritan officials who did so much to shape English policy. However, on his return the Scottish Parliament, in the 'Black Acts' of 1584, reaffirmed episcopal government. After a year and a half, as a result of a further political change, the government began a policy designed to conciliate the Presbyterians, and episcopacy was gradually eclipsed. Adamson's health had long given him concern, and in his later years he declined into misery and poverty.

Lennox, Esmé Stewart, 1st Duke of (*c.* 1542–1583), played a part in Scottish affairs for only three years, but he was for a brief space the dominant figure in the country. He was the only son of John Stewart, the third son of the 3rd Earl of Lennox, whose two elder sons were Matthew, the 4th Earl, father of Lord Darnley, and Robert, Bishop of Caithness. John was adopted as his heir by the Maréchal d'Aubigny, himself a son of the 1st Earl of Lennox, and spent most of his life in France from at least 1544 until his death in 1567, when he was succeeded in the lordship of Aubigny by his son, Esmé. The young James VI had few near kinsfolk, for Darnley's younger brother, Charles, Earl of Lennox, died in 1576 leaving only a daughter, Arabella; the next male in the Lennox line was Bishop Robert, the King's great-uncle and a man advanced in years, with no family. It was not, therefore, surprising that Esmé should be welcomed by the King, when he arrived in Scotland in September 1579, and James found this French cousin so attractive personally that he showered honours upon him: Bishop Robert was prevailed on to resign the earldom of Lennox in his favour (March 1580), and on 5 August 1581 Esmé was created Duke of Lennox; he also became Chamberlain.

Esmé's object in coming to Scotland may have been mainly to secure his reversion of the Lennox titles and estates and of the claim his family had to the throne as heirs of Darnley, and there is no reason to believe that he had either any strong attachment to the Roman Catholic faith or any great desire to restore the captive Mary (except perhaps under an arrangement which would give her titular sovereignty, with real power in the hands of her son and those who influenced him). But there were Roman Catholic intrigues in which over-optimistic priests cast Lennox for the part of leader of a Counter-Reformation enterprise in which the conquest of Scotland would be followed by that of England, and the ultra-Protestants in Scotland were extremely suspicious, although Lennox did his best to allay their anxiety by subscribing the 'Negative Confession' which abjured all papistry in the most sweeping terms. The fact that he upheld the episcopal system made enemies of the Presbyterians, who used their pulpits against him. It was also true that his administration found places for former supporters of Mary and men of a generally conservative outlook. Lennox's ascendancy came to an end in August 1582, when a party of ultra-Protestant notables seized the King in the Ruthven Raid and separated him from his friend. Lennox, after lingering for a time at Dumbarton, withdrew from Scotland and died in France on 26 May 1583.

By a French marriage Esmé had a son Louis, or Ludovick, who succeeded him as second Duke of Lennox and was advanced by King James to most of his father's honours and properties, and a daughter who married the first Marquis of Huntly, another royal favourite. Ludovick (1574–1624) died without surviving issue, and was succeeded by his brother Esmé, the 3rd Duke, whose family continued the line until 1672, when the death of the 6th Duke without issue caused the dukedom to devolve on King Charles II, who granted it to one of his illegitimate sons.

Gowrie, William Ruthven, 4th Baron Ruthven and 1st Earl of Gowrie (c. 1541–1584), was the son of Patrick, 3rd Lord Ruthven (c. 1520–66). Patrick was the eldest son and heir of the 2nd Lord by Jonet, eldest daughter and co-heiress of Patrick, Lord Haliburton of Dirleton, and he succeeded his father in 1552. The family alignment was with the Reformation and the English alliance, and the Ruthven policy was further shaped by something of a personal feud with the reigning house, which began when the 3rd Lord took a prominent part in the murder of Riccio. After that crime he had to flee to England, where he died (13 June 1566). His eldest son had died before 1565, and his second son, William, succeeded.

The 4th Lord had been with his father at the Riccio murder and in his English exile, but survived to be pardoned at the end of 1566. Under the regency for James VI he was appointed Treasurer (1571), and, after acquiring much of the property of the abbey of Scone, he was created Earl of Gowrie in 1581. The creation was a remarkable one, for it is hard in that period to parallel the elevation to an earldom of a man not of royal blood, and it suggests that Ruthven had some quite extraordinary influence, possibly through the indebtedness of the crown to him for the subventions to the royal finances which he, as Treasurer, advanced from his own pocket. The royal debt to Gowrie may have been one reason for his leading the 'Ruthven Raid' which in 1582 put James under the control of the pro-English and ultra-Protestant faction. One of Gowrie's associates in this affair was Sir Thomas Lyon of Baldukie (*c.* 1546–1608), Master of Glamis: when it was made plain to the King that he was in effect a captive and the boy burst into tears, Lyon said to him, 'Better bairns greet than bearded men.' After James's escape from the 'Raiders', Gowrie was pardoned, but in April 1584 he was involved in a plot by some of the other members of his faction to seize Stirling, and was executed (4 May 1584). By Dorothea Stewart, daughter of Henry, 1st Lord Methven, he had five sons and several daughters.

The eldest son, James, who succeeded as 2nd Earl, died in 1588. John, the second son (*c.* 1577–1600), then became 3rd Earl. He was educated at Perth and at Edinburgh and then went abroad to study at Padua. He returned to Scotland in 1600 and on 5 August of that year was killed in his house at Perth in the mysterious Gowrie Conspiracy, along with his next brother, Alexander. Two other sons of the 1st Earl fled to England, and the family was forfeited. The truth about the Gowrie affair has never been cleared up, but it is easy to see certain elements in the situation. The 3rd Earl inherited his family's feud with the royal line, and also inherited the debt still outstanding from the time of Treasurer Gowrie; he was also attached to the ultra-Protestant faction, whom King James had so suppressed that only desperate measures could restore it; his family had a well-established position in Perth, where they had an almost hereditary right to the office of Provost. Recent opinion on the whole inclines to the view that the 3rd Earl may have been planning a *coup* like the Ruthven Raid, and scouts the view that James invented the whole thing as a device to rid himself of a creditor.

Andrew Lang, *James VI and the Gowrie Mystery*, 1902.
William Roughead, *The Riddle of the Ruthvens*, 1919.

Arran, James Stewart, Earl of (*c.* 1545–1596), was the second son of Andrew Stewart, 2nd Lord Ochiltree, who was the son of Margaret Hamilton, the only child of James, 1st Earl of Arran, by his first wife. It is evident from subsequent remarks about him that Stewart received an education which made him a man of learning and culture, but his early career was a military one on the continent. He returned to Scotland at the end of 1577 or early in 1578, possessing, it is said, nothing except his horse, but his experience and address almost at once attracted the favourable attention of James VI, and he was entertained by Robert, Bishop of Caithness, the

King's great-uncle. Although Esmé Stewart, later Duke of Lennox, who had arrived from France in September, became the leading royal favourite, James Stewart had grants of various lands in 1580 and was appointed a gentleman of the bedchamber in October. It was he who, on 31 December 1580, before the Privy Council, accused Morton of the murder of Darnley.

Stewart became a Privy Councillor in February 1581 and Captain of the King's Guard in March. He caused considerable scandal by marrying Elizabeth Stewart, the widow of Lord Lovat, who had married the Bishop of Caithness in January 1579 but obtained a divorce from him on the grounds of impotence in May 1581, after prolonged litigation. She married James Stewart on 6 July 1581 and bore a son six months later. When Lennox was the dominant figure after Morton's fall, Stewart was in high favour. 'He and Lennox ruled the King and Council as they pleased,' it was reported. He was appointed tutor to James Hamilton, 3rd Earl of Arran, who was insane, and on 22 April 1581, on the somewhat flimsy ground of his descent from the 1st Hamilton Earl of Arran, he was created Earl of Arran, to the exclusion of the 3rd Earl's brothers.

When the Ruthven Raiders overthrew Lennox, Arran was a prisoner, but on their fall in June 1583 he was soon at the head of the administration and ruled Scotland for over two years. When an attempt was made to overthrow him in April 1584 he was denounced as 'that godless atheist, bloody Haman and seditious Catiline'. After acting as Chancellor from May 1584 he was formally appointed to the office in September. He was keeper of the castles of Edinburgh and Stirling, and Provost of Edinburgh. His policy was strongly anti-Presbyterian, but he worked with some success for an understanding with Elizabeth (to the fury of her Puritan advisers). In August 1584 he had conversations with Lord Hunsdon, who was greatly impressed by his charm, eloquence and splendid array: there were remarks about 'a princely presence' and Arran was thought 'very wise and learned'. He managed to formulate an alliance with England in the summer of 1585, but at the end of July there was a scuffle at a day of truce on the Borders, when the son of the Earl of Bedford was killed, and Arran's enemies blamed him for this and used it to rouse Elizabeth to frighten James into dismissing Arran from court. In November 1585, when the leaders of the ultra-Protestant faction, who had been exiled in England, came back to bring about a *coup d'état*, Arran's administration collapsed. He was banished from court and did not appear there again except briefly in 1592, but spent most of his time wandering in Ireland, Ayrshire and the Highlands. He was murdered on 2 November 1596 by a nephew of the Earl of Morton.

James Fergusson, *The Man behind Macbeth*, 1969.

Maitland, Sir John, of Thirlestane (1543–1595), like his brother, William Maitland of Lethington, inherited some of the opinions of their father, Sir Richard. He was at St. Andrews University in 1555 and then in France for an uncertain period, possibly during most of Mary's personal reign. In February 1567 he became Commendator of Coldingham and on 20 April was appointed Keeper of the Privy Seal, on his father's resignation. For the next six years he followed his brother William, going over to Mary's party in the war with the Regents for James VI, losing his office in 1570 and being taken prisoner on the fall of Edinburgh Castle in 1573. From 1574 he enjoyed a conditional liberty, which became absolute (after the end of the regency of Morton) in September 1578.

As an ex-Marian Maitland was an obvious candidate for advancement after Morton's final fall from power in 1580, he was on friendly terms with the King's favourite, Esmé, Duke of Lennox, and was made a Lord of Session in 1581. In the eyes of the ultra-Protestant 'Ruthven Raiders', who overthrew Lennox, he was suspected as a 'papist'. In 1583 he married Janet Fleming, the only child of the 4th Lord Fleming and niece of the wife of his brother William. This gave him a connexion through marriage with the Hamiltons, who had been exiled by Morton. After the fall of the 'Ruthven Raiders' Maitland was able to return to court, he became a Privy Councillor and a most assiduous attender to business. In May 1584, under the régime of James Stewart, Earl of Arran, he was appointed Secretary, but did not wholly approve of all Arran's policy and began to work against him.

When the lords of the ultra-Protestant faction came back from exile in England to bring about Arran's fall, they were accompanied by the Hamiltons, and a kind of coalition government was formed, in which Maitland was soon the leading figure. In May 1586 he became Vice-Chancellor and in 1587 Chancellor. He retained the office of Secretary until he resigned it in favour of his nephew in April 1591. King James himself said that some thought he was 'led by the nose' by Maitland, but, while he was sometimes irked by his Chancellor, there is no doubt of his reliance on him and of Maitland's great part in shaping James's policy. It was said that he 'kept the King on two grounds sure, never to cast out with the Kirk or with England', and he was responsible for some of James's temporary concessions to the Presbyterians as well as for maintaining good relations with Elizabeth. But there were many other aspects of Maitland's work. He helped to steer James through the difficulties with the Earl of Huntly and the Roman Catholic faction on one side and Francis Stewart, Earl of Bothwell, who sometimes headed the militant ultra-Protestants, on the other; he made administration more efficient; he helped to work out the policy whereby the ecclesiastical property was used to appease the nobles; legislation during his term of office attempted to reform civil and criminal justice, to pacify the Highlands and Borders and to encourage trade and manufactures. He accompanied James to Norway and Denmark in 1589–90 on his trip to bring home his bride, and on the day of Anne's coronation in May 1590 he was created Lord Thirlestane.

But Maitland had aroused a good deal of jealousy: he was the first Chancellor in the century who was neither a prelate nor a peer, his measures for good government did not commend him to all, and he was not on good terms with the Queen. In March 1592 James dismissed him from the court (partly to throw on him the blame for unpopular measures), but Maitland retained some influence and the office of Chancellor, and he was back at court in the last two years of his life. It has been neatly said that he had trained a successor in the King himself.

Maurice Lee, *Maitland of Thirlestane*, 1959.

Huntly, George Gordon, 6th Earl and 1st Marquis of (1562–1636), was the eldest son of the 5th Earl (d. 1576) by a daughter of the Duke of Châtelherault. Characteristically of the generally conservative traditions of his house, he was educated in France, and shortly after his return (c. 1581) he was able to join King James on his escape from the ultra-Protestant 'Ruthven Raiders' and to be a member of the Privy Council under the administration of James Stewart, Earl of Arran (1583–5). When Arran fell from power, Huntly continued to be associated with the government, and in 1588 he at once demonstrated his own standing in James's eyes and strengthened his position by marrying Henrietta, daughter of Esmé, Duke of Lennox, once the King's favourite. In the previous year Huntly had received a gift of the abbey of Dunfermline, and now he was made Captain of the King's Guard.

The Earl had made a profession of the reformed faith at the time of his marriage, but for years he was under suspicion for plotting with continental Roman Catholic powers, in association with Francis Hay, 9th Earl of Errol (c. 1566–1631). In 1589 he suffered

101

a very brief imprisonment and on his release it seemed that there might be a rebellion, but he could not or would not muster a force to meet the King in the field, and he surrendered, to be placed in easy confinement for a few months. In February 1592 he was responsible for the murder of the Bonnie Earl o' Moray, who was the darling of the Protestants and also the hereditary rival of the house of Huntly. Again the consequence was only a nominal imprisonment. In 1592, after the discovery of the 'Spanish Blanks', mysterious papers signed by Huntly and Errol, it was believed that these earls had offered to aid Spain in an invasion. The King marched north and the earls fled before him. But they were not forfeited, and James secured an act of oblivion for them, on condition that they submitted to the Reformed Church. In 1594, however, they were forfeited, and yet again the King marched against them; they checked Argyll, in command of the van of the royal army, at Glenlivet, but again they would not face the King in person. They now promised to go abroad and did so in March 1595.

In June 1596 the earls returned secretly and came to terms with the King. Twelve months later they were formally received into the Reformed Church, their forfeiture was rescinded, and this marked the end of the threat from this quarter to the stability of James's kingdom. Huntly became a Privy Councillor, a Marquis, and Lieutenant and Justiciar for the north, in 1599. He showed his cultivated taste by his building at Ruthven Castle, Aboyne and Bog of Gight and his town houses in Elgin and Aberdeen. There was still intermittent suspicion about his sincerity in renouncing Rome, but he was received into the Church of England by the Archbishop of Canterbury in 1612 and was absolved by the General Assembly in 1616. However, even shortly before his death, he seems to have been again under suspicion, and Charles I—though as part of a general policy of clipping the wings of the nobility—deprived him of some of his jurisdictions. Errol had been less pliant than Huntly, for he was excommunicated in 1608 and in his will, in 1628, he declared himself a Roman Catholic.

Bothwell, Francis Stewart, 5th Earl of (1563–1612), was the son of Lord John Stewart, Commendator of Coldingham (an illegitimate son of James V), by Jean Hepburn, sister and heir of James, 4th Earl of Bothwell. His father died very soon after his birth, and Queen Mary (who was his godmother and gave him the name of her first husband) took much interest in him. In 1566 he received certain property forfeited by the Earl of Morton, and in April 1567, when

Mary married the 4th Earl of Bothwell, Francis was created Commendator of Kelso. In 1581 he was created Earl of Bothwell and in 1589 was one of the governors of the realm selected to act during the King's absence in Norway and Denmark.

Francis's father, Lord John, had, like the other sons of James V, been well educated, partly in France, and it appears that Francis spent a good part of his youth on the continent. He was a man of intelligence and culture, of which he left a visible memorial in the remarkable Italianate façade which he erected in the courtyard of his castle at Crichton. Yet, from 1590 onwards, his actions suggest a streak of something little short of lunacy. He was accused of dealing with witches during the King's voyage back from Denmark, and for a matter of four years he led one attack after another on royal residences, to the terror of the King, who yet seems to have admired his cousin's dash and verve too much to take effective action against him. Bothwell's actions seem to have been quite aimless, though for a time he did represent the militant Protestants in their objections to the King's leniency towards the Earls of Huntly and Errol, and he was certainly applauded by some of the more extreme ministers. On the other hand, there were two occasions on which he collaborated with Huntly. Finally, in 1595, he was forfeited, and fled to France. Later he settled in Naples, where he died.

Bothwell married a daughter of the 7th Earl of Angus and had a son, Francis, who was rehabilitated but never recovered any property and died a poor man in 1639. He in his turn had two sons, Thomas (d. 1647) and Robert. The Earl's younger son, John, was the grandfather of Francis Stewart, who became a lieutenant of dragoons in 1678 and a captain in 1679 and who served in the royal army at Bothwell Brig. This Francis was the original of the 'Sergeant Bothwell' who figures in Scott's *Old Mortality*.

Stewart, Lord Robert (1533–1593), was an illegitimate son of James V by Euphemia Elphinstone, daughter of the 1st Lord Elphinstone, who later married John Bruce of Cultmalindie. Like other sons of James V, he evidently had a good education, and was abroad from 1553 onwards, but he was back in Scotland by 1561 at latest and threw in his lot with the Reformers, as did his brothers James, Earl of Moray, and John, Commendator of Coldingham. Robert had been made Commendator of Holyrood in 1539, and is sometimes styled 'of Strathdown'. He was much about the court during Mary's personal reign. On 19 December 1564 he received a lease of the crown lands of Orkney and Shetland and on 26 May 1565 a feu charter of the islands. He greatly strengthened his position in the north when in 1568 he compelled Adam Bothwell, Bishop of Orkney, to make over to him the properties of the bishopric, in exchange for the abbey of Holyrood. Robert thus held crown, earldom and bishopric lands and rights in the northern isles and ruled like a semi-independent potentate. From time to time he was suspended, on suspicion of treasonable dealings with the King of Denmark, who claimed that he had never relinquished sovereignty over the islands, but Robert always succeeded in regaining his position, and on 28 October 1581 he was created Earl of Orkney; a charter of the bishopric followed on 9 June 1585. He and his followers were accused of tyrannizing over the people of the islands, and he left a memorial of his rule in the 'palace' he built at Birsay on the mainland of Orkney.

Earl Robert married Lady Jane Kennedy, daughter of Gilbert, 3rd Earl of Cassillis, in 1561. His eldest son, Henry, predeceased him, and he was succeeded by his second son, Patrick, who had been well educated by Patrick Vaus of Barnbarroch, a Senator of the College of Justice, and had been appointed Commendator of Whithorn in 1581. Patrick had a fresh charter of the earldom of Orkney on 1 March 1600 and one of the bishopric on 15 May following. He is a somewhat controversial figure, who lives in popular memory as a worse oppressor than his father and who certainly made use for his own advantage of the Norse legal system which survived in the islands. At the same time, it is hard to prove that he was arbitrary in his proceedings, and there is some ground for believing that he may have been more popular with the native inhabitants than with the many Scots who had recently settled in the islands. There is, at any rate, no doubt about his standards of culture, for his palace at Kirkwall has been authoritatively pronounced to be the finest Scottish domestic building of the period, and his castle at Scalloway in Shetland foreshadows the refinement and sophistication of the tower-house in its final phase. Whatever the truth about Patrick's rule, agitation against him came from James Law, who was presented to the bishopric of Orkney in 1605 and, by a statute of 1606, became entitled to the Bishop's lands. Earl and Bishop made a contract in 1607, but Law continued to pour complaints into the King's ear, with the result that Patrick was imprisoned in 1609. In 1615, after his son had raised a rebellion in the islands, he was executed.

G. Donaldson, *Shetland Life under Earl Patrick*, 1958.

Lindsay, John (1552–1598), statesman, second son of the 9th Earl of Crawford, was educated with his brother, Sir David Lindsay of

Edzell, in France and at Cambridge. As a boy he was presented to the parsonage of Menmuir, and he is regularly styled 'parson of Menmuir' although he was not a cleric. After becoming an advocate, he was elevated to a judgeship of the Court of Session in 1581 with the judicial title of Lord Menmuir. He became a Privy Councillor in 1589 and 'master of the metals' in 1592. In 1596 he was Keeper of the Privy Seal from March to May, and in that month he became Secretary of State, a Lord of the Exchequer and Keeper of the Signet. He resigned the secretaryship in January 1598.

Lindsay's accession to so many offices in 1596 is accounted for by the fact that he was one of the 'Octavians', a group of eight administrators who were employed in that year to reorganize the royal finances and some of whom remained the chief figures in King James's government for years. Besides Lindsay, they were Alexander Seton, Earl of Dunfermline, and Thomas Hamilton, Earl of Haddington (each the subject of a separate notice in this volume), David Carnegie of Culluthie, James Elphinstone (c. 1553–1612), who became Lord Balmerino and Secretary of State, Sir John Skene (c. 1543–1617), a lawyer much interested in the codification of the law, who became Lord Clerk Register, Walter Stewart, Commendator of Blantyre, and Peter Young, who had been one of the King's preceptors.

There can be no doubt that, but for his early death, Lindsay's talents would have given him a prominent place in King James's administration in later years, comparable to that attained by some of the other Octavians. He is best remembered for his 'Constant Platt', in which he endeavoured to solve the problems which had surrounded ecclesiastical endowment since the Reformation and which were not settled until the reign of Charles I. His plan for the provision of adequate stipends for the ministers commended itself to them, but King James was always reluctant to approve of measures which would inevitably alienate the many lay holders of church property, and only piecemeal modifications were made instead of the comprehensive scheme Lindsay had outlined.

Dunfermline, Alexander Seton, Earl of (1555–1622), was the fourth and third surviving son of George, 5th Lord Seton. He was a godson of Queen Mary, from whom he received a gift of the priory of Pluscarden in 1565. His family was on the Roman Catholic side, and Alexander was sent to Rome to be educated for the Church, but he turned to civil and canon law, which he studied in France for seven years. He became an advocate in 1577, a Lord of Session in

1586 and President of the Court of Session (1593–1605). He became a peer as Lord Urquhart, possibly in 1591, and was created Lord Fyvie in 1597. His administrative ability was already marked, and in 1596 he was one of the 'Octavians' who managed the country's finances. He was Provost of Edinburgh, no doubt as a royal nominee, from 1598 to 1608, in 1604 he became Chancellor and in 1605 was created Earl of Dunfermline. After the King went to England in 1603, Dunfermline, as Chancellor, was something like a viceroy in Scotland. Like others among the King's ministers, Seton was conservative in his views, and it was thought that he had never shaken off the influence of his Roman Catholic upbringing, though he conformed publicly to his master's Church. Characteristic in so many ways of Jacobean Scotland, Dunfermline displayed a fine taste in architecture, with his house at Pinkie and his castle at Fyvie.

George Seton, *Memoir of Alexander Seton, Earl of Dunfermline*, 1882.

Haddington, Thomas Hamilton, 1st Earl of (1563–1637), the grandson of an Edinburgh merchant and the son of a Lord of Session, was educated at the High School of Edinburgh and at Paris University. He became an advocate in 1587 and a Lord of Session in 1592, with the title of Lord Drumcairn. In 1593 he was a Privy Councillor and in 1596 one of the 'Octavians' who tried to introduce a new efficiency to government. He apparently commended himself by his personality, as well as his ability, to the King, who referred to him familiarly as 'Tam o' the Cowgate', from the part of Edinburgh where he had his house. After James went to England in 1603, Hamilton kept in touch with him by frequent visits to London as well as by correspondence.

Hamilton was appointed Lord Advocate in 1596 and was knighted in 1603. In 1612 he was appointed Lord Clerk Register, but within two months exchanged that office for the much more influential one of Secretary of State. In 1613 he was created a peer as Lord Binning and in 1616 became Lord President of the Court of Session, while still retaining the office of Secretary. This made him, next to the Earl of Dunfermline, the most powerful agent of James VI's policy in Scotland, and he so warmly supported the King's ecclesiastical policy that Archbishop Spottiswoode referred to 'the good Lord Secretary, the fourteenth bishop of this kingdom'.

After the accession of Charles I, with whom he was, like most Scots, on less intimate terms, Hamilton's influence was reduced. In 1627 he resigned the Lord Presidency, and, when his powers as

Secretary were curtailed because Sir William Alexander, as Secretary in London, had the King's ear, he also resigned the secretaryship, but was appointed Lord Privy Seal. He continued, however, after 1627, to give of his ability as a member of the Commission for the Valuation of Teinds.

In 1619 Hamilton had been created Earl of Melrose, but in 1627 the title was changed to Earl of Haddington, without loss of precedence: the idea seems to have been that it was 'a more worthy title', and it was said that he preferred to take his style from a sheriffdom rather than from an abbey. In the course of his career Haddington had acquired great wealth and considerable estates, including Tyninghame, which became the principal seat of his family.

Sir William Fraser, *Earls of Haddington*, 1889.

Bassendyne, Thomas (d. 1577), printer, was largely responsible for the production of the first Bible printed in Scotland, which is known as the Bassendyne Bible, although it was not completed until after his death. Scottish printing had made very slow progress, perhaps mainly because of the ease with which books could be imported from England, and although a licence to print the Geneva Bible had been issued to Robert Lekprevik in 1568, nothing seems to have been done. Bassendyne had studied the art of printing in Leyden and was in business in Edinburgh by 1567 as a printer and bookseller. In 1568 the General Assembly condemned two books which he had printed—one entitled *The Fall of the Roman Kirk*, in which the King was called 'supreme head of the primitive kirk' and another an edition of the authorized service-book or *Book of Common Order* which was alleged to contain a 'bawdy song'. Bassendyne produced an edition of the *Works of Sir David Lindsay* in 1574. On 30 June 1576, in conjunction with Alexander Arbuthnot (like himself a burgess of Edinburgh) Bassendyne received a licence under the Privy Seal to print the Bible. The New Testament appeared in 1576, but progress thereafter was slow, possibly because of Bassendyne's death. At any rate, Arbuthnot had to call in the assistance of a foreigner—'Salamon Kirknet of Madeburgh' from Flanders—at a cost of 49/- a week, and this suggests a lack of expertise in Scotland. The Bible was completed in 1579. The licensees had been given a monopoly for a ten-year period, the price of the volume was fixed at £4.13s.4d., and it was made obligatory for every 'substantious householder' to possess a copy.

Craig, Sir Thomas (1538–1608), graduated B.A. at St. Andrews (1555) and went to study law in Paris (1555–61). In 1563 he became an advocate, from 1564 to 1573 he was a justice-depute for criminal cases and in 1573 was appointed sheriff-depute of Edinburgh. In 1603 he wrote his *Jus Feudale* (published in 1650), a treatise on Scottish land law which is still an important source of information and which was printed again so recently as 1934. Craig went to England on James's accession to the English throne and in 1604 was a commissioner for the projected union of the two kingdoms. In his *De Unione Regnorum Britanniae Tractatus,* written in 1605 but not published (by the Scottish History Society) until 1909, Craig strongly advocated Union, and his book contains a great deal of thoughtful description of the Scottish economy and Scottish institutions. It is to be remembered that the strongest supporter of Union on the English side at this time was no less a man than Sir Francis Bacon. Craig also produced Latin verses, published in 1566 (on the birth of Prince James) and in 1603 (on James's departure for England and his coronation in London). A *Treatise on the Succession,* written in January 1603, two months before Elizabeth died, was not published until 1703. Craig was a purely professional man, who took no part in Scottish political life. His eldest son, Sir Lewis, became a judge of the Court of Session in 1569 and it is said that when his father appeared before him to plead as an advocate, 'Sir Lewis, as a pious son, uncovered, and listened to his parent with the utmost reverence'.

P. F. Tytler, *Life and Writings of Sir Thomas Craig,* 1823.

Marischal, George Keith, 5th Earl (1553–1623), was the grandson of the 4th Earl, whom he succeeded in 1581. After education at King's College, Aberdeen, he went off at the age of eighteen to the continent, where he spent at least seven years, visiting Paris, Germany and Italy and studying under Theodore Beza at Geneva. Despite his intellectual interests, he was involved in family feuds and deeds of violence, and politically he aligned himself with the militant ultra-Protestants.

In 1583 Marischal had been a member of a commission set up to superintend a 'new erection' or new constitution for King's College in Old Aberdeen, but the proposed reforms were never adopted in their entirety, and this stimulated the Earl to found a rival college in New Aberdeen in 1593. The main innovation was that the teachers were to specialize in their various subjects instead of, as was the usual Scottish practice, each conducting a group of students throughout all their curriculum. At the same time, the new foundation must be seen against the background of Marischal's somewhat radical ecclesiastical views, and it is noticeable that in 1601 he sent his son to Paris, Orleans, Tours and Saumur, which indicates not only an interest in learning, but an association with the more extreme Scottish Protestants who found a refuge in the Huguenot seminary at Saumur. Marischal endowed his college with some ecclesiastical property which had come into his possession, and it remained a distinct university until 1860, when it was united with King's.

Robert S. Rait, *The Universities of Aberdeen*, 1895.

Napier, John, of Merchiston (1550–1617), inventor of logarithms, was the son and heir of Sir Archibald Napier (1534–1608), laird of Merchiston, on the outskirts of Edinburgh, and the fifteenth-century tower-house where he was born has been fittingly preserved as the nucleus of the buildings of Napier College. John was educated first at St. Andrews University (from 1563) and then abroad, until he married in 1571. He then spent a comparatively retired life at Gartness in Stirlingshire (which his father had acquired) and later at Merchiston after he succeeded his father. With a strongly Protestant background, Napier took an interest in the scriptures and, turning his attention to the last book in the Bible, he produced *A Plaine Discovery of the Whole Revelation of St. John* (1593), which went into five editions in English by 1645 besides others in French, Dutch and German. The Revelation was, of course, interpreted as anti-Roman propaganda, but it may be significant in connexion with other interests of Napier that it is also a book much concerned with enumeration. Especially in his earlier years, Napier spent much of his time in the pursuit of 'projects' characteristic of his age—a plan for the use of salt as a fertilizer, a device for raising water from collieries by a hydraulic screw, a burning mirror which would destroy enemy ships at a distance, a kind of infernal machine in the way of artillery, designed to sweep a whole field clear of an enemy, and even schemes for the equivalents of tanks and submarines. However, it was in mathematics that Napier earned enduring fame. Working on the basis of the relationship between arithmetical and geometrical progression, he ultimately developed his system of logarithms. In his *Mirifici Logarithmorum Canonis Constructio* ('The Construction of the Wonderful Canon of Logarithms'), written in 1614 but not published until 1619, he produced tables of logarithms and explained their use in numeration and trigonometry. In another work, *Rabdologiae seu Numerationes per Virgulas Libri Duo* (1617) ('Two Books on calculations by means of Rods'), he explained how

I

calculations could be made and multiplication and division carried out by an arrangement of ivory rods and metal plates. This device, known as 'Napier's Bones', was the first attempt to produce a calculating machine. Like some others among his contemporaries who had scientific interests, Napier had a reputation for dabbling in the occult, and his retired mode of life fostered this. He was alleged to have a 'jet-black cock' as his 'familiar'.

Mark Napier, *Memoirs of Merchiston*, 1834.
Ernest W. Hobson, *John Napier and the invention of logarithms*, 1914.
Priscilla Napier, *A difficult country: the Napiers in Scotland*, 1972.

Pont, Timothy (*c.* 1565–1614), cartographer, was the eldest son of Robert Pont (*c.* 1530–1606), minister of St. Cuthbert's Church in Edinburgh and a Lord of Session. He was educated at St. Leonard's College, St. Andrews (1579–83), and became minister of Dunnet, in Caithness, in 1601. He must have spent much of the period between 1583 and 1601 in travelling over the length and breadth of Scotland and making what was, so far as is known, the first survey of the country of anything like a scientific kind, and he compiled a remarkable series of maps, the original MSS. of many of which are still extant in the National Library of Scotland. Thanks to the patronage of King James VI and Sir John Scott of Scotstarvet, his maps were preserved. Sir James Balfour of Denmilne bought them in 1629 and received £100 from Charles I as a reward for the service he had rendered. The maps were revised and added to, with editorial matter, by Robert Gordon of Straloch (1580–1661) and his son James Gordon, parson of Rothiemay (1615–86), who also enjoyed the patronage of Charles I. The revised work, consisting of three general maps of Scotland and forty-six maps of counties or regions, was published, as part of a great atlas, by Johan Blaeu of Amsterdam in 1654 and in later editions. Several of the maps had, however, been engraved long before 1654 and some had been reproduced in Mercator's Atlas in 1630. Gordon of Rothiemay is remembered not only for his share in Blaeu's atlas but for the graphic bird's-eye views he made of Edinburgh (1647) and Aberdeen (1661). In Robert Gordon's 'Epistle', prefaced to Blaeu's Atlas, it is said of Pont: 'He travelled afoot over the whole kingdom, which no person before him had done. He visited all the islands, inhabited for the most part by a barbarous and uncivilized people with a language different from ours and where he was often despoiled by cruel robbers—as I have heard him relate—and suffered all the hardships

110

of a difficult and dangerous journey without growing weary or ever losing his courage.'

D. G. Moir and R. A. Skelton, 'New Light on the First Atlas of Scotland', in *Scott. Geog. Magazine*, vol. 84, No. 3 (Dec. 1968).

Heriot, George (1563–1624), goldsmith and founder of a famous school, was the son of an Edinburgh goldsmith who trained his son in his craft and, on his marriage in 1586, set him up in business for himself. In 1594 he was Deacon Convener of the Incorporated Trades of Edinburgh. In 1597 he was appointed goldsmith to Queen Anne and in 1601 goldsmith to the King. In this capacity he frequently lent the royal pair money, on the security of their jewels, and in his growing wealth he came to be known as 'Jingling Geordie'. In 1601 he was appointed to a commission set up to issue a new currency. Heriot followed the King to London in 1603 and at the new court he was again jeweller to Their Majesties. On the death of his first wife in 1608 he returned to Scotland, where he married the daughter of James Primrose of Carrington, grandfather of the 1st Earl of Rosebery, but in 1609 he returned to London and spent the rest of his life there, with a steadily expanding and profitable business. At one time Queen Anne is said to have owed him £18,000. In 1620 he was granted a three years' imposition on sugar, no doubt by way of repaying him for the manner in which he accommodated the King in his financial needs. In the year before his death he executed a deed assigning his fortune to the Town Council of Edinburgh for the education of fatherless boys, sons of freemen of the town of Edinburgh, and in his will he made more detailed provision for his proposed 'Hospital'. The foundation stone of the building was laid in 1628, but it was not completed until 1659, and at first housed thirty boys. Heriot died in London and was buried in St. Martin's in the Fields.

William Steven, *Memoir of George Heriot*, 1845.

Montgomery, Alexander (*c.* 1550–*c.* 1602), poet, was the son of the laird of Hazelhead in Ayrshire. He had part of his upbringing in Argyll, but very little else is known of his life. He is said to have been a captain in the army under the Regent Morton, and the fact that in 1583 the crown granted him a pension of 500 merks from the archbishopric of Glasgow suggests both that he had rendered some substantial services to the government and also that he was about the court when James VI began to assemble a coterie of poets around him. The poet complained of prolonged lawsuits about his pension, and alludes to the devious ways of lawyers. It seems that he later fell out of favour, evidently because he had become a Roman Catholic, and his career remains obscure and controversial.

Montgomery's work was quoted by James VI in his *Reulis and Cautelis to be observit in Scottis poesie* (1584). His best-known poem is *The Cherry and the Slae*, which was first printed (though not in its entirety) in 1597 and long remained popular, though modern judgment is that it is a rather clumsy allegory with a rhyme-scheme unfortunate for a work of its length, and that Montgomery's merit lies rather in his lyrics and sonnets. He was a conscious imitator, using Wyatt and Ronsard as models and sources, and there were three main influences on him: the technique of the French *rhétoriqueurs*, as expounded by Molinet in his *Art de Rhétoric* and exemplified by Du Bartas, who was in Scotland in 1587; the revived interest in music at the court of James VI; and classical humanism, which was inspiring the continued output of much Latin verse in Scotland. Yet, within the bounds of established conventions, Montgomery evolved verse of a new and more popular type.

His work should be seen in the context of a group of courtly poets, perhaps the first and one of the most polished of whom was Alexander Scott (?1530–84), who wrote a number of love lyrics and *Ane New Yeir Gift to the Quene Mary quhen scho come first hame*. Two of the best known, of a later generation, are Sir William Alexander, Secretary of State and Earl of Stirling, and William Drummond of Hawthornden, who are the subjects of separate notices in this volume. Another was William Fowler (c. 1560–1610), who translated the *Triumphs* of Petrarch in 1587 (published 1644) and was something of a pioneer in abandoning Scots for English in his verse, as Alexander and Drummond also did: Fowler was the uncle of Drummond, Secretary to Queen Anne and a close friend of Alexander. Yet another was Sir Robert Ayton (1569–1638), who, after education at St. Andrews, spent some time in France and in 1603 published at Paris a Latin panegyric on King James. This brought him royal favour, and he returned to Britain to become a gentleman of the bedchamber, secretary first to Queen Anne and later to Henrietta Maria. His poems, for which he used sometimes English, sometimes Latin, are not numerous, but are of considerable merit, and he has been called 'the father of the Cavalier lyric'.

The Poems of Scott were edited by D. Laing in 1821 and again by Alexander Scott in 1952; those of Alexander Montgomery were issued by the Scottish Text Society in 1886–7 and 1910, those of Fowler by the S.T.S. in 1914–40, and those of Ayton by the S.T.S.

in 1963. *Cf*. Helena M. Shire, *Song, Dance and Poetry of the Court of Scotland under King James VI*, 1969.

Charles I, King of Scots (1600–1649), the second son of James VI, born at Dunfermline on 19 November 1600, became heir apparent after the death of his elder brother, Henry, in 1612. He succeeded his father on 27 March 1625 and on 1 May following he married Henrietta Maria, daughter of Henry IV of France. Charles had little knowledge of Scottish affairs except what he derived from anglicized Scots about the court, and the Privy Council in Edinburgh had little sympathy with, or even understanding of, their master's motives. His policy in Scotland was marked by a solicitude for the Church and a disregard for the interests of the nobility. One of his first measures was an Act of Revocation, annulling all gifts made since 1540 of properties which the crown could claim, and this included the vast ecclesiastical revenues which had fallen into lay hands before and after the Reformation. The aim was to reduce the power of the nobles and to set up machinery which would provide adequate stipends for the clergy, but the measure, partly because its introduction was badly handled, aroused a general fear for the security of property.

Episcopal government had been revived by James, but with Charles episcopacy was an article of faith, and he treated the bishops with a veneration which few of his subjects were disposed to concede. The advancement of prelates to high office and their influence in Council and Parliament aroused much jealousy. A patron of the arts as well as a believer in the value of ritual in worship, Charles was responsible for the restoration and adornment of many cathedrals and of the abbey church at Holyrood (where he was crowned in 1633), and in 1637 he insisted on the acceptance of a new Prayer Book which has won high praise from liturgical experts but which seemed to many of the Scots to be popish in its character. Meantime he had alienated his people by taxation on an unprecedented scale, and had made an enemy of his Scottish capital by insisting that Edinburgh should build a costly new Parliament House and reconstruct the church of St. Giles as a cathedral for a new bishopric (1633).

The introduction of the Prayer Book led to a riot in the cathedral on 23 July 1637 and to widespread agitation which soon took on an organized shape. The multifarious grievances against the King found expression at the end of February 1638, in the National Covenant, which professed loyalty to the crown and asked for a return to ecclesiastical and constitutional practice as it had stood before Charles's innovations, but which in reality made a clash inevitable, especially as Charles was by temperament obstinate and the Covenanters very soon went beyond their professed aims. A General Assembly met at Glasgow (November 1638) with the King's reluctant consent and, after his Commissioner had withdrawn, proceeded to abolish episcopal government. Military operations followed which revealed the King's weakness and forced him to approve of the abolition of episcopacy. Neither side was disposed to adhere to the conditions of the 'Pacification' made at this stage, and a second 'Bishops' War' followed which led to the virtual capitulation of the King, whose English subjects were now increasingly restive. Charles visited Scotland in the autumn of 1641 and gave way to all the demands made on him, but this did not gain him the support of his Scottish subjects after the English civil war started in 1642. In 1643 the Scottish Parliament decided, by a majority, to support the English opposition, on the understanding, formulated in the Solemn League and Covenant, that Presbyterianism would be imposed on England and Ireland.

The Scottish army gave considerable assistance to the English parliamentarians, and, after the King's cause was crushed at Naseby (1645) and Charles surrendered to the Scots (1646), he was handed over to the English. But it became increasingly apparent that the English Parliament lacked the power, even if it had had the will, to maintain a Presbyterian Church in England, for the victorious English army was dominated by Independency (Congregationalism). Disquiet among the Scots about the alliance with the English Parliament had already caused a Royalist rising under the Marquis of Montrose in 1644–5, and there were now deeper divisions because of doubts about the prospects for Presbyterianism in England and apprehension about the King's future. In 1648, therefore, by the Engagement, the more moderate Covenanters undertook to restore the King on condition that he would reaffirm Presbyterianism in Scotland and give it a three years' trial in England. An army of 'Engagers' invaded England, but was cut to pieces at Preston in August 1648. This intervention further harmed the King's cause in England and was soon followed by his trial and execution (30 January 1649)—an outcome abhorrent to the vast majority of the Scots.

C. V. Wedgwood, *The King's Peace*, 1955 and *The King's War*, 1958.
G. Donaldson, *Scotland: James V to James VII*, 1965.

Spottiswoode, John (1565–1639), Archbishop of St. Andrews, was the son of John Spottiswoode (1510–85) and the brother of James, who became Bishop of Clogher in Ireland. The elder John Spottiswoode, after studying at Glasgow, had gone to England to escape prosecution as a heretic and had been ordained there, but returned to Scotland to become parson of Calder (1548) and superintendent of Lothian (1561). John the younger, after being educated at Glasgow University, became assistant to his father at Calder in 1583, and he married a daughter of David Lindsay (*c.* 1531–1613), minister of Leith and later Bishop of Ross. With his background and relationships, John could hardly have been other than Episcopalian in his outlook, and by 1596 it was plain that he favoured King James's policy of curbing the excesses of the Presbyterian faction. This brought him royal favour: he went on an embassy to France in 1601 in company with the Duke of Lennox, he accompanied the King to London in 1603 and he was nominated to the archbishopric of Glasgow in the same year.

Spottiswoode was Moderator of the General Assembly at Glasgow in 1610, when the revival of episcopal administration was approved, and later in the same year, along with the bishops of Brechin and Galloway, he was consecrated at London, thereby restoring to the Scottish episcopate the 'Apostolic Succession'. He was translated to St. Andrews in 1615, and proved an able and energetic administrator, mild but firm in his methods. Already in 1615 he had drawn up suggestions for a measure of liturgical reform, and he was Moderator of the General Assembly at Aberdeen in 1616 which appointed a committee to revise the existing service-book, *The Book of Common Order*, and to draw up a new Confession of Faith. He was Moderator again of the Assemblies at St. Andrews in 1617 and Perth in 1618 and helped to carry through the Five Articles which embodied the King's changes in Scottish usage— observance of the Christian year, private Baptism and Communion, Confirmation by Bishops and kneeling at Communion. But, although Spottiswoode pressed for obedience to the King's wishes, and although he was strenuous in his defence of episcopacy (for example, in his *Refutatio Libelli de Regimine Ecclesiae Scoticanae,* a reply to the Presbyterian Calderwood), he was not enamoured of all the King's proposals and did his best to ignore the widespread failure to observe the Five Articles.

Although Spottiswoode had long been a Privy Councillor, and although Charles I made him Lord Chancellor in 1635, he was in truth less influential under Charles, who relied more on the advice of English churchmen. Consequently, it was almost with dismay that the Archbishop saw the introduction of the Code of Canons of 1635 and the Prayer Book of 1637. When strenuous opposition to the latter became apparent, Spottiswoode remarked that it would be better 'to lay aside that book and not to press the subjects with it any more'. When the King's obstinacy led to the outbreak of something like rebellion, Spottiswoode exclaimed, 'Now all that we have been doing these thirty years is cast down in a moment,' and he retired to London, where he died. He was buried in Westminster Abbey.

Spottiswoode's *History of the Church of Scotland* was first published in 1655. It is a work of considerable merit in style and composition and is rather less strongly partisan than contemporary Presbyterian histories, but it is far less valuable to historians than Calderwood's work, because the latter reproduces so many original documents.

The archbishop's son, Sir Robert (1596–1646), after education in Glasgow, Oxford and France, became a Lord of Session in 1622 and Lord President in 1633. A supporter of Montrose's rising on behalf of the King, he was captured at Philiphaugh and executed. His *Practicks* were published by his grandson, John, in 1706.

'Life of the Author', in the Spottiswoode Society edition of the *History*, 1865.

Forbes, John (1593–1648), theologian, was the second son of Patrick Forbes of Corse (1564–1635). Patrick, son and heir of the laird of Corse, had studied under Andrew Melville at Glasgow and St. Andrews and had clearly aimed at the Presbyterian ministry, until he was recalled by his father to the life of a laird. His reputation for learning and piety, however, was such that he was pressed to accept ordination and ultimately did so, at the age of forty-eight. He became Bishop of Aberdeen in 1618 and won general approval for both his pastoral and his educational work.

John was educated first at King's College, Aberdeen, and then went to the continent to study theology, first at Heidelberg and from 1615 at Sedan, where Andrew Melville was Principal. He long remained on the continent, was ordained at Middelburg by his uncle, John Forbes (1568–1634), and married a Dutch lady, Soete Roosboom. Shortly after his return to Scotland, he was appointed Professor of Divinity at King's College (1620). He was perhaps the most able of the 'Aberdeen Doctors' who were famous for their scholarship but whose work was shattered by the troubles between

116

Charles I and his subjects. Though far from being fanatical, Forbes believed that he knew where the truth lay and, though a man of peace, he found himself in a position were he had to sacrifice peace—as well as his own material comforts—to the truth. In 1638 he published a tract against the National Covenant, *A peaceable warning to the subjects in Scotland*, and he took part in a disputation between the Doctors of the University and a committee from the General Assembly headed by the Earl of Montrose. In 1639, when subscription to the Covenant became compulsory, Forbes refused to submit and was deprived of his Chair. Worse was to come, for on his refusal to accept the Solemn League and Covenant of 1643 he was forced into exile (1644). At Amsterdam in 1645 he wrote *Instructiones Historico-Theologicae de Doctrina Christiana* ('Doctrine of the Christian Church, historically considered'). In 1646 he returned to Scotland and lived in seclusion on his estate at Corse. His *Instructiones* has been described as one of the most important theological works of its century, and some would claim Forbes as Scotland's greatest theologian. He was a man of vast learning, which he deployed skilfully and accurately, and he combined it with simplicity, piety and charity.

D. Macmillan, *The Aberdeen Doctors*, 1909.

Alexander, William, Earl of Stirling (?1567–1640), poet, courtier and Secretary of State, was born at Menstrie Castle, near Stirling, was educated at Glasgow and Leyden and was on the continent as tutor to the Earl of Argyll. As a result of unrequited love in a romance which had started before his departure, he composed a hundred love sonnets, which were published in London in 1604 as *Aurora, containing the first fancies of the author's youth*. He had probably already come to the notice of King James, and he went to London shortly after James succeeded to the English throne. In his *Monarchick Tragedies* (1607), he criticized vanity, power and riches, and in 1612 he wrote an elegy on Prince Henry. In 1614 he produced *Doomsday or the Great Day of Judgment*.

Already something of a courtier, Alexander had become an usher to Prince Charles in 1613 and in 1614 he was knighted and appointed Master of Requests. From this point his literary work was partly effaced by a kind of political careerism which did nothing to endear him to his fellow-countrymen. In 1621 he obtained a gift of Nova Scotia, designed as an area of Scottish colonization, and in 1625 wrote *An Encouragement to Colonies*. But the colonization came to very little, the few settlers were ultimately turned out by the French, and the venture degenerated into little more than a money-making scheme whereby Nova Scotia baronetcies were sold to men who had no intention of ever seeing America. In 1626 Charles I made Alexander Secretary for Scotland, in 1630 he was created Viscount Stirling, and in 1633 Earl. Another scheme which brought unpopularity to Alexander was a patent to issue base coins or 'turners'. For some years he had been involved with King James in the preparation of a new metrical version of the Psalms, and in 1627 Charles I gave him a monopoly to print *The Psalms of King David translated by King James*, the first edition of which appeared in 1631. As verse these psalms are often vastly superior to other metrical versions, though they may be less close to the original language, but any prospect they might have had of acceptance was ended when they were bound up and issued with the new Prayer Book of 1637, which was the occasion of the revolt against Charles I. In the same year, 1637, Alexander's collected works were published as *Recreations with the Muses*.

T. H. McGrail, *Sir William Alexander*, 1940.

Drummond, William, of Hawthornden (1585–1649), poet, belonged to a cadet branch of the family of Lord Drummond. He was the son of John Drummond, who had been a gentleman usher to James VI and who had acquired the Hawthornden property. His mother was a sister of the poet William Fowler, his sister married Sir John Scott of Scotstarvet, and William himself became a close friend of another poet, Sir William Alexander. His whole background was the courtly circle of poets and *literati* associated with the court of James VI. From the High School of Edinburgh Drummond went to Edinburgh University, where he graduated M.A. in 1605, and he then continued his education, with the aim of qualifying as a lawyer, in London, Bourges and Paris. He returned home in 1609, but was in London again in 1610. In that year his father died, and he abandoned the idea of a legal career.

Drummond was already a great reader, especially of poetry and drama in many languages, and he had started writing verse. His first publication was an *Elegy* on Henry, Prince of Wales (1613). A volume of *Poems* followed in 1616, *Forth Feasting* commemorated James VI's visit to Scotland (1617) and *Flowers of Sion* followed in 1623. Ben Jonson, on his visit to Scotland in 1618–19, spent two or three weeks with Drummond at Hawthornden. Other aspects of Drummond's manifold interests appeared in 1627—a gift by him of 500 books to the library of his old university and a curious series of patents for mechanical inventions, several of them related to armaments. In 1633 Drummond was responsible for the composition of some of the many verses required on the occasion of Charles I's visit to Scotland, and in the same year he began work on his *History of the Five Jameses* (descendants of Robert III's Queen, Annabella Drummond, whom the poet claimed as a kinswoman).

Charm of style, rather than profound poetic feeling, marks most of Drummond's verse, for much is conventional. But he has an attractive lightness of touch and the power to create a sense of lingering melancholy. In *Flowers of Sion* he uses the teachings of Christianity to combat his fear of death, and an essay, 'The Cypress Grove', appended to the *Flowers*, has been pronounced an unsurpassed piece of English prose.

With his aristocratic and conservative sympathies, Drummond was on the whole at ease in Charles I's Scotland, though he was critical of some of the King's policies and was, like most people, antagonized by the highhanded action of the King in trying Lord Balmerino for treason in 1634 because he had been in possession of a supplication intended for Charles. From the outset, Drummond was aloof from the covenanting movement, and wrote a pamphlet *Irene* criticizing it. As the movement developed, and proceeded to extremes, Drummond was especially irritated by the growing clericalism, on which he poured scorn in a series of squibs in verse and prose, and he wrote a tract, *Skiamachia* (1643), condemning Scottish intervention on the side of the English Parliament.

David Masson, *Drummond of Hawthornden*, 1873.
Robert H. MacDonald, *The Library of Drummond of Hawthornden*, 1972.

Urquhart, Sir Thomas, of Cromarty (1611–1660), author and translator, was educated at King's College, Aberdeen, and then travelled in several countries, including France, Spain and Italy, where he collected many books. He returned to take the Royalist side in the quarrel between Charles I and his subjects, and fought against the Covenanters at Turriff in 1639. He then went to London, as the King's cause seemed to have no future in Scotland, and he was knighted (1641). His *Epigrams, Divine and Moral* (1641), though of mediocre quality, have flashes of wit. Sir Thomas was in Scotland in 1642, when he succeeded his father in the estate, but abroad again from 1642 to 1645. With the divisions among the Covenanters, prospects for the King seemed to improve, and Urquhart returned to Scotland, to spend some years at Cromarty. In 1649 he supported the proclamation of Charles II as King in succession to his father. At the battle of Worcester (1651), Urquhart was taken prisoner and sent to the Tower of London, but was released on parole in 1652. He then apparently went again to the continent, where he died.

Urquhart is best known for his translation of *Rabelais*, the first part of which was published in 1653 and a second part in 1693, but he was the author of a number of other works. Some of them were designedly serious, notably a *Treatise on Trigonometry* (1645) and *An Introduction to the Universal Language* (1653), though even these had some fantastic elements. His quaintness emerged in *A Peculiar Promptuary of Time* (1652), in which he traces his descent from Adam, and in *The Discovery of a most exquisite Jewel ... found in the Kennel of Worcester Street* (1652), which gives an account of the Admirable Crichton (James Crichton, *c.* 1560–85) and is also largely concerned with Urquhart's pedigree. It was characteristic of much in this hearty Royalist that he died of laughter when he heard of the restoration of Charles II.

J. Willcock, *Sir Thomas Urquhart*, 1899.
Hugh MacDiarmid, *Scotttish Eccentrics*, 1936.

Balfour, Sir James, of Denmilne and Kinnaird (*c.* 1598–1657), antiquary, was the eldest son of Michael Balfour of Denmilne, who was comptroller of the royal household under Charles I and was knighted in 1630. He attended St. Andrews University (1610–14) and was at first inclined to poetry, but his genius lay along different lines, and from an early age he had almost a passion for collecting and transcribing—and occasionally forging—historical MSS. He travelled on the continent from 1626 to 1628 and then spent some time in London, where he made the acquaintance of Sir Robert Cotton and Sir William Dugdale, who were both antiquaries and collectors of MSS., and of Sir William Segar, Garter King of Arms. To Dugdale's *Monasticon Anglicanum* Balfour contributed a section on Scottish religious houses. In 1630 he was knighted and appointed Lyon King of Arms, and settled in Scotland, where his father gave him the estate of Kinnaird. He was a member of the circle of cultivated men who adorned Charles I's Scotland, with Drummond of Hawthornden, Sir William Alexander, Archbishop Spottiswoode and the editors of Pont's maps. He was created a baronet in 1633, when he was responsible for the ceremonial at the coronation of Charles I.

On the outbreak of the troubles between the King and his subjects, Balfour's position was that, while he saw the defects of Charles I's

policy, he was too much of a Royalist to go along with the Covenanters as they proceeded to more extreme courses, and he largely
withdrew from public life except when his services as Lyon were
required. He officiated at the coronation of Charles II at Scone in
1651—the only Presbyterian coronation service. Balfour devoted his
time mainly to inspecting, copying and describing state documents,
registers and charters and the archives of the monasteries. While the
tradition of reproducing documents was already well established in
Scotland, Balfour was a pioneer in concentrating on those of periods
much earlier than his own days. He wrote up much history from
his collections, and his *Annales*, in four volumes, extending from
the reign of Malcolm III, were intended as a supplement to earlier
histories, using new material, rather than as a comprehensive work;
they are especially valuable for his own time. He surveyed his native
sheriffdom of Fife as a contribution to the revision of Timothy
Pont's work, and when Pont's maps were published the Lorne sheet
was dedicated to Balfour. In 1699 the bulk of what remained of his
collections was acquired by the Advocates' Library, now the
National Library of Scotland, where it was used by Thomas Ruddiman in the eighteenth century and later by the historical clubs,
whose debt to Balfour is very considerable.

J. D. Mackie, *The Denmilne MSS.*, Historical Association of Scotland, 1928.

Scott, Sir John, of Scotstarvet (1585–1670), son of Robert Scott of
Knightspottie in Perthshire, acquired the estate of Scotstarvet, near
Cupar in Fife, in 1611. He was educated at St. Andrews University
and in 1611 became Director of Chancery, an office previously held
by his father and his grandfather. He was knighted by King James
on his visit to Scotland in 1617, became a Privy Councillor in 1622,
and a Lord of Session, with the judicial title of Lord Scotstarvet, in
1632. In 1628 he was on a commission for revising the laws and in
1629 was one of the justices appointed to go on circuit for criminal
cases. He acted on behalf of the gentry in the negotiations following
the Act of Revocation whereby Charles I planned to annex church
lands to the crown, and his absence from the Council from 1633 onwards suggests that he disapproved of the King's policy. He signed
the National Covenant in 1638, reappeared on the Council in 1639
and was evidently one of the more extreme Covenanters, for he
opposed the Engagement in 1648. With the Cromwellian conquest
of Scotland he lost his offices, in 1652.

Sir John married three times and had nineteen children. His first wife was a sister of Drummond of Hawthornden, the poet, and his second a grand-daughter of Sir James Melville, who wrote *Memoirs of his own Time*. Scott fitted into the contemporary cultural scene, for he himself composed Latin verses and had a hand in the preparation of the *Delitiae Poetarum Scotorum*, an anthology published at Amsterdam in 1637. He was also involved for many years in the collection for Blaeu of Amsterdam of maps for his *Atlas*, and by providing Timothy Pont's maps he deserves credit for the excellent treatment Scotland received. However, Scott's writings were mainly related to his professional and political interest. Thus, he wrote (but did not publish) a translation of Sir Thomas Craig's *Jus Feudale*, and he composed memoirs of a kind in the shape of a 'Trew Relation of the principal affairs concerning the state', which also remained unpublished. This work deals with three aspects of Charles I's policy; his proposal to exclude the Lords of Session from the Privy Council: his dealings with the Earl of Menteith, who asserted his claim to the earldom of Strathearn in virtue of his descent from the second and unquestionably legal mariage of Robert II and who was demoted by the King to the earldom of Airth; and the affair of the Act of Revocation.

Scott's best remembered work is *The Staggering State of Scots Statesmen*, written between 1650 and 1663 and published in 1754. The theme of the book has nothing to do with drunkenness, and shows no love of scandal for its own sake: the argument is that Scottish statesmen had lost balance through their pursuit of gain and that they had always met with retribution either in their own persons or in their families. It is therefore predominantly a somewhat melancholy book, but contains some illuminating information. Scott includes an account of himself: 'Albeit he was possessor of the place of Chancery above forty years, and doer of great services to the King and country, yet, by the power and malice of his enemies, he has been at last thrust out of the said places in his old age, and likewise fined in £500 sterling [by Cromwell] and one altogether unskilled placed to be Director. ... For his majesty's and predecessor's service had been twenty-four times at London, being 14,400 miles, and twice in the Low Countries for printing the Scots poets and the Atlas: and paid to John Blaeu a hundred double pieces for printing of the poets.'

T. G. Snoddy, *Sir John Scott, Lord Scotstarvet*, 1968.

Jamesone, George (1589/90–1644), portrait-painter, was the son of Andrew Jamesone, a master-mason in Aberdeen, and Marjory

Anderson. His birth is not recorded but must fall between mid-1589 and mid-1590. In 1612, he was apprenticed in Edinburgh to the decorative painter John Anderson, himself an Aberdonian. The circumstances in which Jamesone turned to portraiture remain unclear, but from 1620 he fulfilled a rapidly growing demand for portraits from the academic and burgess circles of Aberdeen and the nobility of the north-east. Interesting portraits of this decade include the poet Arthur Johnston (in Aberdeen University), the Countess Marischal, painted in 1626 (National Gallery of Scotland), and the marriage portrait of the future Marquis of Montrose in 1629 (Kinnaird Castle). While these portraits show a rather provincial amalgam of features derived from the late Jacobean court-portraiture of Marcus Gheeraerts and the painting of the Dutch-inspired Cornelius Johnson, Jamesone infuses a personal warmth of perception.

In the following decade Jamesone worked mainly in the south of Scotland but his personal life still centred in Aberdeen. About 1625 he had married Isobel Tosche, who was to bear him five sons and four daughters, but none of the sons survived childhood. In 1633 Jamesone painted a series of decorative pictures of Scottish monarchs for Edinburgh's reception of Charles I, and from 1635 he rented rooms near the Netherbow. The following year he took as apprentice the Londoner Michael Wright, later one of the more individual painters working in England. These were Jamesone's busiest years, his principal patron being Sir Colin Campbell of Glenorchy, who commissioned the vast Glenorchy Family-tree (Scottish National Portrait Gallery). His dealings in landed property are evidence of considerable wealth, and his part as an emissary of Aberdeen to the forces of the Covenant indicates his social standing. The latter episode led to his confinement in Edinburgh for some months in 1640.

As the political situation deteriorated Jamesone's paintings declined in number and quality. There is a sad fall from the powerful portrait of the Earl of Southesk (Kinnaird Castle), painted in 1637, to the weakly constructed portrait of the Countess of Lothian (Monteviot) of 1644. There are interesting self-portraits of the late 30s at Cullen House and Aberdeen Art Gallery.

Jamesone died late in 1644, his widow surviving until 1680. Though a minor painter, he remains a landmark in the history of Scottish art, while seen in a British context he must count as one of the earliest representatives of a purely native tradition.

Duncan Thomson, *The Life and Art of George Jamesone's* (in the press).

Hope, Sir Thomas (*c*. 1580–1646), son of a burgess of Edinburgh, was admitted advocate in 1605. In 1606 he defended six ministers who were prosecuted for having met in a General Assembly at Aberdeen in defiance of the King, and this has been held, rightly or wrongly, to indicate that Hope already had the sympathy with Presbyterianism which he showed so plainly later in his career. He built up a very successful practice at the bar, and how lucrative it was is indicated by his acquisition of many estates—Edmonston (1612) and Prestongrange (1616) in East Lothian, Graighall in Fife (1619) and Easter Granton in Midlothian (1620). If Hope was all along unsympathetic to the Episcopalian establishment, he must have concealed his views, for Charles I appointed him Lord Advocate in 1626 and made him a baronet in 1628. His ability as a lawyer may have made him indispensable to the King when he was carrying through his delicate and complicated negotiations over the revocation to the crown of ecclesiastical property, but Scott of Scotstarvet, in his *Staggering State of Scots Statesmen, says* plainly: 'Sir Thomas Hope, a notable lawyer who was believed to understand that matter beyond all men of his profession, though in all respects he was a zealous puritan, was made King's Advocate, upon his undertaking to bring all the church lands back to the crown: yet he proceeded in the matter so slowly that it was believed he acted in concert with the party that opposed it.' If this is so, then lack of principle alone can explain why Hope had no scruples about leading the prosecution of Lord Balmerino for having in his possession a supplication which criticized the King's proceedings at the Parliament of 1633 and which was conspicuously antagonistic to the political influence of the bishops as well as to the King's insistence on the use of the surplice.

Hope was a member of the Privy Council which approved the Prayer Book of 1637, but he carefully absented himself from meetings at which the Council had to try to enforce what was clearly an unpopular policy, and, while retaining his office, he put obstacles in the King's way and encouraged the opposition by declaring that the National Covenant was not unlawful. At the Glasgow Assembly in 1638 he refused to defend episcopacy. Royal displeasure followed, and Hope was for a time sent to his private house, but he was soon recalled when Charles saw how few Scots he could rely on and therefore tried to conciliate the opposition. In 1643 Hope was commissioner for the King to the General Assembly.

Hope's *Diary* (Bannatyne Club, 1843), consists essentially of brief and businesslike entries, from which, none the less, much can be inferred about his outlook. He wrote a volume of *Minor Practicks*, published in 1726, and another of *Major Practicks*, which remained in MS. until it was printed by the Stair Society in 1937. These volumes are valuable accounts of Scots law as it stood at the time, and as it was seen by a practising lawyer.

Sir Thomas's eldest son, Sir John (*c*. 1605–54), was knighted and became a Lord of Session in 1632 and was president of Cromwell's Committee of Justice in 1652. It was Sir Thomas's sixth son, Sir James (1614–61), a Lord of Session in 1649 and one of Cromwell's judges in 1652 and 1654, who carried on the family and was the ancestor of the Earls of Hopetoun.

James A. Clyde (ed.), *Hope's Major Practicks*, i, 1937.

Johnston, Archibald, of Wariston (1611–1663), a native of Edinburgh, was a kinsman of the Johnston family who became Earls of Annandale and Hartfell, and his mother was a daughter of Sir Thomas Craig, the lawyer. His parents had little wealth, and Johnston, unlike some contemporary lawyers, was so far from making a fortune from his profession that financial difficulties contributed to some of his vicissitudes. Educated at Glasgow University, he became an advocate in 1633. From his early years he was religious to the point of being neurotic: his *Diary* relates how he 'roared', 'youled [howled] pitifully' and 'skirled' [screamed] in his devotional torments, and it has been said of him that he was no mere religious fanatic but a man 'walking on the dizzy verge of madness'.[1] Yet he found the existing Episcopalian establishment congenial enough, for he listened with profit to the sermons of High Churchmen and assiduously attended Communion. The Prayer Book of 1637, however, threw him on to the side of the opposition, and he was largely responsible for the framing of the National Covenant, which led to his becoming completely obsessed with the concept of a perpetual contract between the people of Scotland and 'Scotland's God'. He was soon eager to go beyond the professed aims of the Covenant, and his production of the old records of the General Assemblies was decisive in leading the Assembly at Glasgow in November 1638 to condemn episcopacy.

In 1641, when Charles I came to Scotland to try to conciliate the Covenanters, Johnston was knighted and made a Lord of Session, with the title of Lord Wariston, from his small estate near Currie. Enthusiastic for the extension of Presbyterianism in England, and for co-operation with the English parliament against the King, he

1. C. V. Wedgwood, *The King's Peace*, p. 185.

K

was a member of the Committee of Both Kingdoms and of the Westminster Assembly, was made Lord Advocate by the Covenanting administration in 1646, and Lord Clerk Register in 1649. Being an extremist, he opposed the Engagement in which the moderates came to terms with Charles I, and when Cromwell arrived in Edinburgh in January 1651 Wariston found it easy to reach agreement with him on an anti-Royalist platform. He distrusted Charles II and did not favour the decision of the Scots to fight for him in 1650–1. On the English occupation of Scotland in 1651, Wariston lost his offices, but as an anti-Royalist he later came to terms with Cromwell, who restored him to the office of Lord Clerk Register and made him a commissioner for the administration of justice in Scotland (1657). He sat in the upper house of the two last Parliaments of the Protectorate. At the Restoration, as he knew that his support of Cromwell endangered him, he fled abroad. He was condemned to death in his absence (May 1661), but was arrested at Rouen in 1663, brought back to Edinburgh and, although obviously broken in mind and body and crying piteously for mercy, was hanged (22 July). Johnston's *Diary*, in so far as it survives, has been published by the Scottish History Society.

Hamilton, James, 3rd Marquis and 1st Duke of (1606–1649), was the son of the 2nd Marquis (whom he succeeded in 1625) and Anne Cuningham, daughter of the Earl of Glencairn. His marriage at the age of fourteen to a daughter of the Earl of Denbigh, brother-in-law of the royal favourite Buckingham, brought him into the inmost court circles. Educated at Oxford, he became Master of the Horse and a Privy Councillor in 1628. In 1631 he led a force to support the Protestant cause in the Thirty Years War, and collaborated with Gustavus Adolphus in Germany, but returned to court in 1633.

On the outbreak of the Covenanting troubles in Scotland, Charles I appointed Hamilton his Commissioner to the General Assembly which met at Glasgow in November 1638, and after Hamilton had left the Assembly it remained in session and went on to abolish episcopacy. In the military operations between the King and the Covenanters in 1639, the command of a fleet on the east coast was assigned to Hamilton, but neither his nor any other part of the King's strategy was successful. In 1641 he sided with Argyll against Montrose when the latter began to question the more extreme courses being followed by the Covenanters, but in 1642, when Argyll favoured Scottish intervention on behalf of the English Parliament,

Hamilton opposed him and tried to outmanoeuvre and outvote him in the Scottish Parliament, without success. He was created Duke on 12 April 1643. On his refusal to sign the Solemn League and Covenant he had to leave Scotland, but his tortuous methods no longer commended him to Charles, who had come to approve of Montrose's more militant policy, and Hamilton was imprisoned on the King's orders in St. Michael's Mount, where he remained until it was captured by the parliamentary army.

When Charles surrendered to the Scots in 1646, Hamilton took part in the negotiations with him. After the Scots had given the King up and began to be apprehensive about his future, Hamilton renewed his attempt to defeat Argyll in the Scottish Parliament, this time with success. He obtained approval of the Engagement, an undertaking to intervene on behalf of Charles, and led an army into England in July 1648. Defeated at Preston, he was captured on 25 August, was tried in England (as Earl of Cambridge) and was executed on 9 March 1649. He was succeeded as Duke by his brother William (1616–51), who had been created Earl of Lanark in 1639 and who died of wounds received at the battle of Worcester.

Huntly, George Gordon, 2nd Marquis of (*c.* 1592–1649), son and heir of the 1st Marquis, was brought up at the English court, became a Knight of the Bath in 1610 and a member of the Privy Council in 1616, but from 1623 spent a long time in France, where he served in the French army, and he may not have returned to Scotland until after his father's death in 1636. His long absence, added to the family tradition established by his father's earlier attachment to Roman Catholicism and his continued equivocal attitude to the ecclesiastical establishment, meant that when the troubles between Charles I and his subjects began Huntly was somewhat detached from the main stream of affairs. The city of Aberdeen and the surrounding area, where Huntly's power lay, were in the main well disposed to the Episcopalian cause and hostile to the National Covenant. The Covenanters tried in vain to win Huntly over by offering money to relieve his financial embarrassment. Huntly, with his wife and children, was loyal to episcopacy (though his mother was a practising Roman Catholic) and showed his defiance of the Covenanters and their agents by celebrating Christmas in 1638. In the King's plans for his 1639 campaign, Huntly was intended to co-operate, but the Earl of Montrose intervened to prevent a gathering of his men and shortly afterwards he decoyed Huntly to Edinburgh, where he was placed under arrest. In any event, Huntly had shown himself too reserved and aloof to be a candidate for effective leadership of an anti-Covenanting party.

After the Covenanters began to divide and something of a Royalist party took shape, under Montrose, Huntly was reluctant to cooperate, partly because he had not forgiven Montrose for his action in 1639, partly because Montrose was a younger man and one of far less standing, and partly because Huntly's own heir, Lord Gordon, was for a time on the Covenanting side. He did take up arms early in 1644, but retired in face of Argyll's advance and did little to help Montrose in his subsequent brilliant campaign. After Montrose's rout at Philiphaugh, another attempt was made to arrange joint action, but the negotiations were still indecisive when, in June 1646, the King ordered both of them to disband. Huntly was soon arrested, and, after being kept a long time in prison, was executed on 22 March 1649. It was ironical that a Royalist like Huntly should go to the scaffold after the Covenanters had decided to acknowledge Charles II as their King, but in the peculiar circumstances of the time those who had fought for Charles I were in general disqualified for fighting for Charles II.

Leslie, Alexander, 1st Earl of Leven (*c.* 1580–1661), general, was the illegitimate son of George Leslie, captain of the castle of Blair Atholl, and—so at least cavaliers said—'a wench in Rannoch'. He entered the Dutch service in 1605 and the Swedish in 1608. In the campaigns of Gustavus Adolphus in the Thirty Years War he won renown especially for his defence of Stralsund against Wallenstein, and ultimately became a Field Marshal. On his return to Scotland in 1638 he joined the Covenanters, and his first exploit was to capture Edinburgh Castle without losing a man. He led the army which marched south to confront the King at Duns Law in 1639, and in 1640, after a victory at Newburn, he lay with his army in England for a year to put pressure on the King to summon the English Parliament. When Charles came to Edinburgh in 1641 in an attempt to conciliate the Scots, Leslie was created Earl of Leven (11 October). When the Scots decided to support the English Parliament in the civil war, Leslie led the army which crossed the Tweed in January 1644 and took part in the parliamentary victory at Marston Moor in July. He opposed the Engagement made by the moderate Covenanters with Charles I in 1648, but supported the agreement whereby, after that King's execution, they undertook to fight for Charles II, and he was at the latter's coronation in 1651. The army which was routed at Dunbar in 1650 was commanded not by him but by David

Leslie, and Alexander did not go on the Worcester campaign in the following year. He was a member of the Committee of Estates when that body was captured by General Monck at Alyth on 28 August 1651, but was soon liberated on parole, at the request of the Queen of Sweden, and in 1654 he was able to return to Scotland. He was succeeded by his grandson Alexander as 2nd Earl.

C. S. Terry, *The Life and Campaigns of Alexander Leslie*, 1899.

Leslie, David (d. 1682), general, was the fifth son of Patrick Leslie, Commendator of Lindores, who was a son of the 5th Earl of Rothes. After serving under Gustavus Adolphus and becoming a colonel of horse, he returned to Scotland in 1643 to join the army of the Covenant. In the invasion of England in 1644 under Alexander Leslie, David had the rank of Major-General, and the charge of his cavalry at Marston Moor went a long way to make that battle a victory over the King. He was recalled to Scotland to deal with Montrose, who had defeated all the Covenanting forces in Scotland, and surprised and routed him at Philiphaugh (1645). Subsequently he mopped up the remnants of resistance in the north-east and in Argyll. Like Alexander Leslie, David opposed the Engagement, with the result that the army which the Duke of Hamilton led into England on Charles I's behalf in 1648 lacked Scotland's best generals, but after the Scots had proclaimed Charles II as their King he commanded the army which defended the country against Cromwell. Leslie completely outmanoeuvred the English in prolonged operations around Edinburgh, so that Cromwell was forced to fall back on Dunbar. There, although Leslie's army had been purged at the instance of the Kirk and he had lost his best officers, he had Cromwell in what was virtually a trap. What could have been a resounding victory was, through mismanagement, turned into a rout known as 'Dunbar Drove'. Leslie fought at Worcester in 1651 and after that battle he was taken prisoner. He spent nine years in the Tower of London. He was created Lord Newark in 1661.

Calderwood, David (1575–1651), historian, has a more obscure background than almost any other notable Scot of the time, for nothing is known with certainty about his ancestry, birth or earlier life, though he appears to have been educated at Edinburgh. The first fact about him that is beyond doubt is that he became minister of Crailing, in Roxburghshire, in 1604. The drift towards the revival of episcopacy had already begun, but Calderwood was a convinced Presbyterian, and in 1608 he refused to submit to the jurisdiction of the Archbishop of Glasgow. So that he would not prove a disturbing element in meetings of presbyteries and synods, he was confined to his parish. In 1617, however, he was able to attend a General Assembly, and joined in a protest against a proposed act empowering the King to legislate for the Church—an act which was first modified and later dropped. James declared that no such act was necessary, as he already had sufficient power by his prerogative, but he was none the less enraged by the strength of the opposition, and he called Calderwood before him to receive a rebuke. The minister showed no inclination to be browbeaten, and was sentenced to banishment. He went to Holland in 1619 and there he published a massive defence of Presbyterianism in his *Altare Damascenum*, as well as an edition of the *First and Second Books of Discipline* (1621). Some time after James's death in 1625 Calderwood returned to Scotland and spent his time quietly collecting material bearing mainly on the history of the Scottish Church since the Reformation.

After the resistance to Charles I began in 1637, Calderwood was eminently fitted to serve the Covenanting cause, with its appeal to earlier practice, and at the Glasgow Assembly of November 1638, when the debate about church government turned largely on arguments based on history, Calderwood was the power behind the throne, or at any rate behind the Moderator's chair: 'The Moderator caused read some papers, ... I think of Mr. D. Calderwood's penning, who lived all the time of the Assembly privily beside the Moderator's chamber, and furthered what he could by his studies all our proceedings.'[1] He was restored to the ministry, and inducted to the parish of Pencaitland, East Lothian. In 1643 he was made a member of the Committee on the Directory of Public Worship, and pressed in vain for the retention of the usages of the Scottish Reformers as against the adoption of those of the English Puritans. When defeated on the issue of the singing of the doxology at the end of psalms, the old man consoled himself with the assurance that he would sing it again in heaven. In 1651, when Cromwell was operating in the Lothians, Calderwood retired to Jedburgh, where he died. His *History of the Church of Scotland*, consisting largely of documents and of extracts from the registers of the General Assemblies, was first printed in 1678.

Preface to vol. viii of Calderwood's *History of the Kirk of Scotland* (Wodrow Soc.), 1849.

Henderson, Alexander (1583–1646), divine, a Fife man, was educa-

1. Robert Baillie, *Letters and Journals*, i, p. 138.

ted at St. Andrews University and taught there for a short time before being appointed by the Archbishop of St. Andrews to be minister of Leuchars (1612). Like many others, he was alienated from the established régime by the Five Articles of Perth, and was reported for failing to obey the article requiring kneeling at Communion. In 1637 he was conspicuous for his hostility to the new Prayer Book and within a few weeks of the outbreak of the troubles he had become one of the leaders of the resistance to Charles I. He was one of the authors of the National Covenant, and preached when it was first signed in Greyfriars' Church, Edinburgh, at the end of February 1638. Henderson was elected Moderator of the Glasgow Assembly (November 1638) and encouraged it to continue in session after the King's Commissioner withdrew, and to proceed to the abolition of episcopacy. In January 1639 he became minister of the church of St. Giles, Edinburgh, and in 1640 Rector of Edinburgh University. When the Covenanters had prepared for war against the King, in 1639, Henderson had written a pamphlet, *Instructions for Defensive Arms,* and in 1639 he accompanied the Covenanting army as a chaplain. Both in 1639 and in 1640–1 he was engaged in negotiations with the King. The second round of negotiations took him to London, where he preached, wrote *The Government and Order of the Church of Scotland* and *Desires concerning Unity in Religion and Unity of Church Government,* and was in close touch with the English Puritans, who misled him about the strength of Presbyterianism in England. Again Moderator of the General Assembly in 1641, he was chaplain to the King when he visited Scotland in the autumn of that year and—although he rebuked Charles for playing golf on Sunday—was appointed Dean of the Chapel Royal. By this time he was obsessed by the idea of Scotland's mission to spread Presbyterianism, and negotiations with the King early in 1643 broke down over this issue. As Moderator of the Assembly for the third time in August 1643 he warmly supported the policy which led to the Solemn League and Covenant and to the Westminster Assembly. To that Assembly he went as one of the Scottish commissioners, and he preached before the English Parliament in 1643 and 1645. He was again involved in negotiations with the King in 1645 and once more in 1646, after Charles had surrendered to the Scots. The King, we are told, had 'an uncommon esteem for Mr. Henderson's learning, piety and solidity'. Henderson is generally regarded as one of the more statesmanlike and less fanatical of the Presbyterian ministers of the time. R. L. Orr, *Alexander Henderson,* 1919.

Baillie, Robert (1602–1662), divine, was born in Glasgow, son of a merchant who was a younger son of Robert Baillie of Jerviston and was connected with many minor landed families. From Glasgow High School he went on to Glasgow University in 1617 and graduated M. A. in 1620, then continued his studies in Divinity. He became a regent in 1625. In 1631 he was presented to the parish of Kilwinning through the influence of Lord Montgomery, one of his students, whose father was patron. Baillie had already been ordained by the Archbishop of Glasgow, and he was favourable to episcopal government. His acquiescence in the ecclesiastical régime was shaken by the Prayer Book of 1637, which aroused his deepest hostility and suspicion, and he supported the Covenanting movement which followed it. He did not, however, believe that the National Covenant had condemned episcopal government, and at the General Assembly at Glasgow in November 1638 he stood out against the decision to 'abjure' episcopacy. Yet he was with the army which marched to Duns Law in 1639 to oppose the King, and in 1640, after another campaign, he took part in negotiations with the King. By this time he was a man of some note because of such writings as *The Canterburians Self-Conviction* (1640) and *A Parallel of the Liturgy with the Masse-Book*, and in 1642 he became Professor of Divinity at Glasgow. From 1643 to the end of 1646 he spent much of his time in London as one of the Scottish commissioners who 'assisted' the English Assembly of Divines at Westminster in its attempt to make the Church of England presbyterian, and he preached before the English Parliament in 1644 and 1645. When the Covenanting party began to divide over its attitude to the monarchy, Baillie was one of the moderate 'Resolutioners', and in 1649 he was a member of the deputation sent to Holland to negotiate with Charles II. In 1650 he fled from Glasgow on the approach of Cromwell's army, but soon returned, to an unhappy situation, for Patrick Gillespie, one of the 'Protestors' or extremist party, was appointed as Principal. After the King was restored in 1660, Gillespie was deprived, and Baillie was Principal in the last year of his life. Baillie's *Letters and Journals*, one of the most important sources for the period, were published by the Bannatyne Club in three volumes in 1841–2.

David Laing, 'Memoirs of the Life of Robert Baillie', in vol. iii of the *Letters and Journals.*

Gillespie, George (1613–1648), divine, son of the minister of Kirkcaldy, attended St. Andrews University and became chaplain first

132

to the rigid ultra-Protestant Viscount of Kenmure and then to the Earl of Cassillis, also of a strongly Protestant family. Gillespie was in the forefront of the opposition to Charles I's innovations in worship, and in 1637 he published anonymously his *Dispute against the English Popish Ceremonies Obtruded upon the Church of Scotland*. In April 1638, at a time when episcopal government had not yet been abolished, he received ordination from a presbytery and was inducted to the parish of Wemyss. In 1641 he preached before Charles I on his visit to Scotland, and in 1642 he was translated to the parish of Greyfriars, Edinburgh. Gillespie went as one of the Scottish agents to the Westminster Assembly of Divines, and argued against the participation of the lay authority in ecclesiastical government. He preached before the English Parliament in 1644 and 1645. In 1647 he presented to the General Assembly the Confession of Faith prepared by the Westminster Assembly, and it was adopted by the Church of Scotland. He was Moderator of the General Assembly in 1648 and was chosen minister of the High Church of Edinburgh. It is significant of Gillespie's prestige that on his deathbed he was visited by the Marquis of Argyll, the Earl of Cassillis, Lord Elcho (son of the Earl of Wemyss) and Archibald Johnston of Wariston.

George's brother, Patrick (1617–75), who became minister of Kirkcaldy in 1642 and of the High Church, Glasgow, in 1648, continued his brother's work and became a leader of the extreme Covenanters. He opposed the Engagement with Charles I and, after the defeat of the extremists at the battle of Dunbar (1650), he sided with the western Whigs who issued the Remonstrance against the agreement of the moderates with Charles II and against making terms with 'malignants' or Royalists. He was deposed by the moderate majority in the General Assembly and in 1651 became leader of the 'Protestor' minority. As Principal of Glasgow University from 1653 he was the nominee of Cromwell's government and he succeeded in obtaining from Cromwell favourable terms for the University as well as a greatly augmented salary for himself, but he was largely an absentee, preoccupied with affairs of state, and, while new buildings were erected, the university did not flourish. In 1660, on the restoration of Charles II, he was deprived and imprisoned.

Rutherford, Samuel (*c.* 1600–1661), divine, born in the parish of Crailing, Roxburghshire, was a student at Edinburgh University from 1617 to 1621 and served as a regent there from 1623 to 1625. In

1627 he was appointed to the parish of Anwoth in Galloway, on the presentation of Viscount Kenmure, a rabid ultra-Protestant, and had great influence as an evangelical preacher. With the death of Kenmure in 1634 and the appointment of a High Churchman, Thomas Sydserf, to the bishopric of Galloway (1635), Rutherford found himself in difficulties, especially as his *Exercitationes Apologeticae* (Amsterdam, 1636) attacked the new Arminian theology. In 1636 he was suspended and ordered to Aberdeen. It was in this period of comparative silence that he wrote most of his famous *Letters* (first published in 1664), which helped to bind together the critics of Charles I's ecclesiastical policy. When the King's administration began to break down, Rutherford returned to Anwoth (February 1638) and was a member of the Glasgow Assembly. In 1639 he became Professor of Divinity at St. Andrews and in 1643 was appointed one of the Scottish commissioners to the Westminster Assembly, where he served for four years. He preached before the English Parliament in 1643 and 1645. He published several works in defence of the Presbyterian position: *The Due Right of Presbytery* (1644), *The Divine Right of Church Government* (1646), *A Survey of the Spiritual Antichrist* (1647) and *A Free Disputation against Liberty of Conscience* (1649). He became Principal of St. Mary's College in 1648 and was invited to the universities of Harderwyck and Utrecht, but declined. He aligned himself with the more extreme Covenanters who opposed the Engagement with Charles I and denounced the subsequent agreement with Charles II. He was deprived at the Restoration, and his *Lex Rex* (which, published at London in 1644, argued for the right of the people to depose their king) was burned. Rutherford is best remembered for his *Letters*, which formed popular reading in Scotland for generations. They sometimes show deep spiritual insights, but the highly emotional, and frequently erotic, imagery is often unsuitable to his theme.

R. Gilmour, *Samuel Rutherford*, 1904.

Montrose, James Graham, 5th Earl and 1st Marquis of (1612–1650), succeeded his father, the 4th Earl, in 1626, was educated at St. Andrews and married a daughter of the Earl of Southesk. After signing the National Covenant in 1638, he was soon in action in Aberdeenshire against opponents of the Covenant, led by the Marquis of Huntly, and he served against the King in both the First and Second Bishops' Wars. But before the second of those wars there were signs of a divergence between him and the more extreme

Covenanters, led by Argyll, for Montrose distrusted the policy of stripping the King of all his influence in Parliament and was suspicious that Argyll was using the Covenant for his own private ends. Accused of intrigues against Argyll, Montrose was imprisoned in Edinburgh Castle for a time in 1641.

When the question arose of Scottish intervention in the English civil war, Montrose opposed the decision to take the side of Parliament. Therefore, when a Scottish army entered England, he was commissioned in February 1644 as the King's lieutenant-general in Scotland and was created a Marquis in May. An attempt at invading the country from the south failed, and in August Montrose made his way, almost alone, to the Highlands, where he raised the clans for the King and was joined by an Irish force under Alasdair MacDonald. Alasdair was a near kinsman of the Earl of Antrim and a son of MacDonald of Colonsay; the latter bore the name Coll Ciotach, or 'left-handed', which is sometimes transferred to his son, Alasdair, as 'Colkitto'. There followed a spectacular series of victories—Tippermuir, Aberdeen, Inverlochy, Auldearn, Alford and Kilsyth—rendered possible by Montrose's unparalleled mobility and the dash with which the clansmen served him. But although after Kilsyth there was no Covenanting army still in the field in Scotland, his position was not strong. His Highland forces were apt to melt away after each victory, the Irish had quarrels of their own to pursue in the far west, the Lowlanders who were sympathetic to the Royalist cause were alienated by the descent on them of Highland and Irish irregulars, while Huntly, the leading figure in the conservative north-east, stood aloof. An army sent from England, under David Leslie, routed Montrose at Philiphaugh, near Selkirk (13 September 1645).

The Marquis failed to reassemble a fighting force in Scotland, and went to the continent, where he wandered in attempts to gain help, with very little success. He landed in Orkney in March 1650 and crossed to the mainland with a few troops, but he had been unable to rally many men to his standard when he was routed at Carbisdale (27 April). He was captured, and hanged on 21 May, protesting to the end that he was a true Covenanter and Presbyterian as well as a loyal supporter of the King.

M. Napier, *Memoirs of the Marquis of Montrose*, 1856.
John Buchan, *Montrose*, 1928.
Margaret Irwin, *The Proud Servant*, 1934. (H.N.)
They Saw It Happen vol. 1, pp. 156-8.

Argyll, Archibald Campbell, 8th Earl and 1st Marquis of (1607–1661), who succeeded his father in 1638, was known as 'Gillespie Gruamach' because of his squint. Educated at St. Andrews, he became a Privy Councillor in 1628 and an Extraordinary Lord of Session in 1634, but was compelled in 1628 to surrender his hereditary office of Justice-General, though reserving his rights as justiciar of Argyll. Although a Privy Councillor, he carefully avoided identifying himself with Charles I's unpopular policy in 1637–8, and his father, shortly before his death, warned the King that Archibald was a potential centre of disaffection. In November 1638 Argyll joined the Covenanting party, which at this point carried the abolition of episcopal government. In the wars with the King which followed, he had in the first place the task of defending his own part of the country against a descent from Ireland, and he next took action against families in the central Highlands and in Angus who had supported the King, especially if they happened to be his own hereditary enemies. His self-seeking was denounced by the Earl of Montrose in August 1640. He took his place among the more radical Covenanters when he supported sweeping constitutional changes in the Parliament of 1640 and again at the time of the King's visit in 1641, but Charles, as part of his policy of attempting to conciliate the opposition, made him one of the Commissioners of the Treasury and created him a Marquis (15 November 1641). Argyll supported the policy of intervention in England on the side of Parliament in 1643, and was therefore an obvious target for attack when the Marquis of Montrose conducted his campaign in Scotland on the King's behalf in 1644–5. Three times Argyll had to flee ignominiously before the victorious Montrose—at Inveraray in December 1644, at Inverlochy in February 1645, and once more after Montrose's final victory at Kilsyth in August 1645.

With his record, it was inevitable that Argyll should oppose the Moderate party who made the Engagement with the King, and after the defeat of the Engagers at Preston in August 1648 he was a member of the government which reached an accommodation with Cromwell in October. Nevertheless he was, like nearly all Scots, antagonized by the execution of Charles I, which caused a new breach with Cromwell, and, after the cause of the extremists had been ruined by the defeat at Dunbar (3 September 1650), he prepared to come to terms with Charles II. It was from Argyll's hands that Charles received the Scottish crown on 1 January 1661. Argyll did not take part in the campaign on the King's behalf which ended disastrously at Worcester (3 September 1651), and after the subsequent conquest of Scotland by Cromwell he played a devious part. At the Restoration, the fact that he had crowned the King did him no good, for he was arrested and executed on the grounds of his compliance with the English army of occupation and the assistance he had given to the force which put down the Royalist rising of 1653–4.

J. Willcock, *The Great Marquess*, 1903.
Neil Munro, *John Splendid*, 1898. (H.N.)

Lauderdale, John Maitland, 2nd Earl and 1st Duke of (1616–1682), the son of the 1st Earl (whom he succeeded in 1645) by a daughter of the Earl of Dunfermline, was a grandson of John Maitland of Thirlestane and a grand-nephew of William Maitland of Lethington. After the Second Bishops' War, he took part in the negotiations of the Covenanters with Charles I at Ripon, in 1642 he was appointed to treat with the English Parliament and in 1643 he became one of the framers of the Solemn League and Covenant and a Scottish commissioner to the Westminster Assembly. Between 1644 and 1647, when he was several times involved in abortive negotiations with the King, he moved towards the Royalist side, and was one of the Scots who made the Engagement with Charles at the end of 1647. Already, before the Engagers' policy met with disaster at Preston (August 1648), Lauderdale was in touch with the future Charles II and was evidently won to a personal devotion to that prince which helped to determine his future policy. After the death of Charles I he helped to persuade Charles II to come to terms with the Scots, he sailed with him to Scotland, took part in the expedition which ended at Worcester and was captured after that battle (1651). He remained a prisoner in England until the spring of 1660.

After the King returned, Lauderdale was appointed Secretary of State for Scotland (1661), an office which he held until 1680 but which he at first exercised in London, while authority in Scotland lay with Middleton and Rothes in turn. Lauderdale's own preference would have been for a Presbyterian settlement in Scotland, along the lines foreshadowed in the Engagement, but he was too devoted to the King and too careful of his own interests to make a stand against the prevailing drift towards episcopacy: when he agreed to renounce the Covenants, he said he would take a cartful of such oaths rather than lose office. However, when the repressive policy of the government in Scotland provoked the Pentland Rising (1666), Lauderdale welcomed the opportunity to experiment with a more

137

lenient policy, which was pursued, under his direction, from 1667 until 1674. Attempts at reconciliation had only limited success, and in 1674 there was a return to repression.

In 1669 Lauderdale became the King's Commissioner to the Scottish Parliament, and in more than one session he anticipated some of the techniques of the eighteenth-century 'managers', though in the face of growing opposition on personal as well as political grounds. He did not maintain his position without a good deal of corruption, and was the author of many swindles in the interests of his clients and kin. His second wife, Elizabeth Murray, daughter of the Earl of Dysart and Countess in her own right, was noted for her venality. Equally, Lauderdale's brother, Charles Maitland of Haltoun (d. 1691), who later succeeded as 3rd Earl of Lauderdale, was Master of the Mint and a Privy Councillor and his proceedings were too outrageous even for that lax age. The corruption of the government intensified opposition and when the repression of the Covenanters led to the Bothwell Brig Rising in 1679 this was used to discredit Lauderdale. He was superseded and retired to Tunbridge Wells, where he died on 24 August 1682. He had been created a Duke in 1672.

W. C. Mackenzie, *John Maitland, Duke of Lauderdale*, 1923.

Middleton, John Middleton, 1st Earl of (*c.* 1608–1674), son of a small laird in Kincardineshire, began his military career as a pikeman in the French army, and returned to become a Major in the army of the Covenant in 1639. He was in the force under Montrose which scattered the Aberdeenshire Royalists at the Bridge of Dee. For a time he was in the English parliamentary army, but in 1645 rejoined the Scots and was second in command against Montrose at Philiphaugh. However, he supported the Engagement whereby many of the Scots undertook to rescue Charles I, and was Lieutenant General of the cavalry in the army which invaded England in 1648. At Preston he was captured, but escaped. In 1649 he was with the Royalist forces which operated for a time in the Highlands before the main body of Covenanters came to terms with Charles II, and he was excommunicated by James Guthrie (*c.* 1612–61), a leading minister in the party which opposed an agreement with Charles. As an officer in the army which invaded England in 1651, he was taken prisoner at Worcester, but escaped from the Tower of London in the next year and joined the King in France. He returned to Scotland to lead a Royalist rising in 1653, and on its collapse rejoined Charles at Cologne. He was created Earl of

Middleton in 1656, an act ratified after the King's Restoration, when he was made Commander-in-Chief in Scotland, Governor of Edinburgh Castle and King's Commissioner to the first Restoration Parliament—the 'Drunken Parliament'. He showed little statesmanship, there was jealousy of him as a *parvenu*, and he was deprived of office in 1663. In 1667 he was made Governor of Tangier, where he died as a result of falling downstairs when he was drunk.

Rothes, John Leslie, 7th Earl and 1st Duke of (1630–1681), was the son of the 6th Earl (*c.* 1600–41). The elder Rothes had voted against King James's Five Articles of Perth in 1621 and had complained about Charles I's measures at the Parliament of 1633. In 1638 he had naturally emerged as a leader of the Covenanters (although he was a man notorious for his loose life), but he showed sufficient moderation to gain a degree of royal favour and, had he lived, might have emerged as a mediator. The 7th Earl in his youth aligned himself with the royalist wing of the Covenanters: he carried the sword of state at the coronation of Charles II at Scone in 1651 and was in the army which invaded England later that year. He was captured at Worcester and remained a prisoner until 1658. When the King was restored, Rothes was appointed President of the Privy Council (1660), an Extraordinary Lord of Session (1661) and Treasurer (1663). He became the King's Commissioner to the Scottish Parliament in 1663, an office which made him virtually head of the administration in Scotland. It has been said that he 'inherited his father's licentiousness without his gift of commending himself to the godly', and as Commissioner Rothes pursued a policy of severe repression of the Covenanters which provoked the Pentland Rising in 1666. That rising discredited the policy of Rothes, who in 1667 was displaced as Commissioner and Treasurer, but was made Chancellor, an office for which he was, on his own admission, unfitted because of his 'ignorance'. In 1673–4 Rothes was associated with the opposition to Lauderdale, who had succeeded him as Commissioner. Lauderdale remained in office until 1681, but in 1680, when his power was declining, a dukedom was conferred on Rothes and his heirs male. As he had no son, the dukedom died with him, but his daughter succeeded as Countess.

Hamilton, William Douglas or Hamilton, 3rd Duke of (1635–1694), the eldest son of the 1st Marquis of Douglas, was created Earl of Selkirk on 4 August 1646. In 1656 he married Anne, daughter of

139

the 1st Duke of Hamilton and Duchess in her own right, and in 1660 he was created Duke of Hamilton for his lifetime. He played a conspicuous part in Scottish politics in 1673–4, when he headed an opposition to the Duke of Lauderdale's administration and took the lead in proceedings in the Scottish Parliament which challenged the government's proposals in an unprecedented way, by demanding that the state of the nation should be considered and grievances redressed before supply was granted. In 1678–9 he repeatedly sought an audience of the King to protest against Lauderdale's proceedings. Owing to his opposition to the administration he had been excluded from the Council, but in 1682, after Lauderdale's fall, he was made a Knight of the Garter and in 1686 he was restored to the Council and became a Commissioner of the Treasury and an Extraordinary Lord of Session. However, as early as 1674 he had been suspected of correspondence with the Prince of Orange, and at the Revolution he led the group of Scottish notables in London who invited William to assume the administration of Scotland and to summon a Convention there. His election by that Convention as its President was a clear indication that William's party had a majority.

Mackenzie, Sir George, of Tarbat (1630–1714), son of Sir John Mackenzie of Tarbat, was born in Fife and educated at King's College, Aberdeen, and then at St. Andrews University. He took part in the Royalist rising against Cromwell in 1653–4 and then went into exile until the Restoration. Charles II's first Commissioner to the Scottish Parliament was the Earl of Middleton, under whom Mackenzie had served in the rising of 1653–4, and Mackenzie, raised to the bench as a Lord of Session in 1661 and a member of Parliament for Ross in the same year, worked with Middleton in an attempt to bring about the overthrow of Lauderdale. With the fall of Middleton in 1663 Mackenzie lost his seat on the bench, and as long as Lauderdale dominated Scottish politics he was out of office. In 1678, when Lauderdale's power began to wane, Mackenzie, who again came to Parliament to represent Ross, was appointed Lord Justice General and a Privy Councillor, and in 1681, after Lauderdale's fall, he was appointed Lord Clerk Register and was again a Lord of Session. He was thus a leading member of the government in the last years of Charles II and subsequently under James VII. At the Revolution he was arrested, but soon made his peace with King William and served him in attempts to mediate with the Episcopalians and to pacify the Highlands. He then held a succession of offices—Lord Clerk Register 1692–6, Secretary of

State 1702–4 and again Lord Justice General 1705–10. Although he continued to profess an attachment to Jacobitism and Episcopacy, he did little when in office to assist either of those causes, and in the last years of a career notable for its inconsistency and lack of principle he supported the Union of 1707. He had been created Viscount Tarbat in 1685 and Earl of Cromartie in 1703.

Mackenzie was one of the original members of the Royal Society and published many works on a remarkable variety of topics. The following examples show his versatility: *A Vindication of Robert III from the imputation of bastardy* (1695), *The Mistaken Advantage of Raising of Money* (1695), *Friendly Response ... on the matter of the Union* (1706), *A Short and Plain Explication of Daniel's Prophecy and of St. John's Revelation* (1707), and *Historical Account of the Conspiracy of the Earl of Gowrie* (1713).

Moray, Sir Robert (*c.* 1600–1673), a son of Sir Mungo Moray of Craigie, was educated at St. Andrews and in France and served for some years in the French army before returning in the 1640s to join the Royalist side. He was knighted by Charles I in 1643 and, in an attempt to save the Royalist cause, negotiated with France on the King's behalf. He made plans for Charles's escape from Newcastle in 1646, but they failed. He returned to France and in 1650 carried on negotiations with Charles II. When the latter was crowned King of Scots, Moray was in Scotland and was appointed Justice Clerk, a Lord of Session and a Privy Councillor, but the Royalist effort met with disaster at Worcester (3 September 1651). Moray was one of those who did their utmost to resist the Cromwellian occupation in Scotland, but when the rising of 1653–4 collapsed he joined the King in Paris. Later he spent part of his exile at Maastricht, where he devoted much of his time to the study of chemistry. At the Restoration he took a moderate line which was not agreeable to Middleton, under whom he had served in 1653–4, and, with Lauderdale, he was one of those whom Middleton tried to exclude from office. However, this attempt failed, and Moray became again Justice Clerk (1662), a Lord of Exchequer and Deputy Secretary (1663). He worked closely with Lauderdale and the King until 1670, and remained a moderating influence, but he 'had no stomach for public employments'. He is best remembered not for his political manoeuvrings but for his interest in science—geology, chemistry, mathematics and natural history. He was one of the founders of the Royal Society and its first president, and was highly esteemed, both for his intelligence and his character, by almost all contem-

141

L

poraries, including the King (who often visited him in his laboratory), Bishop Gilbert Burnet, John Evelyn and Samuel Pepys.

A. Robertson, *Sir Robert Moray*, 1922.

Gregory, James (1638–75), mathematician, was born at Drumoak, Aberdeenshire, where his father was minister, and was educated at the Grammar School and Marischal College, Aberdeen. A mathematical streak in his family derived from his maternal grandfather, David Anderson of Finyhaugh, nicknamed 'Davie-do-a'-thing', and James's elder brother, David (1627–1720), had three sons who were distinguished mathematicians. David encouraged James's talents, and in 1663 there was published his *Optica Promota*, describing the principle of the reflecting telescope which he had invented in 1661. From 1664 to 1667 he was in Padua, where he published *Vera circuli et hyperbolae quadratura* (1667), which dealt with the areas of the circle, ellipse and hyperbola and drew him into controversy with the Dutch mathematician Christian Huygens. Returning to London, Gregory was made a Fellow of the Royal Society, and in 1668 published *Exercitationes Geometricae*, in which he extended his methods to the cissoid and conchoid. He became professor of mathematics at St. Andrews (1668) and then at Edinburgh (1674). He corresponded with Isaac Newton about the merits of their respective telescopes. In his last years he was doing pioneering work in astronomy, related to the parallaxes of Mercury and Venus and the distance of the stars from the earth. He carried out many of his experiments in the Parliament Hall at St. Andrews, where there is preserved an astronomical clock made to his orders.

H. W. Turnbull (ed.), *James Gregory Tercentenary Memorial Volume*, 1939.

Gregory, David (1661–1708), was the son of David Gregory of Kinnairdie in Banffshire (1627–1720), who had many scientific interests, extending from practising medicine to inventing an improved type of cannon. David the younger, born on 24 June 1661, was educated at Marischal College and the University of Edinburgh, where he graduated M.A. in 1683. In 1684 he published *Exercitationes Geometricae*, and in the same year, at the age of twenty-three, he became professor of mathematics at Edinburgh. His lectures included geodesy, optics and dynamics, and his *Catoptricae et Dioptricae Elementa*, though not published until 1695, contained the substance of the lectures he gave in 1684. After the Revolution he refused to take the Presbyterian Confession of Faith, and, ousted from his chair, he went to London in 1691, to be warmly welcomed by Newton, of the truth of whose theories he had become convinced. He became a Fellow of the Royal Society, and in 1692 was appointed Savilian Professor of Astronomy at Oxford. His work on the reflection and refraction of spherical surfaces prepared the way for the improvement of telescopes. In 1702 he published *Astronomiae Physicae et Geometricae Elementa,* a kind of digest of Newton's *Principia* and the first text-book of the principles of gravitation. He also produced an edition of Euclid (1703). He died on 10 October 1708. David had two brothers who also became Professors of Mathematics—James at Edinburgh and Charles at St. Andrews— and his uncle, James, had been Professor of Mathematics at St. Andrews and Edinburgh.

W. G. Hiscock (ed.), *David Gregory, Isaac Newton and their circle,* 1937.

Stair, James Dalrymple, 1st Viscount (1619–1695), born in the parish of Barr, Ayrshire, son of the laird of Drummurchie, was educated at the parish school of Mauchline and the University of Glasgow (1635–7). He went to Edinburgh intending a legal career, but he joined the army of the Covenant and in 1641, when a captain, was appointed a regent in philosophy in Glasgow. He turned his attention once more to the study of law, resigned his chair in 1647 and became an advocate in 1648. He acted as secretary to the commissioners who negotiated with Charles II in 1649 and 1650. In 1657, on the recommendation of General Monck, who described him as 'a very honest man, a good lawyer and one of considerable estate', he was appointed one of the Cromwellian commissioners for the administration of justice in Scotland. Despite Dalrymple's association with the Cromwellian régime, Charles II, on his restoration, knighted him and raised him to the bench. In 1663 he resigned office rather than take an oath renouncing the possibility of rebellion, but the King prevailed on him to take it with a qualifying clause and he returned to office in 1664. In the same year he was made a baronet. He became Lord President of the Court of Session in 1671, member of Parliament for Wigtownshire in 1672 and a Privy Councillor in 1674, but demitted his office in 1681 rather than take the Test Oath, which would again have committed him to repudiate resistance. It was in 1681 that his *Institutions of the Law of Scotland* was published—a work which, as 'Stair's Institutes', has been familiar to Scots lawyers ever since and which, with its combination of the practical and the philosophical, attempted to erect Scots law into a system, on a model far superior to the many earlier 'Practicks' or dictionaries of decisions. When Dalrymple's wife was prosecuted for attending conventicles and he himself threatened with arrest, he went to Holland (1682), and two volumes of *Decisions*, edited by him, were published in 1684 and 1687, besides *Physiologia nova experimentalis* (1686). In 1688 Dalrymple returned with William of Orange, was reappointed Lord President and made a Viscount (1690). He died at Edinburgh on 25 November 1695.

Stair's eldest son, John (1648–1707), knighted in 1667, became an advocate in 1672. He defended the Earl of Argyll at his trial in 1681, and, prejudiced by his father's withdrawal to Holland, he was imprisoned and fined in 1683. However, he came to terms with James VII and was appointed Lord Advocate in 1687; in 1688 he was appointed Lord Justice Clerk when his predecessor as Advocate, Sir George Mackenzie, was reinstated. Despite his record, Dalrymple ingratiated himself with William of Orange, who reappointed him Lord Advocate in 1689, and in 1691 he was joint Secretary of State. In this capacity he is believed to have borne a heavy responsibility for the massacre of Glencoe (1692). Despite much censure on him for exceeding his instructions, the King defended him, and he remained Secretary until he resigned in 1695. He was created Earl of Stair in 1703 and died on 8 January 1707.

A. J. G. Mackay, *Memoir of Sir James Dalrymple*, 1873.

Mackenzie, Sir George, of Rosehaugh (1636–1691), a nephew of the Earl of Seaforth, was born at Dundee and educated at the grammar school there before going on to the Universities of St. Andrews, Aberdeen and Bourges. He became an advocate in 1659 and was briefed to defend the Marquis of Argyll at his trial in 1661. In the same year he was appointed a justice for criminal cases. He became a member of Parliament for the sheriffdom of Ross in 1669 and at first opposed Lauderdale's administration, but later supported it and was appointed Lord Advocate in 1677. It fell to him, in his official capacity, to conduct prosecutions of Covenanters and plotters. He boasted in 1680 that he had never lost a case for the King, and his names lives as 'the Bluidy Mackenzie'. He refused to countenance James VII's policy of toleration, and was removed from office in May 1686, but was restored from February 1688 to May 1689. At the Revolution, he was one of the five Jacobite members who remained in the Convention to oppose the resolution that James VII had forfeited the throne, but he then withdrew to England and died at Westminster on 8 May 1691. He was buried in Greyfriars' Churchyard, Edinburgh.

Mackenzie's 'bluidy' reputation reflects the wrong emphasis which distorts so much of Scottish history. He deserves to be remembered rather as the founder of the Advocates' Library, now the National Library of Scotland, which had its beginnings when Mackenzie was Dean of the Faculty of Advocates in 1682, and he delivered a lecture inaugurating the library in 1689. His numerous writings range through fiction (*Aretina*, 1661), ethics (for example, *A moral paradox* [1667]), political philosophy (*Jus Regium* [1684], which argues in favour of the royal prerogative) and an *Institution of the Law of Scotland* (1684), which is brief compared with the similar work of Stair. His *Vindication of the government of Scotland during the reign of King Charles II* (1691) and his *Memoirs of the affairs of Scotland from the Restoration of King Charles II*, not published until 1821, are valuable historical sources. He has been highly praised for the elegance of his English prose.

Andrew Lang, *Sir George Mackenzie*, 1909.

Bruce, Sir William, of Balcaskie and Kinross (1630–1710), architect, was born in Kinross, the son of Robert Bruce of Blairhall. A strong Royalist, he was concerned in negotiations between Charles II and General Monck in 1660 and was rewarded with the lucrative appointment of Clerk to the Bills (1662). He was created a baronet in 1668, and in 1671 was appointed King's Surveyor and Master of Works. As architect to Charles II he restored and extended the palace of Holyroodhouse (1671–8), leaving it in the shape it has retained ever since. He acquired the lands of Balcaskie and Drumardie, in Fife, and later, from the Earl of Morton, the lands and barony of Kinross. He was a member of Parliament for Fife from 1669 to 1674 and for Kinross-shire from 1681 to 1686. He became a Privy Councillor in 1685 and held various other official positions. Apart from Holyrood, his best known work is Kinross House, which he is said to have intended for James, Duke of York, should he be excluded from the succession, but the truth appears to be that its erection (1685–92) was from the first intended for Bruce himself. Bruce also built Harden House, in Teviotdale, and Moncrieffe House, in Perthshire. In 1698 he designed the central part of Hopetoun House, and it fell to his pupil, William Adam, father of the famous Adam brothers, to complete that building. Through his influence not only on Adam but also on James Smith, who began his work under James VII and succeeded Bruce as royal architect,

Bruce has some claim to be regarded as the founder of a school of architecture.

Hubert Fenwick, *Architect Royal*, 1970.

Sibbald, Sir Robert (1641–1722), physician, naturalist and antiquary, descended from a Fife landed family, was born in Edinburgh on 15 April 1641 and attended the grammar school of Cupar before going to the High School and University of Edinburgh. He then went to Leyden, where he graduated M.D. in 1661. He studied also at Angers, Paris and London. When he settled in Scotland, late in 1662, he divided his time between Edinburgh and the country, where he devoted himself mainly to the study of botany. In 1667, in conjunction with Dr. Andrew Balfour, he started the Physic Garden, later the Royal Botanic Garden, first on a small plot of ground near Holyrood and then on a site near Trinity College. In 1681 Sibbald was one of the founder members of the Royal College of Physicians of Edinburgh, in 1684 he was its President and in 1685 he became the first Professor of Medicine in Edinburgh University. In 1682 Charles II appointed him his physician and also Geographer Royal for Scotland.

The King commanded Sibbald to compile a description of Scotland, geographical and historical. Sibbald very soon produced *Scotia Illustrata* (1684), in which he was assisted by John Adair as a cartographer, but something much more ambitious was planned, and the whole project, had it been completed, would have anticipated the Statistical Account prepared by Sir John Sinclair more than a century later. Sibbald himself wrote a *History Ancient and Modern of the sheriffdoms of Fife and Kinross* (1710) and a similar work on Linlithgowshire and Stirlingshire (1710), and he published a *Description of Orkney and Shetland* (1711) which was a reissue of an earlier work by another hand. Some other writers were stimulated to produce comparable volumes. Among Sibbald's own other writings were *The Liberty and Independency of the Kingdom and Church of Scotland asserted from Ancient Writings* (1703), various works on Roman monuments in Scotland, and a large number of papers which were collected after his death in *A Collection of several treatises concerning Scotland* (1739). Sibbald, always much of a courtier, was also something of a vicar of Bray, and at the persuasion of his patron, the Earl of Perth, who was Chancellor of the Kingdom, he was a Roman Catholic in the reign of James VII but subsequently reverted to Protestantism.

Sir Robert Sibbald, *Memoirs*, ed. E. P. Hett, 1932.

Sharp, James (1618–79), Archbishop of St. Andrews, was a native of Banffshire and was educated in Aberdeen. His background was therefore that of the predominantly Royalist and conservative north-east, and when the Covenanters abolished episcopal government in 1638 he went to England. He returned in 1643 and, after teaching for a time at St. Andrews University, became minister of Crail in 1649. He had already gained considerable repute, and was soon called to Edinburgh, but the disturbances caused by the war with Cromwell prevented his translation. By this time the Covenanters had divided into two factions, and Sharp had joined the more moderate and Royalist Resolutioners. In 1657 he represented that party in discussions with Cromwell in London and showed conspicuous ability as their spokesman. Robert Baillie described him as 'that very worthy, pious, wise and diligent young man' and Cromwell—perhaps more perceptive—said he should be designated 'Sharp of that ilk'.

In 1660, before the King's return in May and after it, he again represented his party in London and soon realized that the conservative reaction in England would affect Scotland and bring about a revival of episcopacy there. On his return to Scotland in August he was appointed Professor of Theology at St. Andrews. As the leader of the moderate party, he was the obvious choice for the archbishopric of St. Andrews, and was consecrated on 15 December 1661. To those who adhered to the Covenants, Sharp was a scheming Judas who had betrayed the cause, and he therefore bore the odium for many unpopular measures which in truth emanated from the Privy Council. The real charge against him is that he was too compliant with the government's policy, simply because he was determined to retain his position, and therefore did not make a stand against measures of which he disapproved, like the Act of Supremacy of 1669, which, by giving the King complete authority in the Church, cut at the roots of any sincere belief in episcopacy.

An attempt was made on Sharp's life in 1668. His assailant, James Mitchell, was arrested six years later and, after confessing the crime on the promise of his life, was executed in 1678. This intensified resentment against the primate, and a gang of fanatics hacked him to death in his daughter's presence, after dragging him from his coach on Magus Muir, three miles from St. Andrews (3 May 1679). The Archbishop's assailants had in fact set out to murder another of their persecutors, but on the appearance of Sharp's coach had concluded that he had been providentially delivered into their hands.

T. Stephen, *Archbishop Sharp*, 1839.

Leighton, Robert (1611–1684), Bishop of Dunblane, was the son of the violently puritanical Alexander Leighton (1568–1649), who practised as a physician in England and wrote *Zion's Plea against Prelacy* (1630), for which he had an ear cut off by order of the Court of Star Chamber. Robert was presumably born in London, but educated at Edinburgh University, where he graduated in 1631. For ten years thereafter hardly anything is known of him, but there is a strong presumption that he spent much of his time in France and came under the influence of the Jansenists, with their marked devotional piety and their tolerant attitude. In 1641 he became minister of Newbattle, but was highly critical of the extremes to which Covenanting policies led in the late 1640s. He therefore supported the Engagement with Charles I, but preferred a retired and saintly life to meddling in politics, and when he was censured for not preaching 'to the times' he protested that when all the other ministers preached to the times it might be permissible for him to preach Christ and eternity. In 1652 he asked to be relieved of his charge, and in 1653 became Professor of Divinity and Principal of Edinburgh University.

In 1661 Leighton agreed with some reluctance to accept the bishopric of Dunblane, and was consecrated in England, but his real desire was for a healing of schism in the Church and he devoted himself quietly and piously to the welfare of his diocese. He worked out plans for an 'accommodation' with the Presbyterians and had them ready in 1667, when the first period of repression of the Covenanters came to an end. When the government thus adopted a conciliatory policy—though it took the form of 'indulging' the Presbyterians outside the Church rather than incorporating them within it—Leighton was appointed to supersede the unyielding Episcopalian Burnet as Archbishop of Glasgow. However, his attitude was not acceptable to intransigents on either side, and he found that he could make no headway against the bigotry of the south-western radicals. He therefore resigned his office in 1674 and retired to England. He died in London, and left his library to the clergy of Dunblane.

D. Butler, *The life and letters of Robert Leighton*, 1903.

Barclay, Robert (1648–1690), was born at Gordonstoun on 23 December 1648, the son of Colonel David Barclay of Urie (1610–86) and a daughter of Sir Robert Gordon of Gordonstoun, the historian of the house of Sutherland. David, Robert's father, had served under Gustavus Adolphus, but returned to take part in the wars of the

Covenant, and for a time, alienated by the more extreme wing of the party, he supported the moderate policy of the Royalist 'Engagers'. However, he was prepared to come to terms with Cromwell after the English conquest of Scotland, and sat in Cromwell's Parliaments of 1654 and 1656, with the result that after the Restoration he suffered a brief imprisonment. In prison he encountered James Swinton, a strong supporter of Cromwell who had been converted to Quakerism, and David Barclay declared himself a Quaker in 1666.

Robert, David's son, who had been for a time at the Scots College in Paris, returned to Scotland in 1664. Shocked at the religious animosity in Scotland, he was in a suitable frame of mind to follow his father's example, and he became convinced of the truth of Quakerism (1667). He preached in England, Holland and Germany, sometimes in the company of William Penn and George Fox, and he wrote several books, including *Truth cleared of Calumnies* (1670), *A Catechism and Confession of Faith* (1673) and *An Apology for the True Christian Divinity* (1676), which is one of the ablest defences of Quaker principles. He engaged in debates with the students of Aberdeen and suffered imprisonment more than once. In time, however, he won such wide respect that he was left in peace. He had dedicated his *Apology* to Charles II, and, like Penn, was on good terms with James VII, whom he visited in London and from whom he received several favours. In 1679 he had a charter of barony of the lands of Urie, which his father had purchased in 1648. In 1682 he was a party to the scheme for a Quaker colony in East New Jersey, of which he was appointed governor, but he never visited the settlement.

D. Elton Trueblood, *Robert Barclay*, 1970.

Argyll, Archibald Campbell, 9th Earl of (1629–1685), son and heir of the 1st Marquis, travelled on the continent between 1647 and 1649, and returned in 1650 to become a Colonel in the Covenanting army which had undertaken to fight for Charles II. He took part in the battles of Dunbar and Worcester and after his escape from the latter disaster he maintained resistance to Cromwell for a time. He joined the Royalist rising led by Glencairn and Middleton in 1654 and in consequence was excepted from the general oblivion contained in Cromwell's Act of Grace. Once again he continued resistance after others had laid down their arms, and on his submission he was kept under surveillance and for a time imprisoned in Edinburgh Castle (1657–60). His record was such that he naturally enjoyed royal favour at the Restoration, when his father was executed, but Middleton tried to involve him in his father's downfall and he was imprisoned and sentenced to death, though not executed. However, in 1664, after Middleton's fall, he became a Privy Councillor and as such identified himself with the prosecutions of the Covenanters. He also showed his approval of the government's policy by raising a militia regiment in 1670.

In 1681, when conscientious difficulties were caused to Scots of many shades of opinion by the Test Act (designed to ensure that there would be no resistance to the royal will), Argyll declared himself prepared to swear the prescribed oath 'in so far as it was consistent with itself'. This piece of flippancy was taken seriously by the government, and Argyll found himself tried for treason and convicted. He escaped from Edinburgh Castle disguised as a page, made his way to London and ultimately reached Holland. There he associated not only with other Scottish malcontents but with the Duke of Monmouth, the illegitimate son of Charles II whom the most bigoted opponents of the accession of a Roman Catholic sovereign proposed to set up as King in preference to James VII and II. It was arranged in 1685 that, while Monmouth invaded England, Argyll would invade Scotland. He landed in Orkney with a small force and made his way to the Firth of Clyde, but found little support, for King James had been generally accepted in a flush of loyalty to hereditary monarchy, and the Covenanting dissidents, although they did not acknowledge James, would not support Argyll, who was not himself a Covenanter. With about 500 men he set out to march on Glasgow, but was taken prisoner and was executed in terms of the sentence of 1681.

The Earl's eldest son, Archibald (c. 1651–1703), offered to serve against his father in 1685, but he afterwards went to Holland and accompanied William of Orange to England. He took his seat in the Scottish Convention in 1689, and his father's forfeiture was rescinded in 1690. He was created Duke of Argyll in 1701.

John Willcock, *A Scots Earl of Covenanting Times*, 1907.

Cameron, Richard (1648–80), Covenanting leader, was the son of a small shopkeeper in Falkland. He became schoolmaster and precentor of the parish, but was converted to Presbyterian views by one of the covenanting field preachers. He had therefore to give up his parochial appointments, and was for a time a tutor to the family of Sir Walter Scott of Harden, until his refusal to attend the parish church led to his dismissal. He was then licensed as a preacher by John Welch and another Covenanting minister. His denunciation of the Presbyterian clergy who had accepted the measure of toleration offered by the Indulgences was so severe that he broke completely with the majority of the Presbyterians, and only a small number would agree with him. He therefore went to Holland, where he was ordained by some exiled ministers, and returned in 1680 to act as a field preacher at the head of the extremist remnant who came to be known as Cameronians. At Sanquhar on 20 June 1680, with a small party of about twenty persons, he made a public renunciation of the King's authority. This led the Privy Council to put a price of 5,000 merks on his head. Pursued by the military, he was defeated and killed in a skirmish at Airds Moss on 20 July 1680.

John Herkless, *Richard Cameron*, 1896.

Cargill, Donald (1619–1681), Cameronian preacher, a native of Rattray in Perthshire, studied at the Universities of Aberdeen and St. Andrews and became minister of the Barony Church, Glasgow, in 1650. With the restoration of episcopal government in 1661, he was ordered to remain north of the Tay, but he did not obey and in 1668 he was called before the Council and the sentence repeated. The Covenanters were now divided on their attitude to the Indulgences, and Cargill, who strongly condemned the Indulgences and those who accepted them, became one of the most extreme of the field preachers. He was wounded at the battle of Bothwell Brig in 1679 and took refuge for a time in Holland but soon returned. He was presumably one of the authors of the Queensferry Paper (1680), which, among other statements, repudiated the idea that the Church should be governed 'after a carnal manner, by plurality of votes', and on 22 June 1680 he associated with Richard Cameron in disowning the King by the Sanquhar Declaration. After Cameron's death at Airds Moss a month later, Cargill became the leader of the Cameronians and for a time the only active field preacher remaining in Scotland. At a conventicle at the Torwood in September 1680 he solemnly excommunicated the King, the Duke of York (afterwards James VII), the Dukes of Monmouth, Lauderdale and Rothes, Sir George Mackenzie of Rosehaugh and Sir Thomas Dalyell. A price of 5000 merks was put on his head and he was apprehended at Covington Mill, in Lanarkshire, in July 1681. Before his execution in Edinburgh he exclaimed, 'This is the most joyful day ever I saw in my pilgrimage on earth'. The Cameronians, though now without a minister, preserved their organization until they obtained the services of James Renwick (1662–88), who had attended Edinburgh

University but could not graduate because he refused to take the necessary oaths. He threw in his lot with the Cameronians, and crossed to Holland, where, after studying for a few months at Groningen, he was ordained by a Dutch *classis* (the equivalent of a presbytery). He returned to Scotland in 1683 to lead a hunted life as a field preacher and took part in the Sanquhar Protestation of 1685, in which the Cameronians disowned King James VII. He was arrested in Edinburgh early in 1688 and, convicted of denying the King's authority, adhering to the Covenants, refusing to pay taxes and maintaining the lawfulness of defensive warfare, was executed on 17 February.

P. Walker and A. Shields, *Biographia Presbyteriana*, 1827.

Turner, Sir James (1615–?1686), the eldest son of Patrick Turner, minister successively of Borthwick and Dalkeith, graduated M.A. at Glasgow University in 1631, but rejected the idea of a career in the Church and in 1632 entered the service of Gustavus Adolphus. After taking part in many operations in Germany, he returned to Scotland to join the army of the Covenant and served with it in England and Ireland as well as in Scotland. In 1647 he was Adjutant-General. Turner had already shown evidence that he was more Royalist than the bulk of the Covenanters, and when they divided in 1648 he was on the side of the moderates who supported the Engagement with Charles I. Taking part in the invasion of England under the Duke of Hamilton, he was a prisoner for a time after the defeat at Preston, but was released on condition that he would go abroad for a year, and this he did. Subsequently he returned and fought as a Colonel for Charles II at Worcester (1651). He was again captured, but escaped and made his way to Paris, where he joined the King, and he was then employed for several years on various missions on behalf of the Royalist cause. At the Restoration he was knighted and in July 1666 he was put in command of the forces which operated against the Covenanters in the south-west. In November he was captured by a party of Covenanters at Dumfries, and this episode sparked off the Pentland Rising. Turner escaped when his captors were involved in their engagement at Rullion Green, but his severities were blamed for the outbreak of rebellion and he found himself out of favour when the government decided to adopt milder measures. He spent most of the rest of his life in retirement. Contemporaries testified to the varied facets of his character. Gilbert Burnet described him as 'naturally fierce' and 'mad when he was drunk, and that was very often', but added that he was 'a learned man'; and Robert Wodrow, who was no more apt than Burnet to praise persecutors of the Covenanters, said that Turner was 'very bookish'. He wrote *Pallas Armata* (1683), a series of essays on the art of war in ancient and modern times, and also *Memoirs*, which were published by the Bannatyne Club in 1829. He is often thought of as the original of Dugald Dalgetty in Scott's *A Legend of Montrose*.

Dalyell, General Sir Thomas, of the Binns (*c.* 1599–1685), was the son of Thomas Dalyell of the Binns, an estate in West Lothian. At an early stage in his military career he took part in the English expedition against La Rochelle (1628), and then held various military appointments, some of them in Ireland, where he was in charge of the town and castle of Carrickfergus in 1649. He was back in Scotland to join the expedition which ended at Worcester (1651), where he was taken prisoner. He escaped from the Tower of London and went abroad, but returned to take part in a rising in the Highlands in March 1654. After this, he then went further afield than most Scots who followed military careers on the continent, for he entered the Russian service, in which he became a General in wars against the Poles and Turks. At the Restoration he was still in the Czar's service, reorganizing his army, but Charles II recalled him and gave him command of the forces in Scotland (1666). Dalyell's first action was to defeat the Covenanters at Rullion Green. He remained Commander in Scotland until his death, except for a brief period in 1679 when he was superseded by the Duke of Monmouth. He was also a Privy Councillor, a member of Parliament for Linlithgowshire (1678–85) and a Commissioner of Justiciary for dealing with the Covenanters after their second rebellion had ended at Bothwell Brig. He raised the Royal Scots Greys Regiment in 1681. Dalyell had shown his royalist principles by making, and keeping, a vow never to cut his beard again after the execution of Charles I. In later years, with his white, bushy beard reaching almost to his girdle, a bald head which he refused to cover with a wig, and eccentric dress, he attracted much attention from small boys when he paid his occasional visits to London. Dalyell's death, shortly after the accession of the Roman Catholic James VII, saved him from the need to choose between his loyalty and his religion.

Graham, John, of Claverhouse, Viscount Dundee (1648–1689), the son of William Graham and Lady Magdalen Carnegie, succeeded his father in 1653. Educated at St. Andrews, he served in the French and Dutch armies as a volunteer until he returned to Scotland in 1677. In September 1678 he was appointed Captain of one of the three troops of horse commissioned to act against the militant conventicles which were now meeting in the south-west. On 1 June 1679, after the murder of Archbishop Sharp had given a stimulus to Covenanting violence, Graham was defeated by a large armed conventicle at Drumclog, and he was present with his troop when the rebellion was crushed at Bothwell Brig (22 June). His subsequent activities against the Covenanters took place in 1682 and for a few months in each of the years 1684 and 1685. The image of 'Bloody Clavers' which lives in folk memory is a distortion. His practice was to make examples of carefully selected victims, not to slaughter indiscriminately, and the number of lives he took in the discharge of his duties did not exceed ten. He became a Colonel in December 1682 and a Privy Councillor in 1683. From 1685 to 1688 he lived mainly at Dudhope Castle, which he had acquired, and he was provost of the nearby town of Dundee. When William of Orange invaded England in 1688, Claverhouse was second in command of the Scottish army which James VII called to England, and he was created Viscount Dundee on 12 November. He in vain urged James to remain in England and fight, instead of fleeing to France. In the following year he withdrew from the Convention in Edinburgh when it became clear that the supporters of William would carry the day, and, after conferring with the Duke of Gordon, who was holding the castle for King James, he moved northwards and was soon raising the clans for him. He showed a mobility and a power of command comparable to those of his namesake the first Marquis of Montrose and on 27 July trapped William's general, Hugh MacKay, a younger son of MacKay of Scourie, in the pass of Killiecrankie. MacKay's force was routed by a wild Highland charge, but Dundee was mortally wounded in the moment of victory. When King William was asked to send additional forces to Scotland, he said, 'Armies are needless: the war is over with Dundee's life.' However the Jacobite army did advance as far as Dunkeld, where it was checked by a garrison raised from the more extreme Covenanters and known as the Cameronian Regiment, under Colonel William Cleland (c. 1661–89). Cleland's defence was successful, but, like Dundee, he did not survive his victory, for he was shot through the head and killed.

C. S. Terry, *John Graham of Claverhouse*, 1905.

Carstares, William (1649–1715), ecclesiastical statesman, was the son of the Presbyterian minister of Cathcart, who was deprived in 1662 and, after the Covenanters' rebellion of 1666, fled to Holland. William, born on 11 February 1649, was educated at Glasgow High School and Edinburgh University (1663–7), and then joined his father in Holland, where, after studying at Utrecht (1669–72), he entered the service of William, Prince of Orange. In 1672, when war began between England and Holland, Carstares crossed to Britain to make contact with the disaffected there, and on a second mission he was arrested in London and imprisoned in Edinburgh Castle (1675–9). He became a Presbyterian minister in London in 1680, and was soon involved in plots, both in England and Scotland, against Charles II and James VII. In 1683, after being arrested in Kent, he was sent to Scotland so that he could be examined under torture. He made a number of disclosures, but succeeded in avoiding the incrimination of William of Orange, for which the latter was always grateful. After release in 1684, Carstares returned to William's court and in 1688 accompanied him on his invasion of England.

William was much inclined to maintain episcopal government in the Scottish Church, but he ultimately, in 1690, agreed to establish the Presbyterian system—partly on the prompting of Carstares, who founded his arguments on politics and expediency rather than on any superior claim of presbytery to divine right. Throughout most of William's reign Carstares had apartments at court, he accompanied the King on his continental campaigns, and his influence was such that he was known as 'Cardinal Carstares'. The authorization of Presbyterianism did not by any means solve all problems in Scotland, and there was a struggle between the King and the General Assembly, partly over the conditions on which the Episcopalian ministers might be admitted to the new establishment and partly over the terms of an oath of allegiance which it was proposed to impose on all ministers. This dispute threatened disaster to William's régime, and at one point Carstares saved the situation by abstracting a royal letter from the King's messenger and then persuading William to countermand his orders. Carstares became Principal of Edinburgh University in 1703, and was Moderator of the General Assembly four times.

R. H. Story, *William Carstares*, 1874.
A. Ian Dunlop, *William Carstares*, 1967.

Rose (or Ross), Alexander (?1647–1720), son of a minister and nephew of Archbishop Arthur Ross of St. Andrews, was born at Kinnairney, Aberdeenshire, and graduated at King's College, Aberdeen, in 1667. He was a minister in Perth from 1672 to 1683, when he became Professor of Divinity at Glasgow, and in 1686 he became Principal of St. Mary's College, St. Andrews. He was appointed Bishop of Moray in 1687 and translated to Edinburgh in the following year. When William of Orange had been accepted as King of England, and the future of Scotland was still in some doubt, Rose went to London to negotiate on behalf of the Scottish Church. He learned that William, who had been misled by the exiled Presbyterians in Holland, now realized that episcopacy had considerable support in Scotland and was willing to retain it if the bishops would declare their allegiance to him. In an interview with Rose, William said, 'I hope you will be kind to me, and follow the example of England'. But Rose, who had taken an oath to King James which he felt he could not conscientiously break, replied, 'Sir, I will serve you as far as law, reason or conscience will allow.' William turned away from him, and this decision of Rose went a long way to determine the fate of the Episcopal Church. When the Episcopalians had to vacate the parish churches, Rose, so it is said, led his congregation from the Cathedral of St. Giles down the High Street to Carrubber's Close, where they assembled in a meeting-house which was the ancestor of Old St. Paul's Church. After the death of the Archbishop of St. Andrews in 1704, Rose became the leader of the Episcopalians. He took no part in politics either at the time of the Union or during the 'Fifteen, and indeed showed little militancy of any kind, but he did ensure that the succession of bishops was maintained, though without appointment to sees. Rose outlived all the other bishops of the establishment except John Gordon of Galloway, who had gone over to Rome.

Mary E. Ingram, *A Jacobite Stronghold of the Church*, 1907.

Sage, Bishop John (1652–1711), born at Creich, Fife, was educated at the parish school there and then at St. Andrews University, where he graduated M.A. in 1669. He was a parish schoolmaster, for a time at Ballingry and then at Tibbermore, but became tutor to the sons of Drummond of Cultmalindie, whom he accompanied to St. Andrews and there renewed his contacts with men of learning. In 1684 he was ordained presbyter and became a parish minister in Glasgow and clerk of the presbytery and synod. When he was deprived at the Revolution as an Episcopalian, he carried with him the presbytery records (which were, however, later recovered for the established Church). For the rest of his life Sage was intermittently persecuted and hunted for his attachment to episcopacy and to the exiled Stewarts, and he suffered much hardship, but he was sheltered for a time by Sir William Bruce of Kinross and spent periods acting as chaplain to the Countess of Callendar and to Sir John Stewart of Grantully. He was consecrated a bishop in 1705. His troubled life had not been conducive to sound health, and in 1709–10 he went to Bath and then to London in a fruitless search for a cure. He died at Edinburgh on 7 June 1711.

Sage was perhaps the most prolific, and certainly one of the ablest, of the writers on the Episcopalian side in the fierce controversy with the Presbyterians which followed the Revolution and in the pleas which the Episcopalians made for toleration. Perhaps his best remembered works in those fields are *The Fundamental Charter of Presbytery* (1695) and *The Reasonableness of Toleration to those of the Episcopal Persuasion* (1703). However, Sage used his unquestioned scholarship for other purposes besides controversy, for he associated with Thomas Ruddiman, a fellow Episcopalian, in preparing the works of earlier Scottish writers for publication. In this way he came to write a *Life of Gavin Douglas* (1710) and an introduction to William Drummond's *History of the Five Jameses* (1711). Sage's *Works,* with a memoir, were issued by the Spottiswoode Society in 3 volumes, 1844–6.

Paterson, William (1658–1719), financier, was born in Tynwald, Dumfriesshire, but nothing is known of his early life. From his childhood he evidently lived mainly in England, where he became a merchant and traded to the West Indies. In 1691 he proposed the establishment of the Bank of England, and when it was founded, in 1694, he was one of the directors. Always a man of grand, if not grandiose, ideas, he considered the operations of the bank to be too narrowly conceived, and in 1695 he resigned from it. He then reverted to a scheme, which he had had in mind since 1684, for the establishment at Darien, near Panama, of a settlement which would be a commercial emporium for trade with the Atlantic and the Pacific and with both North and South America. At this point there was founded, though not on Paterson's initiative, The Company of Scotland Trading to Africa and the Indies, which was strongly supported by English merchants who wanted to compete with the East India Company. Paterson himself was an expatriated Scot, and it occurred to him that he could use the Company for his

157

own ends. As it happened, the opposition of the East India Company was so successful that English support was withdrawn and the company became a purely Scottish venture. This increased Paterson's opportunities, and thanks to his exertions in Edinburgh the operations of the Company were directed to Darien, though his wider vision was lost sight of and all that was now planned was the establishment at Darien of a 'plantation' or colony of the usual type. Paterson sailed with the first expedition to the Isthmus in 1698, but he had little influence on the conduct of affairs and he returned to Scotland in 1699 before the venture met with final disaster. In subsequent years he prepared schemes for a Sinking Fund and for the Consolidation of the National Debt, both carried out later. Although he had been an associate of the anti-Unionist Fletcher of Saltoun, he supported the Union of 1707, and his expertise was called in to assist in the framing of its fiscal provisions. He lived in London from 1703 until his death.

J. S. Barbour, *A history of William Paterson and the Darien Company*, 1907.
G. P. Insh, *The Company of Scotland*, 1932.

Clerk, Sir John, of Penicuik (1676–1755), politician, was the son and heir of Sir John Clerk of Penicuik, Bart., whom he succeeded in 1722. He was educated at the University of Edinburgh and at Leyden (where he graduated Doctor of Law in 1697). In all he spent about five years on the continent and visited Vienna and Rome before he returned in 1699. He was admitted an advocate in 1700. As member for Whithorn in the last Scottish Parliament, 1703–7, he was one of the commissioners for the Union. Thereafter he was an M.P. in the British Parliament and from 1708 until his death he was a judge in the Scottish Court of Exchequer. Like many of his contemporaries, he was prompted by his thoughts on the Union to consider economic problems, and wrote *Money and Trade considered, with a proposal for supplying the Nation with Money* (1705). He was fascinated by antiquities: he collected ancient objects, took an interest in old buildings and wrote a Description (in Latin) on 'Certain Roman Monuments found in North Britain' (1750). He became a member of the Society of Antiquaries (of London) in 1727 and a Fellow of the Royal Society in 1729. His *Historical View of the Forms and Powers of the Court of Exchequer in Scotland* was not published until 1820.

Memoirs of Sir John Clerk of Penicuik. Scot. Hist. Soc., 1892.

Cockburn, John, of Ormiston (1679–1758), agrarian improver, was the son of Adam Cockburn, Lord Justice Clerk (d. 1735), by a daughter of the 4th Earl of Haddington. The family had been consistently on the side of Protestantism and the English alliance since the 1540s, and it was appropriate that John, as a member for Haddingtonshire in the last Scottish Parliament, was a Privy Councillor and a commissioner for the Union of 1707. He then sat in British Parliaments as M.P. for Haddingtonshire until 1741 and was for a time a Lord of the Admiralty. John's father, like other lairds in fertile East Lothian, had already set in motion a certain amount of agrarian improvement, by granting leases for as long as eleven years in place of the precarious tenures which had often been customary. John, when he succeeded to the estates in 1714, had seen something of English agriculture, and he introduced some novelties both in land management and in crops. He was one of the most famous agricultural 'Improvers' of the period. He granted long leases on condition that the tenants followed certain rules, he carried out ditching and hedging on his home farm to set an example to his tenants, he sent the sons of tenants to learn husbandry in England, and he brought advisers from England. During his absences in London he directed operations by a stream of correspondence. He encouraged the cultivation of the novel crops of turnips, clover and potatoes, and the village of Ormiston was remodelled as a nucleus of his estate. In addition to his agrarian activities, he established the first bleachfield for linen in East Lothian and he introduced experts from Ireland and Holland to give instruction in that craft. He founded the Ormiston Society of Landowners and Tenants, one of the many societies set up at the time for discussion of agrarian development. While Cockburn's schemes were to the ultimate benefit of the country, they were not a financial success for him personally, and in 1747 he had to sell the estate to the Earl of Hopetoun.

Letters of John Cockburn of Ormiston. Scot. Hist. Soc., 1904.

Breadalbane, John Campbell, 1st Earl of (1635–1717), son of Sir John Campbell of Glenorchy (d. 1686), took part in the Royalist rising against Cromwell in 1654 and in 1657 married Mary Rich, daughter of the 1st Earl of Holland, who brought him a dowry of £10,000 and who died in 1666. As chief creditor of the 6th Earl of Caithness, Campbell obtained a conveyance of the latter's dignities and lands in 1672; after the earl's death he was created Earl of Caithness and Viscount of Breadalbane (1677); and in 1678 he married the earl's widow, so saving the pension he had undertaken to pay her. In 1680 he invaded Caithness and dispossessed the rightful heir to the earldom, but the latter was subsequently confirmed in his title, whereupon Campbell was made Earl of Breadalbane and Holland (1681). He became a Privy Councillor in 1685. Described as having 'neither honour nor religion but where they are mixed with interest' and as being 'cunning as a fox, wise as a serpent but slippery as an eel', he took a non-committal attitude at the Revolution, but after Killiecrankie he was entrusted with money to gain the submission of the Highlands to King William. He met the Jacobite chiefs at Achallader in June 1691 and brought them to terms by devious means which did not (so it was said) include the disbursement of the money. Shortly afterwards, indemnity was offered to chiefs who would take the oath of allegiance to William before 1 January 1692, and the failure of MacDonald of Glencoe to do so led to the Massacre of Glencoe (13 February). Breadalbane was widely suspected of taking the opportunity of bringing about the punishment of a clan which had long been troublesome to his family, but although he was aware that action was planned it appears that he was not himself a party to the arrangements for the massacre. He was imprisoned in 1695, on the ground of his earlier dealing with the Jacobite chiefs, and he was released when the King intimated that he had acted with the royal approval. Breadalbane did not vote for the Union of 1707, but sat as a representative peer in the British Parliament from 1713 to 1715. He maintained contact with the Jacobites and displayed characteristic double-dealing at the time of the 'Fifteen, so that, although some of his men served for a time in the Jacobite army and his son was imprisoned, he himself escaped punishment.

Hamilton, James Douglas or Hamilton, 4th Duke of (1658–1712), was the son of Anne, Duchess of Hamilton in her own right, and her husband the 3rd Duke. In 1698, four years after his father's death, his mother resigned her rights to him and he was created Duke. After education at Glasgow University he went abroad for two years and there showed an extravagance and irresponsibility which were to mark him throughout his life. On his return he was created a gentleman of the bedchamber (1679), but went to France as ambassador in 1683 and then served in the French Army. He returned to Britain in 1685. At the Revolution he refused, unlike his father, to join the party of William of Orange and was so strongly suspected (not without reason) of being involved in Jacobite plots that he was twice confined in the Tower of London, but he was not prosecuted. He won popularity in the Scottish Parliament in 1700 for his defence of the interests of the Company of Scotland, and in 1702 he protested against the illegality of continuing William's Parliament after that King's death. As the premier Scottish peer, and with a record of opposition to King William, Hamilton was the obvious leader for the party which opposed the Union of 1707, but in the crisis he showed the irresolution characteristic of his house and he opposed the suggestion of an armed rising. As he all along preferred life in London to life in Scotland, it is hard to believe that any genuine conviction moved him. His devious ways may have been shaped partly by the knowledge that he was the native of Scotland who stood nearest to the throne, but this cut him off from the Jacobites as well as from the unionists who favoured the Hanoverian succession. At any rate, when the anti-unionists looked to him for leadership, he absented himself from the Parliament House on the plea of toothache. Once the Union was an accomplished fact he accepted it, for in 1708 he opposed the Jacobite invasion scheme and he became one of the Scottish representative peers at Westminster. In 1711 he was created Duke of Brandon in the peerage of the United Kingdom, but by an astonishing decision he and his descendants were not allowed to sit in the House of Lords in that capacity until 1782. In 1712 Hamilton was planning a reconciliation between Queen Anne and her half-brother James, 'the Old Pretender', whereby the latter was to be recognized as Anne's successor, and was about to set out for France when he was killed in a duel with Lord Mohun, on 15 November 1712.

Fletcher, Andrew, of Saltoun (1653–1716), politician, son of Sir Robert Fletcher of Saltoun, was cared for, after his father's early death, by Gilbert Burnet (1643–1715), minister of Saltoun and later Bishop of Salisbury, who instructed him in Whig principles. As a member of the Scottish Parliament, from 1678 onwards, he served his apprenticeship as a politician by taking part in the opposition, first to the Duke of Lauderdale and then to James, Duke of York. Outlawed for refusing to take the Test Oath of 1681, Fletcher went to the continent and then to England. Like other members of the Scottish opposition, such as Robert Baillie of Jerviswoode (*c*. 1634–84) and Sir Patrick Hume of Polwarth (1641–1724), he became involved with the more militant wing of the English Whigs at the time of the Rye House Plot, and, after a period of exile in Holland, he was with James, Duke of Monmouth, in the early stages of his rebellion, before it reached its disastrous end (1685). Forfeited in his absence (1686), he travelled widely in Europe, visiting Spain and serving against the Turks in Hungary, but in 1688 he was in the Hague and in touch with William of Orange before the latter led the expedition which overthrew James VII. Fletcher, whose temperament perhaps made him perpetually 'agin the government', did not support William's administration, but was a member of the 'Club' or opposition which embarrassed it. He encouraged William Paterson in his plans to set up the Company of Scotland, which led to the Darien Disaster.

In the last Scottish Parliament, Fletcher was a leader of the party which in 1703 urged the need to liberate Scotland from domination by the English ministry, and he brought forward a scheme of 'limitations' which would in effect have transferred power from the crown to the Parliament. Some of his projected 'limitations' lay behind the Act anent Peace and War and the Act of Security, in which the Scottish Parliament sought to assert its independence in the making of war and peace and in the choice of a successor to the throne. After commissioners were appointed to treat for a union with England, in 1705, Fletcher was naturally an anti-Unionist, and as his policy was again and again outvoted he became increasingly irascible. He challenged some of his fellow members to duels and at one point went so far as to propose the King of Prussia as an alternative to the Elector of Hanover for a future King. He wrote pamphlets and published speeches expressing his opposition to the terms on which Union was ultimately achieved in 1707. At an earlier stage in his career, Fletcher had shown much concern for the economy of Scotland, and in *Two Discourses concerning the affairs of Scotland* (1698) he urged the use of public funds for the promotion of industry and brought forward a proposal that Scotland's numerous paupers should be absorbed by being made serfs. As an East Lothian laird, Fletcher was interested in agrarian improvements, and criticized the existing methods of working. In 1710 he employed James Meikle, father of the better-known Andrew, to construct a barley-mill on the Dutch model.

W. C. Mackenzie, *Andrew Fletcher of Saltoun*, 1935.

Mar, John Erskine, 11th Earl of (1675–1732), best remembered as a Jacobite leader, but known as 'Bobbing John' because of his facility in changing sides, succeeded his father in 1689. He showed no signs of Jacobite leanings in William's reign or Anne's, and worked for a union with England in 1703 and in 1705–6. He was

Secretary of State in 1705 and one of the Commissioners for Union in 1706. After the Union he was a representative peer in the British Parliament and was again for a time one of the Secretaries for Scotland. Although he was very closely linked with the Tory ministry at the end of Anne's reign, he was prepared to welcome George I, but he found himself repulsed, and was deprived not only of his secretaryship but also of the office of governor of Stirling Castle, which had long been hereditary in his family. Mar therefore turned to the Jacobites. In August 1715 he embarked on a collier in the Thames and made his way in disguise to Deeside, where he organized a meeting of nobles and chiefs to plan a rebellion. On 6 September he raised the standard of James VIII on the Braes of Mar, where the Invercauld Arms Hotel now stands.

Mar soon had 5000 men, against only about 1500 government troops in the country. The latter were concentrated at Stirling by their general, the Duke of Argyll, and increased to 3,300. But Mar's force also increased, and he found himself at Perth with 10,000 men. There he stopped. The Jacobites had almost everything in their favour except leadership. 'Forty years of age and of an inactive disposition, Mar was very far from being a Montrose or a Dundee, and it never seems to have occurred to him that a rebellion on the defensive is already beaten.... Had there been no opposition at all, it is doubtful if Mar would have accomplished anything.'[1] There was also in the field a Jacobite force in south-west Scotland and north-west England, and Mar detached over 2000 men under William Mackintosh of Borlum (1662–1743) to cross the Firth of Forth and join them. Mackintosh showed mobility and initiative, but the combined southern forces, instead of taking Argyll in the rear, moved further into England (losing many Highlanders by desertion) and had to surrender at Preston on 14 November. On the previous day, Mar, who had at length bestirred himself, encountered Argyll at Sheriffmuir, which was tactically a drawn battle but strategically a defeat, for Mar retired, to leave the position covering Stirling to the enemy. Mar now had better reasons for refusing aggressive action, and the arrival of 'James VIII' in person at the end of the year did nothing to re-invigorate the dispirited army. Mar slipped away to France with his king on 4 February, and his estates were forfeited.

James made Mar a Duke, but did not long retain him in his full confidence. Mar was not unwilling to change sides again, and he later abandoned Jacobitism to the extent of giving information

1. Petrie, *The Jacobite Movement*, i, p. 175.

163

against Bishop Atterbury when the latter was engaged in a Jacobite plot in 1722. He died at Aix-la-Chapelle. It is only fair to say that his heart may always have lain in peaceful rather than warlike pursuits, for he was interested in gardening and architecture, he was an advocate of a Forth–Clyde canal, and in 1728 he predicted the future development of the New Town of Edinburgh. The title was restored to his descendant in 1824.

Alistair and Henrietta Tayler, *1715: the story of the Rising*, 1936.

Argyll, John Campbell, 2nd Duke of (1678–1743), was the son of the 1st Duke, whom he succeeded in 1703. He entered the army in 1694 and served in Flanders. After the Scots Parliament had shown itself recalcitrant in its defiance of the government in 1703–4, Argyll was appointed Queen's Commissioner for the 1705 session, when it was agreed that the Queen should nominate the Scottish commissioners to treat for union with England. He was rewarded for his services in supporting the Union with the earldom (which in 1719 became the dukedom) of Greenwich. His political activities in Scotland were intermingled with a continuing military career, for he served under Marlborough at Ramillies, Oudenarde and Malplaquet and in 1711 was in command of the allied forces in Spain. In the later years of Anne's reign he was in opposition to the administration, for he condemned the Malt Tax in 1713 and supported a motion to repeal the Union in the same year.

Argyll helped to secure the peaceful acceptance of George I as King in 1714 and was made Commander-in-Chief in Scotland. In September 1715, after the Jacobite rebellion had broken out, Argyll arrived in Scotland to find himself short of both men and funds to face the substantial Jacobite army, but, fortunately for him, it was commanded by the incompetent Mar. He took up his position at Stirling, but had to detach part of his army to deal with Mackintosh of Borlum's forces, who had crossed the Firth of Forth and threatened Edinburgh, and had then to hasten back to Stirling on a report that Mar was on the move. At the battle of Sheriffmuir (13 November), each side claimed the victory, but Mar retired to leave Argyll in possession of the field, and Argyll was then able to move northwards, as Mar evacuated Perth and Dundee, and to pursue the dispersing Jacobite forces. The government, which had never appreciated the danger in Scotland, deprived Argyll of his offices in 1716, but he was restored three years later.

Although he was created a Field Marshal in 1736, the later part of Argyll's life was spent mainly in building up an 'interest' in

Scotland which secured the supremacy of his faction, the 'Argathelians', and which made him for a time the real master of the country. In association with his brother Archibald (1682–1761), who had been created Earl of Islay in 1706 and who succeeded him as 3rd Duke, he worked in an uneasy partnership with Walpole which was sorely tried when Argyll strenuously opposed the penal measures the government proposed to take with Edinburgh after the Porteous Riot in 1736. From that point Argyll (though not Islay) worked against Walpole, and in the election of 1741 he captured nearly half the Scottish constituencies. This helped to bring about Walpole's fall. Argyll did much to change the organization of his estates by abolishing the tacksman system and run-rig agriculture and commuting labour services, though his objective was not so much economic development or the well-being of his tenants as the increase of the revenues necessary to maintain his expensive mode of living in the south, and his operations had only limited results.

Scott, *The Heart of Midlothian.* (H.N.)
Neil Munro, *The New Road.* (H.N.)

Forbes, Duncan (1685–1747), lawyer and statesman, the second son of Duncan Forbes (1644–1704), succeeded his elder brother as laird of Culloden in 1734. He studied law at Leyden, became an advocate and was appointed sheriff of Midlothian in 1709. He took an active part against the Jacobites in 1715, but showed his patriotism and his regard for the independence of the Scottish legal system by opposing the trial in England of Scots who were arrested during and after the rising. In 1722 he became M.P. for Inverness Burghs and in 1725 Lord Advocate. In the post-Union system of administration, there was considerable scope for the Lord Advocate to exercise powers in the day-to-day administration of law and order–a task which had belonged to the Privy Council before its abolition in 1708. Thus, in 1725, Forbes restored order after the Shawfield Riots in Glasgow against the imposition of a new Malt Tax, though his legal competence to do so was challenged. In 1736, when an Edinburgh mob had hanged John Porteous, Captain of the City Guard, after he had fired on townsmen who had raised a disturbance at the execution of a smuggler, Forbes made a stand against the proposal to inflict harsh penalties on the city. Forbes became Lord President in 1737 and did much to introduce a new efficiency into the work of the Court of Session—transforming, so it was said, the courts of law into the courts of justice and overtaking arrears for the first time in living memory.

In the crisis of 1745 he again assumed wide authority, and, largely through his personal influence and his vigour, was able to prevent most of the northern clans from joining the rising. He said that, had he had more resources at his disposal, he would have prevented any reinforcements at all from joining the original Jacobite army which crossed the Forth. When Prince Charles retreated north through Scotland, Forbes had to retire to Skye until after the defeat of the Jacobites at Culloden. Despite his services, he was insulted by the victorious Cumberland: when Forbes referred to the law, Cumberland retorted, 'The laws of the country! My Lord, I'll make a brigade give laws, by God,' and later referred to Forbes as 'that old woman who talked to me about humanity'.

Like most Scottish lairds of the time, Forbes was interested in agrarian improvements, and as adviser to the Duke of Argyll he brought about the abolition of the tacksman system in Mull and Tiree in 1737, but the scheme was in many ways ill-conceived and the results limited.

George Menary, *Duncan Forbes*, 1936.

Wade, Field-Marshal George (1673–1748), became an ensign in 1690, and during the wars of the 1690s and the early eighteenth century he served in the Low Countries, Portugal and Spain. By 1714 he was a Major-General. In 1724, when he was already turned fifty, he was appointed Commander-in-Chief in Scotland. A statute passed after the 'Fifteen had not been very successful in disarming or demilitarizing the Highlands, and a second statute, in 1725, gave wider powers, which were exercised by Wade. He was given a force of 400 regulars and six Highland companies, each of a hundred men, drawn from the loyal clans; later the number of companies was increased to ten, and in 1739 formed into the Black Watch Regiment. Instead of awaiting the surrender of weapons, arms were now to be searched for and seized, but further measures were necessary if the Highlands were to be controlled. Between 1725 and 1738 Wade carried out most of his road-making, mainly along three routes: from Inverness to Fort William, through the Great Glen; from Inverness by Dalwhinnie and Blair Atholl to Dunkeld; and from Crieff to Aberfeldy, Dalwhinnie and Fort Augustus. Wade's mileage of roads was about 250, and the work involved also the construction of 42 bridges, but many military roads of later date are wrongly attributed to him. He also built barracks at Fort George and Fort Augustus and strengthened those at Fort William and Ruthven. Wade remained in Scotland until 1740. In 1743 he was appointed a Field-Marshal, and at the age of seventy was sent to service on the continent, but in 1745 he was appointed Commander-in-Chief in England. He led a force which sought to deal with the Jacobites when they invaded the north of England, but his enemy was so superior in mobility that it eluded him.

J. B. Salmond, *Wade in Scotland*, 1938.

MacGregor, Rob Roy (1671–1734), freebooter, was the son of a younger brother of the chief of his clan who was noted as a Jacobite at the Revolution. When the act making the name MacGregor illegal was revived, in 1693, he took his mother's name of Campbell. The family had a farm in Balquhidder, and Rob operated quite legally as a dealer in cattle, but he also indulged in a good many illicit pursuits and levied blackmail for the protection of cattle against his and others' depredations. Situated as his headquarters were between the lands of the Earl of Breadalbane and those of the Marquis of Montrose, he played one off against the other, with varying success. In 1715 he proclaimed the Pretender and drank his health, but stood by at Sheriffmuir, possibly out of loyalty to the Campbell Duke of Argyll who commanded the government troops and whom he seems to have regarded as in some sense his chief. Rob's various activities led to several adventures, in which he was more than once captured but escaped, and in 1726 he was in Newgate and was saved from transportation to Barbados only by a pardon. Yet, despite his colourful career, he was a man of education and culture, who subscribed to Bishop Keith's *History*, and his testament, duly recorded, shows that he was also a man of some substance.

One of Rob's sons, Robin Oig, abducted Jean Kay, a wealthy widow, and married her. For this crime both he and his brother, James Mhor, were condemned to death, but James escaped from Edinburgh Castle by changing clothes with one of his daughters, who had entered disguised as a cobbler. James, who had been a Jacobite in the 'Forty-Five and attainted for treason but had by some devious means managed to make his peace with the government, made his way to France and lived until 1789. Robin was hanged (1754). A third brother, Duncan, was found not guilty.

Hamilton Howlett, *Highland Constable: The Life and Times of Rob Roy MacGregor*, 1950.
Walter Scott, *Rob Roy*. (H.N.)

Charles Edward, *de jure* Charles III, otherwise the Young Pretender

(1720–1788), the elder son of 'James VIII' and Clementina Sobieski, born at Rome on 31 December 1720, was trained for an active, military life, and first came under fire when he was with the Spanish army besieging the Austrians in Gaeta (1734). In 1744, when France and Britain were at war, he was invited to France and joined a French fleet designed to invade England, but the fleet was shattered by a storm and the project abandoned.

Charles, determined to try a venture on his own, sailed for Scotland on 12 July 1745 and raised his standard at Glenfinnan on 19 August. He entered Edinburgh (17 September), defeated General Cope at Prestonpans (21 September) and after some weeks advanced into England with an army drawn predominantly from limited areas in the north-east, Perthshire, north Argyll and western Invernessshire. The English Jacobites failed to give support, and at Derby (6 December) it was decided to retreat. Although the government forces were defeated again at Falkirk (17 January 1746), the withdrawal continued and the Jacobites were routed at Culloden on 16 April.

Charles was enabled to escape to France by the help of devoted Highlanders, including Flora MacDonald (1722–90), the daughter of a laird in South Uist. Finding no prospects of help either there or in Spain, he wandered to Aix-la-Chapelle and then to Avignon. For some years almost nothing is known of his life, but he was certainly in London in 1750 and was received into the Church of England, though he reverted to Roman Catholicism in 1759. Supposed visits to Britain after 1750 are not authenticated. There was little that was politic in Charles's actions, and he did not retain the loyalty of his followers. He was severely censured for taking as his mistress, in 1752, Clementina Walkinshaw, whose sister was a lady-in-waiting to the Hanoverian Princess of Wales and who was suspected of being a spy. By Clementina Charles had a daughter, Charlotte (b. 1753), whom he created Duchess of Albany. On James's death in 1766, Charles was not acknowledged as King by either the Pope or France. It did something to revive Jacobite hopes when in 1772 he married Princess Louisa of Stolberg, but there were no children and the pair separated in 1783. Charles had for many years lived mainly at Rome and Florence, and in 1784 he sent for his daughter Charlotte, who cared for him until his death on 31 January 1788.

Charles's younger brother, Henry Benedict (1725–1807), the last male of the house of Stewart, was made a Cardinal in 1747. Henry became very wealthy as a prelate of the Church and was able to assist many needy Jacobites, but he did not formally claim the British throne on Charles's death.

C. H. Hartmann, *The Quest Forlorn*, 1952.
Donald Nicholas, *The Young Adventurer*, 1949.

Murray, Lord George (*c.* 1700–1760), Jacobite general, was a son of the 1st Duke of Atholl. With his elder brother William, the Marquis of Tullibardine (1689–1746), he took part in the 'Fifteen and in another Jacobite effort in 1719, when Tullibardine took command of the small Spanish force which the Earl Marischal had brought over to Scotland and of the Highlanders who joined it. After being defeated at Glenshiel, the brothers fled to France, but Lord George was pardoned in 1726. In 1745, when Tullibardine returned from France with Prince Charles Edward, Lord George joined the rising. As a Lieutenant-General, he shared command, under the Prince, with the Duke of Perth, but he was regarded by some of the Jacobites with suspicion and was at loggerheads with the Prince's Irish followers. At one stage during the march into England he resigned, but was persuaded to resume his duties. The situation was not conducive to efficient direction of a campaign, and there can be little doubt that Lord George, though not a military genius, would have managed better with less interference. His aide-de-camp said, 'Had Prince Charles slept during the whole of the expedition and allowed Lord George to act for him, according to his own judgment, there is every reason for supposing he would have found the crown of Great Britain on his head when he awoke.' Others have described him as 'a defeatist from the moment he joined', and Sir Charles Petrie's assessment is that, while he was competent, he was 'tactless and ungracious'.[1] His services were undoubted: his strategy enabled the Prince to evade Cumberland's army and get between it and London; he beat off the pursuit on the return march; and his wing of the army was successful at the battle of Falkirk. He was highly critical of the decision to fight at Culloden and resigned the following day. He escaped to France and died in Holland. Tullibardine was taken prisoner and died in the Tower.

Winifred Duke, *Lord George Murray*, 1927.
Kathleen Tomasson, *The Jacobite General*, 1958.

Lovat, Simon Fraser, 11th Lord (*c.* 1667–1747), was educated at King's College, Aberdeen, and throughout all his devious career he never lost a taste for letters. In 1696 he prevailed on his cousin, the

1. Petrie, *The Jacobite Movement*, ii, p. 85.

9th Lord, to settle the estate on Simon's father with 5000 merks to Simon himself. When the 9th Lord died shortly afterwards, Simon attempted to carry off his daughter, who was legal heir to the title and estates, and then, failing in this, he forced her mother to go through a marriage ceremony with him. For this he was outlawed in 1698. In 1702 he proclaimed James VIII at Inverness, after the death of William of Orange. He went to the court of the Pretender at St. Germain, and, while he subsequently obtained a pardon for his dealings with James, his outlawry for his proceedings in relation to his kinsfolk was renewed in 1703. Lovat was sent on a mission by Louis XIV to Scotland in 1703, but he betrayed his employer and on his return to France was imprisoned for ten years. He supported the government in the 'Fifteen, and was rewarded by recognition of his right to the Lovat title and estates, because the husband of the 9th Lord's daughter had been on the Jacobite side. It was held that Simon's father had in fact succeeded as 10th Lord Lovat in 1696 and that Simon had become Lord Lovat when he died in 1699. However, he did not fully establish his claims to the title until 1730 and to the estates until 1733.

Lovat was under suspicion for Jacobitism in 1737 and, although he approved of the formation of the Independent Companies of Highlanders who were loyal to the government, and had a command in one, he was dismissed as a suspect. In 1745 he at first sent his son to join Prince Charles while he kept up a correspondence with Duncan Forbes, the leading figure in the government of Scotland, and even after the Jacobite victory at Prestonpans, while he raised his clan for the Prince, he himself remained at home and denounced his son. After Culloden he urged Charles to continue the campaign. He was captured after taking refuge on an island in Loch Morar, and taken to London for trial. He conducted an able defence, in which he enlarged on his services to the House of Hanover, but evidence was given against him by John Murray of Broughton (1718–77), who had been Prince Charles's secretary and earned his own pardon by denouncing Lovat, to his perpetual shame in the eyes of his fellow Jacobites. Lovat was condemned and, although his age and infirmity made it necessary for him to be carried in a litter, was beheaded, completely self-composed and cynical to the end.

W. C. Mackenzie, *Simon Fraser*, 1908.

Stewart, James, 'of the Glens' (d. 1752), was an illegitimate son of the laird of Ardshiel and half-brother of the Ardshiel who led the Clan Stewart of Appin in the 'Forty-Five, when the chief, Stewart of Appin, was a minor. The Ardshiel estate was forfeited after the rising, and in 1748 Colin Campbell of Glenure (1708–52) was appointed factor of the forfeited lands of Stewarts and Camerons. The lands included the farm of Glenduror, which James held as a tenant and from which he was evicted in May 1751, whereupon he moved to Aucharn. James and Glenure almost came to blows at New Year, 1752. Shortly afterwards, Glenure gave notice to many Stewart tenants that they must remove at the next Whitsunday term (15 May 1752). James obtained a legal deferment of the eviction, but Glenure had it withdrawn, and although James made another attempt at legal action, it became evident that it would fail. On 14 May, Glenure, on his way from Fort William to carry out the eviction, was killed by a shot from the hillside of Lettermore. Suspicion fell on James of the Glens and on Alan Breck Stewart, his foster brother. Alan had been at Aucharn early in May, and returned on the 11th to warn James that Glenure was on his way; he left Aucharn on the 12th, but remained in the vicinity. Both were indicted for the murder, but Alan escaped arrest and survived in France until at least 1789. James was confined at Fort William from his arrest on 16th May until he was brought to trial at Inveraray, the headquarters of his hereditary foes, the Campbells (21–25 September). He was hanged above Ballachulish Ferry on 8 November, protesting his innocence and his attachment to the Episcopal Church. His body hung in chains until about 1755, when it was secretly removed, and buried at Keil in Duror. There appears to be general agreement that James was innocent of the actual murder, as indeed was Alan, and the local belief was to the effect that the guilty person was Donald Stewart, nephew of Alexander Stewart of Ballachulish, who was dissuaded from giving himself up by the argument that James would be hanged as an accessory even if he did. It was he who ultimately undertook James's burial at Keil.

David N. Mackay, *The Trial of James Stewart*, 1931.
James Fergusson, 'The Appin Murder Case', in *Scot. Hist. Rev.*, xxxi, 116–30.

R. L. Stevenson, *Kidnapped*. (H.N.)

Forbes, Bishop Robert (1708–1775), born at Rayne, Aberdeenshire, and educated at Marischal College, entered the ministry of the Episcopal Church and in 1735 was ordained by the Bishop of Edinburgh to serve the non-juring, or Jacobite, congregation at Leith, to which he ministered for the remainder of his life. Himself an enthusiastic Jacobite, Forbes set out in 1745 to join Prince Charles's army, but

—perhaps fortunately for himself—he was arrested at Stirling and confined, first in Stirling Castle, then in Edinburgh, until the rising was over. He resumed his ministrations in June 1746, though his chapel had been closed and his work was illegal under the legislation of 1746 and 1748 against the non-juring Episcopalians, and in 1749 a rival congregation of juring, or 'Qualified' Episcopalians was set up, which qualified for toleration under an Act of 1712. Once Jacobitism ceased to be a political danger, Forbes had greater liberty, and wrote with pride in 1763 of his 'fine new chapel, thirteen windows in front, most neatly fitted up with a proper altar . . . and a genteel large vestry, with a fireplace'. Even then, however, his services were liable to interruption by the military, and in 1764 he thought it prudent to take a 'jaunt' to London.

In 1762 Forbes had been elected and consecrated Bishop of Ross and Caithness. He visited his wide diocese (which apparently was considered to include Argyll) twice, in 1762 and 1770, and on his travels collected many reminiscences of the Jacobite movement which, with material found in other ways, he brought together in his *The Lyon in Mourning*, published in ten 8vo volumes, 1747–75, and reissued by the Scottish History Society in three volumes in 1894–6. This constitutes one of the most important sources for Jacobite history. Forbes was in close touch with the English Non-Jurors and, like most Non-Jurors, was a High Churchman. He even rebaptized Presbyterians who had been 'sprinkled by an unauthorised holder-forth', he sometimes used the chrism in Confirmation, and he confirmed one of the English Non-Juring bishops who was doubtful if he had ever received that rite.

Registers of the Episcopal Congregation in Leith, Scottish Record Society, 1969.
J. B. Craven, *Journals of the Episcopal Visitations of Bishop Robert Forbes*, 1886.

Douglas, Archibald James Edward (1748–1827), successful claimant in 'the Douglas Cause', was a nephew of Archibald, 3rd Marquis and 1st Duke of Douglas (1694–1761), who died childless and with whom the dukedom became extinct. Lady Jane Douglas (1698–1753), the Duke's sister and heir, was married quietly, in her home, to Sir John Steuart of Grandtully, Bart., on 4 August 1746, and the marriage was kept secret for two years. On 10 July 1748, when she was fifty, twin boys were born to her. The younger of them died at the age of five, the elder, Archibald, survived, but the Duke refused to acknowledge him as a child of his sister and as his heir. On the

Duke's death Archibald Douglas was invested in the Douglas estates, but his right to them was challenged by the Duke of Hamilton, who was heir male and who succeeded to the older titles of the Angus family, by Lord Douglas Hamilton, as heir of entail, and by Sir Hew Dalrymple of North Berwick, one of the heirs of line. In proceedings which aroused enormous interest and excitement, the Court of Session decided against Douglas by the Lord President's casting vote, but the House of Lords in 1769 reversed this verdict. Douglas was created Baron Douglas of Douglas in 1790. The property which he inherited descended through his eldest daughter to the Earls of Home.

MacLeod, Mary, or Màiri nighean Alasdair Ruaidh (*c.* 1615–1705), poetess, was born in Rodel, Harris. According to tradition she was closely related to the chiefs of the MacLeods of Dunvegan and Harris, and she spent the greater part of her adult life in their household as nurse to no less than five of them. Late in her life she was, for some reason, banished from Dunvegan for a time, probably by Roderick, who succeeded to the chieftainship in 1693 and died in 1699, but she was restored to her position, probably by Roderick's successor, Norman. She was buried in the south transept of St. Clement's church in Rodel.

Mary MacLeod is easily the best known poetess to compose in Gaelic. Twelve of her sixteen surviving poems are eulogies or laments, mainly for MacLeod chiefs and members of their family. In this and in the imagery she employs she was very much a product of the classical school of Gaelic poetry still productive in her time, although in a state of decay. But her style is simple and direct, often lyrical in quality, her language is that of the people, while she introduces an element of personal feeling and emotion which is usually lacking in the compositions of the classical poets. Most important of all, perhaps, she composed in the popular stressed metres, and although neither she nor her contemporary John MacDonald can be described as innovators here, they could be said to have made composition in these metres respectable, thereby opening the door for the remarkable flowering of popular versification in the eighteenth century.

MacDonald, John, or Iain Lom (*c.* 1624–1710), was a poet of whose work almost 3,000 lines are extant, yet we know little of the details of his life. He was closely related to the chiefs of the MacDonalds of Keppoch, and there is a strong tradition that he received his education at the Catholic Seminary at Valladolid in Spain. He was buried in the cemetery of Cill Choiril in Brae Lochaber.

173

His poetry provides us with a remarkable record of an important period in the history of the Highlands in particular and of Scotland in general, seen through the eyes of a Highlander who played a full part in the stirring events of the time, who was a staunch Roman Catholic and wholly committed to the house of Stewart. He was chief Gaelic propagandist for the Royalist party, and it is on record that at the Restoration he was appointed the King's poet laureate in Scotland with an annual pension. His poetry reveals his personal involvement with many of the leading Royalists of the period, including Alexander MacDonald (Alasdair mac Cholla Chiotaich), Montrose, Huntly, and Dundee, for all of whom he composed eulogies or elegies or both. His concern with events affecting the nation as a whole is demonstrated in compositions on the Restoration of Charles II, on the accession of William and Mary, on the union between Scotland and England in 1707, this last a bitter denunciation in which he lays the blame squarely on the shoulders of the Scottish nobility and their greed for gold.

He took a personal interest in the affairs of his clan and was principally responsible for bringing to justice the people involved in the murder in 1663 of the young chief of the MacDonalds of Keppoch and his brother. As a MacDonald he lashes the Campbells at every opportunity, nowhere more effectively than in his graphic eyewitness account of the battle of Inverlochy in 1645. This poem demonstrates well his fine economy of language and terseness of style which is in sharp contrast to the eighteenth-century group of poets headed by such as Alexander MacDonald and Duncan MacIntyre. This and much of his imagery derive directly from the classical school of poetry, the most important contemporary exponents of which were members of the renowned MacMhuirich family. But by eschewing the syllabic metres and esoteric language of the classical bards and by composing in the vernacular and in the popular stressed metres, Iain Lom, along with his contemporary Mary MacLoed, is generally credited with imbuing the composition of Gaelic poetry with a fresh vigour and sense of purpose.

MacDonald, Alexander, or Alasdair mac Mhaighstir Alasdair (*c.* 1700–1770), poet, was probably born in Moidart and was the son of Alexander MacDonald, Episcopalian minister of Ardnamurchan. Following in his father's footsteps, he went to Glasgow University, but he married early and was forced to abandon his classical studies before graduation. By 1729 he was employed in the parish of Ardnamurchan as a teacher by the Society for Propagating Christian

Knowledge. They invited him to compile a Gaelic vocabulary which was published in 1741, the first in the language. He left their employment in May 1745, and, having turned Roman Catholic, was present at the raising of Prince Charles Edward's standard. He was commissioned a captain in the Clanranald regiment and, according to tradition, was entrusted with the duty of teaching the Prince Gaelic.

In 1751 MacDonald published a volume of his own poetry, which is the first book of Scottish Gaelic secular poetry. From the preface it is clear that he intended following this with a volume of poetry by early Gaelic poets and he was almost certainly responsible for much of the material in the valuable collection issued by his son Ronald in 1776. Although copies of his book were ordered by the government to be burnt by the common hangman in Edinburgh in 1752 on the grounds of treasonable content, he himself escaped censure and continued to live in the mainland territory of Clanranald, apparently supported by his chief. He died at Sannaig in Arisaig and was buried in the cemetery of Kilmory.

In propagandist terms, Alexander MacDonald did for the Royalist and Stewart cause in the eighteenth century what John MacDonald had done in the previous century. Although it is reckoned that we possess only about one tenth of his total poetic output, much of that was composed for the express purpose of rallying support for Jacobitism. But he was more than a Jacobite propagandist, he was a Gaelic nationalist; even his book of poetry is entitled *Aisheiridh na Sean Chánoin Albannaich*, 'Resurrection of the Ancient Scottish Tongue', and, as a protagonist of the Gaelic way of life, he urged the Scots of the Lowlands to enter its fold. But, Jacobite or Gaelic nationalist, he is read today for his love poems and, above all, for his poetic representations of nature. His masterpiece and, excluding Ossianic material and translations, perhaps the longest poem in the language, *Birlinn Chlann Raghnaill*, 'The Galley of Clanranald', describes a voyage from South Uist to Carrickfergus. But equally impressive in terms of descriptive detail and technique are his song to the burn *Allt an t-Siucair* and his poems on the seasons. Successfully widening the range of Gaelic poetry, his compositions deeply influenced Duncan MacIntyre. Claims have been made for both as the greatest Gaelic poet of all time. Perhaps Alexander MacDonald deserves the final accolade, if only for the passionate involvement with life which pervades all his poetry.

Ramsay, Allan, poet (1686–1758), was born in Leadhills, the son of the manager of the lead-mines. He learned the trade of wig-maker in

Edinburgh from 1700 onwards and practised it for some years. From 1712 he was contributing verses to the meetings of the 'Easy Club', a Jacobite association, and some of his work was published by the club, of which he became poet laureate in 1715. In that year the Jacobite rising caused the club to lapse. Some minor poetasters had recently begun to revive the Scottish vernacular in verse, and Ramsay was inspired to look into the work of earlier poets. He published an edition of the fifteenth-century *Christ's Kirk on the Green* (1716), with an additional canto by himself in contemporary, and not archaic, Scots, and it was several times reissued. He had by this time taken to bookselling and publishing, and he sold his own verses, in sheets as they were written. In 1720 he obtained subscribers for a collection of his poetry and made 400 guineas by it. It contained the first part of *The Gentle Shepherd*. This success encouraged him to produce a volume of *Fables and Tables* (1722), *The Fair Assembly* (1723) and *Health* (1724). In 1719 he had produced a volume of *Scottish Songs*, from 1724 onwards came four successive volumes of *The Tea Table Miscellany*, a collection of Scottish and English songs, and *The Evergreen* (1724–7) was a collection of older Scottish poetry. The first part of *The Gentle Shepherd* was followed by others, and it finally took shape as a dramatic pastoral in five acts (1725). Ramsay's works were published in London in 1731 and in Dublin in 1733, and several editions of his *Poems* appeared at Edinburgh in rapid succession. He showed his initiative by starting a circulating library and building a playhouse (1736), but the latter was condemned as illegal and probably never functioned. Ramsay attained considerable wealth and was in good standing with men of distinction and birth. He built a house on a magnificent site on the north side of Castle Hill, still commemorated in the name Ramsay Garden.

Burns Martin, *Allan Ramsay*, 1931.

Fergusson, Robert (1750–1774), poet, born in Edinburgh and educated at the High School there, matriculated at St. Andrews in 1765 with the intention of studying for the Church, but after four years gave up the idea; his impulsive and high-spirited pranks, as well as his satirical verse, had indeed made it plain that he was not suited for the eighteenth-century ministry. He found employment as a clerk in the Commissary Office in Edinburgh and remained in it for the rest of his life except when he spent a few months in similar work in the Sheriff Clerk's Office. Meantime he was writing incessantly and drinking heavily to relieve the drudgery of his duties. 'Leith

Races', 'The Rising and Sitting of the Session', 'Caller Oysters' and the like show powers of lively and humorous description of the Edinburgh scene. Some of his verses appeared in Ruddiman's *Weekly Magazine*, and were collected in a volume of *Poems* (1773). One of Fergusson's most important works was 'The Farmer's Ingle', which is often regarded as the prototype of Burns's 'Cottar's Saturday Night'. It gives a realistic impression, useful to the historian, of the old agricultural system, but Fergusson omitted certain aspects of rural life, not least the religious observance, which Burns introduced to his work. Fergusson had never had good health, and latterly, when his mind was affected, he was sent to an asylum, where he committed suicide at the age of twenty-four. His place in the revival of Scottish vernacular verse is an important one, and Burns himself recognized it by raising a monument to his memory over his grave in the Canongate Churchyard, Edinburgh.

A. B. Grosart, *Robert Fergusson*, 1898.

Burns, Robert (1759–1796), poet, was born at Alloway in Ayrshire, the eldest son of William Burness or Burns, a small farmer who was himself the son of a Kincardineshire farmer. Robert was educated partly by a teacher hired by the farmers of the neighbourhood, partly by his father, under whose guidance he became familiar with the works of the English and Scottish poets of the previous generation. His patriotism, like that of many Scots, was stirred by Blind Harry's *Wallace,* and his ambition to develop Scottish poetry was stimulated by reading the works of Allan Ramsay and Robert Fergusson. He learned surveying in 1777 and for a time worked without success at flax-dressing in Irvine. On his father's death in 1784 he and his brother took the farm of Mossgiel, near Mauchline, in Ayrshire.

Burns had long been given to versifying, and his talent had become known to quite a number of his fellow-countrymen through his membership of the Freemasons and of the Tarbolton Club. The first collection of his verses—*Poems chiefly in the Scottish Dialect* —published at Kilmarnock by John Wilson in 1786, included such well-known items as 'The Twa Dogs', 'The Holy Fair', 'Address to the Deil', 'The Cottar's Saturday Night', 'To a Mouse' and 'To a Mountain-Daisy'. The poet's object in issuing the volume had been to raise enough money to enable him to emigrate to Jamaica, at a time when his farming activities were proving unrewarding and many Scots were going overseas, but the attention which his published verses received made him change his plans and altered the whole course of his life. On a visit to Edinburgh in 1786–7 he was much sought after and courted by people of rank and fashion. A second edition of his poems was published by William Creech at Edinburgh in 1787.

Burns had already shown an intemperance in his conduct which was at variance with the strict standards upheld by the kirk sessions, and in the capital, where he was spoiled by success, he fell into habits of conviviality and debauchery. He toured the Borders and Argyll in 1787, revisited Edinburgh and then travelled in the central Highlands. A well-wisher let him have the farm of Ellisland, in Dumfriesshire, and he was also appointed to a position in the Excise (1789). In an attempt to settle down, he married Jean Armour (August 1788) and with her help he made an effort to combine farming with his Excise duties. However, he lacked the stability and habits of application which would have made a success of the farm, which was instead neglected, and, resigning his lease in 1791, he went to live in Dumfries.

Franklyn Bliss Snyder, *The Life of Robert Burns*, 1932.
De Lancey Ferguson, *Pride and Passion: Robert Burns*, 1939.
Maurice Lindsay, *Robert Burns*, 1954.

Tannahill, Robert, poet (1774–1810), the fourth child of a silk-weaver, was born in Paisley and was already composing rhymes when he was at school there. He was apprenticed to the trade of cotton weaving when that branch of industry was in a particularly flourishing and prosperous condition, and he found ample time to pursue other interests, including the playing of the flute and the composing of words to fit tunes which attracted him. His earliest published verses appeared in periodicals. When his apprenticeship was over he moved to Lochwinnoch and in 1800 to Bolton, in Lancashire, where he spent two years. Personally of a retiring disposition, he was fortunate to find influential friends who showed more enterprise and gave him encouragement. The first edition of his *Poems and Songs*, published in 1807, proved very popular. Popularity was somewhat embarrassing to Tannahill, and the consequent conviviality which was forced on him undermined a constitution which had never been strong. He tended to melancholy, especially when he failed to find a publisher for a revised edition of his works, and in a fit of despair he insisted on burning all his manuscripts and finally committed suicide by drowning. Among his best known verses are 'Gloomy winter's noo awa', 'Jessie the Flower o' Dunblane' and 'The Wood of Craigielea'.

MacIntyre, Duncan, or Donnachadh Bàn nan Òran (1724–1812), poet, born in Glenorchy, was gamekeeper first to the Earl of Breadalbane and then to the Duke of Argyll. He fought at the battle of Falkirk in 1746 in the Campbell regiment. Sometime thereafter he married Mary MacIntyre (Mairi Bhàn Òg), and by 1767 they had settled in Edinburgh, where Duncan was enrolled in the City Guard. In 1768 he published the first edition of his poetry, dictated entirely from memory as he could neither read nor write—a remarkable feat, for the latest edition runs to some 6,000 lines. From 1793 to 1798 he served with the Breadalbane Fencibles. Accompanied by his wife, he made numerous journeys throughout the Highlands canvassing subscribers for the second and third editions of his poetry, published in 1790 and 1804 respectively. He died in Edinburgh and was buried in Old Greyfriars churchyard.

No poet composing in Gaelic has been more widely acclaimed than Duncan MacIntyre, and this is not surprising, for his ability to make music with words is unsurpassed, no matter if sometimes the words make little sense. We need not look for a philosophy of life or even depth of feeling in MacIntyre's poetry, nor was he in any sense an innovator. His subject matter was conventional, poems of praise, mainly to Campbells, drinking songs, a finely wrought love song to Mairi Bhàn Òg. But he is chiefly remembered for his nature poetry. Here he is, in the words of his latest editor, 'splendidly sure'. His eye for detail and his comprehensive vision of nature at large can both be seen to greatest advantage in his two best known poems, *Coire a'Cheath-aich* and *Beinn Dóbhrain*, descriptive of places familiar to him as a gamekeeper. If the deer of Scotland need a poet laureate, they have surely found him in Duncan MacIntyre.

Macpherson, James (1738–1796), author, born at Ruthven, Inverness-shire, was educated at Inverness Grammar School and the Universities of Aberdeen and Edinburgh. He was apparently intended for the ministry but soon returned to Ruthven as a schoolmaster. However, in 1758, when he was twenty, he published a poem, *The Highlander*, in six cantos, and began travelling through the Highlands to collect oral poetry and Gaelic MSS., including the *Book of the Dean of Lismore*. In 1760 he published *Fragments of Ancient Poetry, collected in the Highlands of Scotland and translated from the Gaelic or Erse language*, which was so enthusiastically received that the leading literary men of the day—Blair, Robertson, Carlyle and Hume—lent their patronage to the raising of funds to enable

Macpherson to enlarge his collections. In 1762 he produced *Fingal, an ancient epic poem, in six books, with several other poems, composed by Ossian, translated from the Gaelic*. This brought the author wide fame, and it was translated into several languages, though even at this stage there were some signs of scepticism about the authenticity of the ancient verse. In 1763 the author—who must at least be given credit for his industry—produced *Temora, in eight books, with other poems by Ossian*. There was now less enthusiasm and a growing suspicion that Macpherson had not really discovered such a mass of hitherto unsuspected Gaelic verse.

In the ensuing controversy, almost every critic of any significance took part, and opinion among contemporaries was divided. Macpherson's consistent failure to produce the alleged Gaelic originals led ultimately to a general consensus of opinion that he was a fraud. After his death, alleged originals were produced, but they turned out to be translations from his English. Yet Macpherson was not a mere forger. He did use original Ossianic ballads—nine of them in *Fingal*—although none of them can be dated earlier than the eleventh century, and he wove them into works which were substantially his own. When he was translating he was sometimes inaccurate, and it is a serious criticism that he misrepresented the mood of the ancient poetry as one of gloom. His work, though not thought very meritorious now, was enthusiastically received at the time.

After 1763 Macpherson turned his attention to other things. For a time (1764–6) he held an appointment in the colonies and did some travelling, and in 1766 produced *An Introduction to the History of Great Britain and Ireland*, which was severely criticized. In 1773 came a translation of the *Iliad*, which was received with contempt. Almost simultaneously, Macpherson's prestige was further reduced by the critical attitude of Dr. Johnson, who, after his visit to the West Highlands, attacked the authenticity of 'Ossian'. Macpherson issued in 1775 *Original Papers containing the Secret History of Great Britain from the Restoration to the Accession of the House of Hanover*, and was then employed by the government to state its case against the American Colonies, which he did in *The Rights of Great Britain asserted against the Claims of the Colonies (1776)*. Next he was employed by the Nabob of Arcot to write on his behalf. From 1780 he was M.P. for Camelford.

Derick S. Thomson, *The Gaelic Sources of Macpherson's 'Ossian'*, 1952.

Stewart, David, of Garth (1772–1829), soldier and author, the second son of Robert Stewart of Garth, was born at Garth Castle. He succeeded to the estate in 1823, after the deaths of his father and his elder brother. At the age of eleven he became an ensign in the Atholl Highlanders, but it was in 1787, when he joined the 42nd Regiment (the Black Watch) that he began his serious military career, under the Duke of York in Flanders and under Sir Ralph Abercromby (1734–1801) in the West Indies. He was then for a time at Gibraltar and Minorca, and was taken prisoner by the Spaniards but was liberated on an exchange. In 1801, now a captain, he served under Abercromby on the expedition which led to the battle of Aboukir. Promoted to the rank of major, he went with Sir John Moore (1761–1809) to Spain in 1805, but he was soon ordered to Sicily and southern Italy, where he was so severely wounded at Maida that he was never again fit for active service. He retired on half-pay, but was promoted colonel in 1814. In 1825 he was made a Major-General and appointed Governor of St. Lucia, where he died. Stewart had shown from an early stage in his career that he had an unusual understanding of the Highlanders under his command and peculiar powers of appealing to their loyalty and courage. This gift may initially have been instinctive, but he later made a serious study of the subject and in 1822 published his *Sketches of the Character, Manners and Present State of the Highlanders of Scotland, with details of the military service of the Highland Regiments.* Designed as propaganda against emigration, this was the forerunner, and to some extent the foundation, of the many later books on 'The Clans'.

Boston, Thomas (1677–1732), divine, born in Duns, was the son of a nonconformist minister who was imprisoned and took his young son with him to prison for company. However, Boston senior soon decided to conform, and his son attended the parish church for a time. In 1687, with the grant of toleration to Presbyterians by James VII, Thomas began to attend Presbyterian meeting-houses, heard the preaching of a noted Covenanter, Henry Erskine (1624–96), and underwent a conversion. It is notable that Henry Erskine was the father of Ralph and Ebenezer Erskine, who were subsequently to found the Secession Church. Boston received some education at the grammar school of Duns and then—after some delay owing to his father's poverty—went on to Edinburgh University, where he took the Arts curriculum from 1691 to 1694, at a total cost, in fees and maintenance, of no more than £11 sterling. He spent one year in divinity and then engaged in private tuition. He was licensed by the presbytery of Duns in 1697 and in 1699 inducted to the parish of Simprim, from which he moved to Ettrick in 1707 and to Closeburn in 1717.

The earlier influences on Boston had been partly of a moderate Presbyterianism, but partly of an extreme Covenanting tradition, and his views on theology and on ecclesiastical politics were further shaped by his encounters with 'Macmillanites' (the followers of John Macmillan [1670–1753]) and 'Hebronites' (the followers of John Hepburn [c. 1649–1723]), both of whom represented the extreme or Cameronian wing of the Presbyterians. From an early stage, Boston, like the Cameronians, had been critical of the control over the Church which continued to rest with Parliament after 1690, and he declined to take the Abjuration Oath which Parliament demanded of ministers. His conservative views in theology were stimulated when, in the house of a parishioner at Simprim, he found a copy of *The Marrow of Modern Divinity*, an English work dating from 1646 which reiterated traditional Calvinist doctrines of 'election' and emphasised the importance of faith as against works. This book was re-published in 1718 by James Hogg (c. 1658–1734), minister of Carnock, and in 1726 by Boston himself, and it became the centre of doctrinal disputes in the Church between conservatives, or 'evangelicals', and those who were more liberally minded. In 1720 Boston published his *Fourfold State of Man*, which long remained a popular classic of Calvinist theology. He opposed the attitude of the Assembly to men like John Simson (?1668–1740), Professor of Divinity at Glasgow, who taught opinions which seemed heretical to Boston but were only mildly rebuked by the Assembly. Boston, on the other hand, with other 'Marrowmen', was likewise rebuked by the Assembly in 1722. His attitude to church affairs generally meant that he was a member of the party which opposed the rights of lay patrons, which had been restored in 1712. All in all, there is no doubt that Boston's influence made him in a real sense one of the founders of the First Secession Church, which reflected all his principles, though he died before it actually came into being (1733).

W. Addison, *Thomas Boston of Ettrick*, 1936.

Erskine, Ebenezer (1680–1754), divine, was born at Dryburgh, the son of a minister who had served in England until he had to leave that country on the restoration of episcopacy and the Prayer Book in 1662 and who became minister of Chirnside at the Revolution. Educated at the University of Edinburgh, Ebenezer became minister of Portmoak (1703–31) and then of Stirling, and drew great congregations from far and wide by his powerful preaching. During his ministry there were many divisive elements in the Church of Scotland. There was a tendency to a more liberal theology, which some thought heretical, and controversy centred largely on *The Marrow of Modern Divinity*, a book which conservatives defended as putting a due emphasis on faith rather than works and which the more liberal denounced as tending to Antinomianism or the repudiation of the moral law. Erskine was a 'Marrowman', and signed the protest against the condemnation of the *Marrow* by the General Assembly. Another cause of dispute was the Abjuration Oath, renouncing the Pretender, which some ministers, although they were far from being Jacobites, thought the government had no right to impose on them, and which Erskine declined to take. Yet another topic of controversy was the place which the popular rights of congregations should have in the choice of ministers, and in 1731 Erskine came down in favour of popular rights. Erskine's own synod censured him for a sermon on this subject, and his supporters appealed to the Assembly, which upheld the synod's action and suspended Erskine and three of his associates—James Fisher of Kinclaven, William Wilson of Perth and Alexander Moncrieff of Abernethy. In the same year, at Gairney Bridge near Kinross, Erskine and those three ministers renounced 'the prevailing party in the Church' and appealed to 'the first free, faithful and reforming General Assembly'. This act, though veiled, amounted to secession, and from it the origin of the Secession Church is dated. Four more ministers soon joined Erskine's party; in 1740 the eight were formally deposed by the General Assembly and the existence of the Secession thereby recognized. The Seceders renewed the Covenants in 1743.

Shortly afterwards the Secession split between Burghers (who felt that they could accept an oath whereby burgessses acknowledged the ecclesiastical establishment) and Anti-Burghers (who did not); and Erskine took the Burgher side. The Anti-Burgher party was led by Adam Gib (1713–88), called 'Pope Gib', who had been ordained a minister of the Secession in 1741 and served a congregation on the south side of Edinburgh.

Ebenezer's brother, Ralph (1685–1752), became minister of Dunfermline in 1711. He was more devoted than his brother to spiritual matters and less of an ecclesiastical politician, and did not join the

Secession until 1737. Like Ebenezer, he took the Burgher side. He wrote *Faith no Fancy*, *Gospel Sonnets* and *Scripture Songs*.

A. R. Macewen, *The Erskines*, 1900.

Glas, John (1695–1773), founder of the Glassite sect, son of the minister of Auchtermuchty, Fife, was educated at the grammar school of Perth and the Universities of St. Andrews and Edinburgh. He became minister of Tealing, in Angus, in 1719. By forming in the parish a kind of inner congregation or society of the more serious-minded among his flock he showed that he was already out of sympathy with the principles of the established Church. He also began to preach critically against the Covenants as inimical to the rights of the individual's conscience. When he repudiated parts of the Confession of Faith he was deposed by the synod (1728), and, after he had expounded his ideas more fully in his *Testimony of the King of Martyrs*, deposition by the General Assembly followed. First in Dundee, and then (from 1733) in Perth, he drew together a congregation with somewhat radical practices: it had no professional ministry, it repudiated the whole principle of establishment and it adopted certain forms of service imitative of the most primitive, apostolic times. In Perth Glas was joined by Robert Sandeman (1717–71), who later married Glas's daughter, and subsequently developed the sect in America, where it was sometimes known as the 'Sandemanians'.

Anon., *An Account of the Life and Character of Mr. John Glas*, 1813.
Daniel Macintosh (ed.), *Letters and Correspondence between Robert Sandeman, John Glas and their contemporaries*, 1851.

Gillespie, Thomas (1708–74), founder of the Relief Church, a native of Duddingston, was brought up by his mother to frequent the sermons of the more evangelical ministers. She joined the Original Secession when it was founded in 1733, but her son declined to study for its ministry, and instead, after attending classes at Edinburgh University, went to an English dissenting academy, where the theological atmosphere was more liberal. He was licensed as a preacher in England in 1741, but very soon returned to Scotland and was called to the parish of Carnock, near Dunfermline (1742). Already at this stage he protested against the clauses in the Westminster Confession relating to the duty of the civil magistrate to maintain the Church and enforce its decisions. Disputes over the rights of lay patrons were now causing considerable friction, and Gillespie was one of the ministers of the presbytery of Dunfermline who refused to take part in the induction of a minister who had been presented to Inverkeithing against the wishes of the congregation. The Assembly deposed the recalcitrant ministers (1752), and Gillespie formed an independent congregation in Dunfermline. For some years he was an isolated figure, but in 1761 he was joined by the congregation of Colinsburgh, which had in effect withdrawn from the establishment and built a church for its own chosen minister, and also by Thomas Boston, younger, minister of Oxnam, who had been irregularly accepted as their minister by a congregation in Jedburgh. The three ministers formed in 1761 a presbytery 'for the relief of Christians oppressed in their privileges'. This new body, which rapidly gained strength, was not, like the first Secession, reactionary in its theology or its politics, it did not make any claim to be the only true Church in Scotland, and it stood for what came to be known as the 'voluntary principle', that is, the denial that the Church should look to the State for support.

William Lindsay, *Life of Thomas Gillespie*, 1849.

Wodrow, Robert (1679–1734), historian, son of the Professor of Divinity at Glasgow University, went there as a student and from 1697 to 1701 was University Librarian. In 1703 he was ordained minister of Eastwood, and remained there for many years, declining calls to Glasgow and Stirling. He devoted himself to collecting material relating to the history of the Covenanting and Presbyterian opposition in the Church of Scotland between the Restoration and the Revolution. This task required immense labours in the national archives, which were then deposited in unsatisfactory conditions in the Laich Parliament House, adjacent to the Advocates' Library. He published the results of his work in his *History of the Sufferings of the Church of Scotland* (2 vols., 1721–2). The *History* is marked by tendentiousness, sometimes less than honest, but as it contains such a mass of transcripts of original material it has remained the principal quarry from which most later historians have derived their information about the period. The work had a fulsome dedication to George I, addressed to 'the best, as well as greatest, of Kings', and the author was rewarded by a present of 100 guineas from the government. Wodrow's activities as a collector extended to other periods of Scottish Church history besides that covered in his *History*. He left a large number of 'Lives' of Scottish divines of the sixteenth and seventeenth centuries, some of which were published by historical clubs in the nineteenth century. His *Analecta*, relating to the early eighteenth century, was printed in four volumes by the Maitland Club in 1842–3 and his *Correspondence* partly by the Wodrow Society (3 volumes, 1843) and partly by the Scottish History Society (1937). A considerable mass of his MSS. remain unpublished in the National Library of Scotland.

Anderson, James (1662–1728), record scholar, son of a minister who was ejected as a Covenanter in 1662 and who was subsequently imprisoned for preaching illegally, graduated M.A. at Edinburgh in 1680 and became a Writer to the Signet in 1691. He was diverted from normal professional practice by the antiquarian side of legal studies, and as a result was peculiarly well equipped to take part in the historical arguments which arose at the time of the negotiations preceding the Union of 1707. In reply to an English pamphleteer who resurrected the claims of England to superiority over the Scottish crown, Anderson published in 1705 *An Essay showing that the Crown of Scotland is Imperial and Independent*. For this he was officially thanked by Parliament, and the English pamphlet was ordered to be burned by the common hangman. Anderson's studies, both in the preparation of his essay and earlier, had led him much to charters and original records, and he has a high place in the long line of Scottish charter scholars. In November 1706 Parliament granted him £300 for engraving and publishing a series of facsimiles of charters, seals, medals and coins, almost by way of a memorial to the now expiring independent Scottish kingdom. In March 1707, when he had expended in addition £600 of his own, the estates voted him a further £1,050, and one of the last actions of the Scottish Parliament was to commend him to Queen Anne as worthy of a suitable office. He moved to London to proceed with the production of his great work, but it is not clear whether the British government honoured the promise of the Scottish government to pay him the £1,050—though from 1715 to 1717 he held the office of Postmaster General for Scotland. Without resources to complete his major task, he turned his attention to the production of *Collections relating to the History of Mary, Queen of Scots* (1727)—a work still of value for source material. After his death the plates for his collection of charters were sold by auction, and the work was finally published, under the editorship of Thomas Ruddiman, in 1739, as *Selectus Diplomatum et Numismatum Scotiae Thesaurus*. Familiarly known as 'Anderson's *Diplomata*', this handsome and impressive volume contains not only facsimiles and transcripts of a great range of charters, but also facsimiles of medieval forms of letters and abbreviations, making it in effect an early manual of palaeography.

Innes, Thomas (1662–1744), historian, a native of Aboyne in Aberdeenshire, became a student in the Scots College in Paris, where his brother Lewis (1651–1738) was Principal and where Thomas ultimately (1727) became Vice-Principal. Most of his life was spent in Paris, but for three years (1698–1701) he officiated as a priest in Banffshire and later he spent two or three years (*c.* 1722–5) doing research in Scotland. His interest in Scottish history was possibly stimulated by the fact that in Paris he had the custody of the archives of the archbishopric of Glasgow which had been taken away at the Reformation by Archbishop James Beaton, but Innes's interests moved into the dark ages, where there was little historical material available and where his work was inevitably in the main destructive of the fables which had been repeated by generations of Scottish historians. In 1724, when he was in Edinburgh, working industriously in the Advocates' Library, he was described by Robert Wodrow as 'a monkish, bookish person', and, while the stalwart Presbyterian Wodrow could not go so far as to admire a Roman priest, he had to admit that Innes seemed to have no political motives. As a result of his labours, Innes produced in 1729 his *Critical Essay on the Ancient Inhabitants of Scotland,* which coolly eliminated the forty imaginary kings, beginning with Fergus I in 330 B.C., who had been inserted before the historical Fergus, son of Erc, of A.D. *c.* 500. This book, which marked a new approach to dark age studies, contains an appendix of original documents. Innes also wrote a *Civil and Ecclesiastical History of Scotland,* which was edited by George Grub for the Spalding Club in 1853. A large number of his collections and letters are in Edinburgh University Library.

Keith, Robert (1681–1756), historian, born near Dunnottar, the son of a laird who was descended from the 3rd Earl Marischal, was educated at Marischal College and became tutor to Lord Keith, later 10th Earl Marischal, and his brother James. He was ordained deacon in 1710 and presbyter in 1713 by Bishop Haliburton of Aberdeen. As chaplain to the Earl of Errol he visited the continent in 1712, and in 1713 he settled as the pastor of an Episcopalian congregation in Edinburgh to which he continued to minister for the remainder of his life. The Edinburgh Episcopalians tended on the whole to suffer less molestation than those in some more remote parts of the country, and Keith's own qualities and his production ultimately of work which earned him widespread respect seem to have protected him from prosecution under the savage laws passed against Episcopalians after the 'Fifteen and the 'Forty-Five. In 1727 he was consecrated Bishop, as coadjutor to Arthur Millar, Bishop of Edinburgh. He was one of those bishops who supported the concept of a diocesan system, as opposed to government of the Church by a College of Bishops, and it was partly his doing that the two parties reached agreement by a concordat in 1732. Keith for a time had the oversight of the scattered Episcopalians in the old dioceses of Caithness, Orkney and the Isles, but in 1733 his sphere of supervision was changed to Fife. He became Primus in 1743.

It was in 1734 that Keith produced the first (and only) folio volume of his *History of the Affairs of Church and State in Scotland*, which was published by subscription: the wide esteem in which Keith was held is shown by three hundred and fifty individual subscribers (including, incidentally, 'Robert MacGregor *alias* Rob Roy', who is not usually thought of as a patron of literature, but who, as he died in the same year, may never have seen the book). The book itself was the result of painstaking work on record sources, the more creditable when the difficulties of consulting the records at that time are taken into account, and Keith printed the text of many documents and extracts from records, so that his book is still a standard work for historians of the reign of Queen Mary. It was reprinted by the Spottiswoode Society in 1844. In 1755 Keith produced his *Catalogue of Scottish Bishops*, which was also highly creditable in the circumstances of the time, though it has been superseded by later research.

'Biographical Sketch' prefixed to the Spottiswoode Soc. edition of the *History*.

Ruddiman, Thomas (1674–1757), author and publisher, the son of a small tenant farmer in Banffshire, was educated at the parish school of Inverboyndie and at the age of sixteen, after walking to Aberdeen without his father's knowledge and being robbed by gipsies on the way, won a bursary which enabled him to matriculate at King's College in 1690. He graduated in 1694, acted for a time as a tutor and in 1695 became schoolmaster of Laurencekirk. One evening in 1699 he was called to the local inn to provide company for Dr. Archibald Pitcairn, an Edinburgh physician, who had been storm-stayed, and Pitcairn was so impressed that he invited Ruddiman to Edinburgh. He seems at first to have been employed in a very subordinate capacity in the Advocates' Library and in 1706 found employment with the printer and bookseller Robert Freebairn. In 1709 he edited a volume of poems by Arthur Johnston and next year was largely responsible for Freebairn's edition of Gavin Douglas's translation of Virgil's *Aeneid*. To this he added a glossary of old Scots words which, though it has many imperfections, was the first thing of its kind, and the work contributed to the revival of Scots vernacular verse. Ruddiman collaborated with another printer in an edition of the *Works* of Drummond of Hawthornden (1711), and it appears that in 1712 he was in business as a printer on his own account. Subsequently he took his brother, Walter, into partnership in a printing and publishing business which was responsible for Allan Ramsay's *Works* as well as most of the important books on history, antiquities, law and theology which appeared in Scotland at the time. He bought the best-known Scots newspaper, the *Caledonian Mercury*, in 1729.

Ruddiman first attained fame with his *Rudiments of the Latin Tongue* (1714), which went through fifteen editions in his lifetime, and his edition, in collaboration with Freebairn, of George Buchanan's *Opera* (1715). He followed his *Rudiments* with books which treated more fully of the Latin tongue, and in 1722 he edited the two volumes of *Epistolae Regum Scotorum*, giving the texts of letters of James IV, James V and Mary.

In 1728 he was appointed joint-printer to the University of Edinburgh and in 1730 Keeper of the Advocates' Library. He was responsible for the completion and publication of James Anderson's *Diplomata* (1739), and the first volume of his catalogue of the Library of which he was Keeper appeared in 1742. Ruddiman was a convinced Jacobite and Episcopalian and was involved for some years not only in literary controversy, especially about the merits of Buchanan's translation of the Psalms, but also in historical or political controversies concerning the succession to the crown of Scotland. His last major work was a text of Livy in 1751, and failing eyesight made him resign his Keepership in 1752, when he was succeeded by David Hume.

Douglas Duncan, *Thomas Ruddiman*, 1965.

Goodall, Walter (*c.* 1706–1766), historian, son of a Banffshire farmer, went to King's College, Aberdeen, in 1723, but left without taking a degree. In 1730, he became an assistant to Thomas Ruddiman, Librarian of the Advocates' Library, and remained an assistant under David Hume. He died in debt—owing, it is said, to his

189

drunken habits—and his daughter was hardly able to pay for his funeral. Like Ruddiman and Hume, Goodall was a Jacobite, and a sense of *pietas* towards the house of Stewart led to the preparation of his *Examination of the letters said to have been written by Queen Mary to James, Earl of Bothwell* (1754), a two-volume collection of documents, largely from the English archives, which has been indispensable to all later writers on Mary, whether or not they have shared Goodall's view that the Casket Letters were forgeries. Goodall also prepared editions of Scott of Scotstarvet's *Staggering State of Scots Statesmen* (1754) and Sir James Balfour's *Practicks* (1754). He assisted another Jacobite, Robert Keith, with the production of his *Catalogue of Scottish Bishops*. Goodall's most important work was an edition of the *Scotichronicon*, published three years after his death.

Robertson, William (1721–1793), historian, son of the minister of Borthwick, was educated at the grammar school of Dalkeith, which then had a national renown, and he moved to Edinburgh when his father was appointed to Old Greyfriars' in 1733. He spent several years in quiet, retired study, laying the foundations of his scholarship. He was licensed by the presbytery of Dalkeith in 1741 and two years later was presented to the parish of Gladsmuir, East Lothian. An enthusiastic Hanoverian, he joined the volunteers who prepared to defend Edinburgh against the Jacobites in 1745, and then, when it was decided to make no resistance, he offered his services to Sir John Cope, who declined them. He became minister of Lady Yester's Church, Edinburgh, in 1756.

One of Robertson's earliest actions in the General Assembly was to defend his fellow-presbyter, John Home, when he was criticized for producing his drama, *Douglas*, and this shows that he was attached to the 'Moderate' party in the Church which was prepared to make concessions to current trends in thought and behaviour. He was Moderator of the Assembly in 1763 and for many years he was the acknowledged leader of the Moderates, but after 1780 he ceased to take an active part in ecclesiastical politics, though he continued to preach.

In preparing his *History of Scotland during the Reigns of Mary and James VI* (London, 1759), Robertson relied much on the activities of his predecessors, especially Bishop Keith, who had printed records and documents for the period, and he candidly admitted that he had no taste for original research in manuscript sources. Yet the work contained more analysis and interpretation than earlier histories and was so readable that it was received with enthusiasm and the author made £600 out of it. *The History of the Reign of Charles V* (1769) brought him £4,500, supposed to be the largest sum yet paid for the copyright of any book. In 1777 came his *History of America* and in 1791 his *Historical Disquisition concerning the knowledge which the Ancients had of India*. It has been neatly said of Robertson that he 'was not the greatest British historian of his time, but only because he was a contemporary of Edward Gibbon'.

Robertson's *Mary and James VI* brought him advancement— appointment as one of the King's chaplains in Scotland, the office of historiographer royal for Scotland, which then carried a salary of £200 a year, and the principalship of Edinburgh University. His fame inevitably brought distinction to the University and, along with the reputation of other contemporary professors, led to rapid expansion. As Principal from 1762 until his death, Robertson reorganized the Library, raised money for a museum and induced the Town Council to authorize various improvements to the existing buildings and then a completely new building, the present Old College, of which the foundation stone was laid in 1789. The architect, Robert Adam, was the son of Robertson's cousin, William Adam.

Robertson was, inevitably, a leader of the intellectual life of Edinburgh, and founded the Royal Society of Edinburgh (1783). His works brought him international renown as well: he was a member of the Academy of Sciences of Padua and of the Imperial Academy of Sciences at St. Petersburg, and the Empress Catharine of Russia sent him a gold-enamelled snuff-box, set with diamonds.

J. B. Black, *The Art of History*, 1926.

Pinkerton, John (1758–1826), historian, born in Edinburgh, was educated partly at the grammar school of Lanark and then returned to Edinburgh to be apprenticed to a Writer to the Signet, but in 1781 removed to London. His earliest publications were of verse, and in *Select Scottish Ballads* (1783) he passed off compositions of his own as traditional verses. He turned to numismatics with an *Essay on Medals* (2 vols., 1784), and a review of the classical authors, under the title *Letters of Literature* (1785), brought him some renown and the acquaintance of Horace Walpole and Gibbon. In 1786 he published *Ancient Scottish Poems* (2 vols.) in which he admitted his earlier forgeries, and in 1787 *The Treasury of Wit*, a collection of jests and witticisms. But he had already turned his attention to ancient and dark age history and had developed an obsession with 'the Goths' or Teutonic races which carried with it an antipathy to the Celtic peoples. In 1787 he produced *A dissertation on the origin and progress of the Scythians or Goths*. He developed the view that the Picts were 'Gothic' or Teutonic, and in his *History of Scotland preceding the reign of Malcolm III* (1790) he argued that the Picts had conquered the Celtic Scots. Meantime he continued an output of varying quality and nature—*Vitae Antiquae Sanctorum Scotorum* (1789), an edition of Barbour's *Brus* (1789), *The Medallic History of England to the Revolution* (1790), and another collection of Scottish *Poems* (1792). His most important contribution to history came in his *History of Scotland from the accession of the House of Stewart to that of Mary* (1792), in which he used state papers to good effect and which is still valuable for the reign of James V. His miscellaneous works continued: *Modern Geography* (1802), *Recollections of a stay in Paris* (1806), a collection in 19 volumes of *Voyages and Travels* (1807–14) and, in 1811, *Petrology or a Treatise on Rocks*. Pinkerton died in poverty in Paris.

Home, Henry, Lord Kames (1696–1782), the son of George Home of Kames in Berwickshire, was educated privately, apprenticed to a Writer to the Signet in 1712 and admitted an advocate in 1723. He became a Lord of Session in 1752, with the title of Lord Kames, and in 1763 a Lord of Justiciary. Many of his voluminous writings sprang from his professional work and interests: *Remarkable Decisions of the Court of Session from 1716 to 1728* (1728), later continued to 1752 (1765) and to 1768 (1780); *Dictionary of Decisions of the Court of Session* (1741); *Essays upon several subjects in Scots Law* (1732); *Historical Law Tracts* (1757); *The Statute Law of Scotland Abridged* (1759); *Principles of Equity* (1760); *Elucidations respecting the Common Law of Scotland* (1777). Even within the legal field, the antiquarian side of the subject plainly interested him, and it was not a long step to history, in his *Essays upon Several Subjects Concerning British Antiquities* (1747), and *Sketches of the History of Man* (1774). But Home, like many of his contemporaries, was drawn to philosophy as well, and in 1751, in his *Essays on the Principles of Morality and Natural Religion*, he upheld the existence of innate ideas of right and wrong, in opposition to Locke and David Hume. Kames had practical interests also, and it was possibly because he had become in 1755 a member of the Board of Trustees for Manufactures that in 1765 he produced a pamphlet on *Progress of Flax Husbandry in Scotland*. Flax was a crop which linked manufactures with agriculture, and with the latter, too, Kames concerned himself, especially after he succeeded in 1766 to the estate of Blair Drummond on the death of his wife's brother. One of his achievements on his estate was to float a mass of peat-moss into the sea and convert the subsoil to cultivated land. In 1776 he wrote *The Gentleman Farmer*, which went through several editions. In 1762 he published *Elements of Criticism*.

W. C. Lehmann, *Henry Home, Lord Kames*, 1971.
Ian S. Ross, *Lord Kames and the Scotland of his day*, 1972.

Hume, David (1711–1776), philosopher and historian, second son of the laird of Ninewells in Berwickshire, was born at Edinburgh and went to Edinburgh University to study law, which he found uncongenial. From 1734 to 1737 he lived in France, reading, studying and writing, and the fruit was his *Treatise on Human Nature* which he returned to London to publish (anonymously) in 1738–40. The work ranged over the problems of metaphysics and ethics and dealt at length with causality. It was not well received, partly because of its sceptical approach to religion. Hume went on to write *Essays Moral and Political* (1741), which was intended to have a wider appeal and was successful. However, the author was turned down for the chair of moral philosophy at Edinburgh, perhaps owing to dislike of both his scepticism and his Jacobitism, and he continued for the most part to live quietly at Ninewells. In 1747 he was secretary to General St. Clair when he went on an expedition against Port l'Orient, and in the following year he accompanied the General on a mission to Vienna and Turin. Hume had meantime been re-thinking some of his earlier views and he issued his revision in *Philosophical Essays concerning human understanding* (1748) and an *Enquiry concerning the Principals of Morals* (1751). In 1752 he issued *Political Discourses*, which dealt largely with economics. In the same year he was appointed Keeper of the Advocates' Library in Edinburgh and turned his attention for a time mainly to history. The first volume of his *History of England*, dealing with the reigns of James I and Charles I, appeared in 1754, and, after a volume on the period 1649–88, he worked backwards, with two volumes on the Tudor period (1759) and another on the earlier history (1761). Rather oddly for a freethinker, Hume showed High Church and Cavalier bias in his work, a sharp reaction against the Whig view which had predominated since the Revolution. While engaged mainly on his *History,* he produced a *Natural History of Religion*. In 1752 he had been made secretary to the Royal Society of Edinburgh, but, after being censured for purchasing La Fontaine's *Contes* and other

French works, he resigned, and in 1757 he also resigned his appointment at the Advocates' Library. In 1763 he accompanied Lord Hertford to Paris, became secretary of the embassy there and was for a time *chargé d'affaires*. He was highly esteemed in France, where he befriended Rousseau, whom he brought to Britain and for whom he secured a pension. He was Under-Secretary of State for the Home Department from 1767 until 1769, when he returned to Edinburgh, where he spent most of his later days.

John Hill Burton, *Life and Correspondence of David Hume*, 1846.
John Y. T. Greig, *David Hume*, 1931.
Ernest C. Mossner, *David Hume*, 1954.

Smith, Adam (1723–1790), economist, the son of a comptroller of customs, was born at Kirkcaldy (5 June 1723) and attended the grammar school there. In 1737 he went to Glasgow University, where he took a special interest in mathematics, natural philosophy and moral philosophy, and in 1740 proceeded to Balliol College, Oxford, where he remained for seven years. He spent the better part of two years (1747–8) in Kirkaldy, without having found a career, and then went to Edinburgh, where, under the patronage of Lord Kames, he delivered lectures for three years on Rhetoric and Belles Lettres. In Edinburgh he made the acquaintance of David Hume and the other leading literary figures. He was appointed to the Chair of Logic at Glasgow in 1751 and translated four years later to that of Moral Philosophy, which he held until 1764. In 1759 he produced his *Theory of Moral Sentiments*, a work of greater merit from a literary than from a philosophical point of view, but it was based on part of his lectures and he was thus able to devote a larger proportion of them to economics. Glasgow gave him an LL.D. in 1762. Even when holding the chair at Glasgow he managed to spend a good deal of time in Edinburgh, where he was a member of the Poker Club (designed to stimulate public opinion on certain issues) and then of the Select Society, founded in 1754, at which most of the well-known men of the capital met. In 1764–6, with the young Duke of Buccleuch, Smith visited Paris and other parts of France, where he met Quesney, d'Alembert, Turgot and Necker. The influence of French thinkers and an acquaintance with the closely-controlled economy of France were part of the background for Smith's greatest work.

On his return from the continent in 1766, Smith settled at Kirkcaldy, able to live on a pension given to him by Buccleuch and to devote himself for ten years to the preparation of his great work, *An Inquiry into the Nature and Causes of the Wealth of Nations* (1776).

194

This book marked the transition to something like modern economics, for Smith had a clearer grasp than any of his predecessors of what constitutes real wealth, and he took the revolutionary line of advocating free trade as the best means of increasing wealth. He preferred to write of the concrete rather than the abstract, so that his book was easily understood, and it had an immediate influence on William Pitt the Younger, who became Prime Minister in 1784. Controversy over Smith's views went on for two generations, but he became and remained the patron saint of British economic policy until, in the twentieth century, free trade was abandoned and governmental policy reverted to controls and restrictions similar to those which Smith had condemned. For two years after the publication of his book, Smith was in London, enjoying the fame his work had brought him, but in 1778 he was appointed one of the Commissioners of Customs for Scotland and settled at Edinburgh. He was elected Lord Rector of Glasgow University in 1787.

John Rae, *Life of Adam Smith*, 1895.
William R. Scott, *Adam Smith as Student and Professor*, 1937.

Fergusson, Adam (1723–1816), philosopher, son of the minister of Logierait, Perthshire, was educated at Perth and then at the Universities of St. Andrews and Edinburgh. In order to take up a commission as a chaplain to the 42nd Regiment, which he obtained through the patronage of the Duchess of Atholl, he was licensed as a preacher, and went off to Flanders in 1745. He resigned his chaplain's appointment in 1757 and, after a few months as Librarian of the Advocates' Library, was for two years a tutor in the family of the Earl of Bute. In 1759 he became Professor of Natural Philosophy at Edinburgh and in 1764 Professor of Moral Philosophy. His tenure of the latter chair was twice interrupted: from 1773 to 1775 he accompanied Lord Chesterfield on his continental travels, and in 1778, on the nomination of Henry Dundas (afterwards Viscount Melville), he was one of the commissioners sent to America in a fruitless effort to make the colonists reconsider their Declaration of Independence. In 1766 he published his *Essay on Civil Society*, in 1772 his *Institutes of Moral Philosophy* and in 1783 his three-volume *History of the Roman Republic*, all of which went into many editions both in Britain and abroad. He resigned his chair in 1785 and went to live at Manor, near Peebles, where he was able to devote himself largely to farming, in which he had always had an interest. In 1792 he published his lectures, under the title *Principles of Moral and Political Science*. Shortly thereafter he again visited the continent, and was in Berlin and Vienna, but his intention of visiting Rome was frustrated owing to the disturbances caused by the French Revolution. On returning to Scotland, he settled at St. Andrews. As he had considerable means—a government pension of £400 and one of £200 from Lord Chesterfield as well as provision made when he resigned his chair—he was able to purchase a small estate near the city.

W. C. Lehmann, *Adam Fergusson*, 1930.

Carlyle, Alexander (1722–1805), known as 'Jupiter' because of his noble head and impressive person, was the son and grandson of parish ministers and was born in the manse of Cummertrees, Dumfriesshire. His father soon moved to Prestonpans, and it was in East Lothian that most of Alexander's life was spent. He was at the University of Edinburgh from 1735 to 1742, and then studied at Glasgow and Leyden before being presented in 1746 to the parish of Inveresk, where he remained for fifty-seven years. His ministry covered the period of the rule of the Moderates in the Church and the peak of the Scottish 'Enlightenment', and he was in many ways typical of both moderation and enlightenment. He liked to boast of the intellectual achievements of Scottish ministers and their works on history, rhetoric, drama, mathematics and agriculture, but, while he was a friend of many of the men of letters of his day, he did not seek personal distinction, and his own tastes led him to lighter accomplishments and pastimes which had not hitherto been thought fitting for Presbyterian divines—dancing, billiards, golf and the theatre. He was said to be the first minister to play cards 'with unlocked doors', and he did his best to demonstrate that Charles II had been wrong when he pronounced that Presbyterianism was 'no religion for gentlemen'. He paid many visits to London, and both there and in Edinburgh he dined and wined in the best company. On the other hand, he spent much time in his parish, he was a kind friend to his parishioners, even the poorest among them, and his concern for action, rather than 'high speculation', made him something of a forerunner of believers in the 'social gospel'. In church affairs he was an advocate both of patronage and of higher stipends because he naturally thought that by these means men of intellect and social standing would predominate in the ministry. It is to his credit that he was much more tolerant, even of Episcopalians, than had been customary. Although he mixed with all the literary men of his day, he published nothing of his own of any significance, but he wrote an *Autobiography*, which was published in 1860.

Monboddo, James Burnett, Lord (1714–1799), was born on the estate of Monboddo in Kincardineshire. He graduated M.A. at Aberdeen and then proceeded to study law at Edinburgh and at Groningen, where he spent three years. On his return to Edinburgh he became an advocate (1737). He was prominent as a counsel in the Douglas Cause in 1762. In 1767 he became a Lord of Session. Monboddo was one of the 'characters' of the Edinburgh of his day and was noted for his eccentricities. But he was possessed of great learning and eloquence and was an entertaining host or guest. He held 'learned suppers' for men of kindred interests and was a member of the Select Society of Edinburgh *literati*. Monboddo's own writings were massive: in the six volumes *Of the Origin and Progress of Language* (1773–92) he propounded the theory that the orang-outang was a class of the human species and he even believed that human infants were born with tails; his *Ancient Metaphysics* was another six-volume work (1779–99). Samuel Johnson visited him at Monboddo in 1773 and remarked, 'Monboddo is as jealous of his tail as a squirrel'. Monboddo regarded coaches as effeminate, and insisted on riding on horseback, even to London, until he was eighty.

E. L. Lloyd, *James Burnett, Lord Monboddo*, 1972.

Home, John (1722–1808), dramatist, son of the town clerk of Leith, was educated at the grammar school there and at Edinburgh University. He fought on the government side in the 'Forty-Five, was taken prisoner at Falkirk, but escaped. He became minister of Athelstaneford, East Lothian, in 1746. In 1749 he wrote a tragedy, *Agis*, which he took to London and offered to Garrick, who rejected it. He gained notoriety as well as fame when he wrote another play, *Douglas*, in 1755, for this was to become well known at a time when it was generally considered highly improper for a minister of the Church of Scotland even to attend the theatre. Home took *Douglas* to London, where Garrick pronounced it totally unfit for the stage. However, it was produced in Edinburgh in 1756, and won great praise at the time, though later generations have not thought highly of it. The attitude of the presbytery, which suspended ministers who attended the Edinburgh performances, made it necessary for Home to resign his parish, but he went to London and through the patronage of the Duke of Argyll and the Earl of Bute he was able to have his play performed there (1757), with some success. His *Agis* too was performed, and also a later play, *The Siege of Aquileia*. Home was appointed secretary to the Earl of Bute, who was tutor to the Prince of Wales (later George III) and who became Prime Minister (1761–3). He was also given the sinecure of Conservator of the Scottish privileges in Flanders and received a government pension of £300. Home's later plays were less successful, and in 1779 he returned to Edinburgh, where he died. Besides his plays, he wrote a *History of the Rebellion of 1745*, published in 1802. His *Works*, edited by Henry Mackenzie, were published in 3 volumes in 1822.

Alice Edna Gipson, *John Home*, 1917.

Stewart, Dugald (1753–1828), philosopher, son of Matthew Stewart (1717–85), Professor of Mathematics at Edinburgh University, was educated at the Royal High School and the Universities of Edinburgh and Glasgow. At the age of nineteen he began to assist his father in his teaching, and in 1785 was appointed his father's successor. Already, however, in 1778, he had temporarily taken the place of Adam Fergusson in the teaching of moral philosophy, and in 1785 he carried through an exchange with Fergusson, who retired on part of the salary of the Chair of Mathematics while Stewart succeeded to the Chair of Moral Philosophy. He showed extraordinary versatility: not only did he, like Adam Smith, include political economy in his moral philosophy course from about 1800 onwards, but he sometimes acted as a substitute in natural philosophy and occasionally taught Greek and logic. He proved himself an accomplished and masterly speaker and extempore lecturer, and, although much given to clearing his throat, it was remarked that 'there was eloquence in his very spitting'. His *Philosophy of the Human Mind*, vol. i, was published in 1792, followed by a second volume in 1814 and a third in 1827. In 1793 he wrote a *Life of Adam Smith* and in the same year produced, for the use of his students, *Outlines of Moral Philosophy*. In 1810 came his *Philosophical Essays*. His collected works were published in 11 vols., 1856–60. Stewart was of such liberal opinions that the Whigs regarded him as an ornament of their party, and when the French Revolution made radical views suspect, some parents forbade their sons to attend his lectures. But current practices which are now commonly regarded as corrupt opened a way to reward and recognize his genius: in 1806 an office of 'gazette writer for Scotland', a sinecure worth £300 a year, was created for Stewart's enjoyment during his lifetime. This enabled him to retire from the University in 1810 and to settle at Kinneil House, near Bo'ness, lent to him by the Duke of Hamilton.

Foulis, Robert (1707–1776), was educated at Glasgow and at first apprenticed to a barber, but he attended the lectures given at the university by Francis Hutcheson (1694–1746), the Professor of Moral Philosophy, who suggested that he should become a printer. With his brother Andrew (1712–75), he visited Oxford and France, collecting rare books, from 1738 to 1740. Shortly after he had started business as a bookseller and printer in Glasgow he was appointed official printer to the university (1741) and showed his skill by at once producing a Greek book—*Demetrius Phalereus de Elocutione.* He produced editions of Horace, Cicero and Caesar, and his great edition of Homer (1756–8), which was carefully checked six times, is a monument of literary and typographical accuracy. In 1753 Foulis founded an Art Academy in Glasgow, but this ran into financial difficulties, and, combined with the unremunerative character of his high-quality printing, caused Robert to die in debt. The work of the Foulis press gained wide applause, and Robert was awarded the Silver Medal of the Select Society for his Callimachus and his Homer. Among English works, the press produced an edition of Gray (1768) and *Paradise Lost* (1770). The Foulis collection of books was sold in 1777, but most of them are now in the Mitchell Library in Glasgow.

David Murray, *Robert and Andrew Foulis and the Glasgow Press,* 1913.

Webster, Alexander (1707–84), divine and demographer, son of the minister of the Tolbooth parish in Edinburgh, entered the ministry and, after serving at Culross (1733–37), was appointed to his father's former parish. He was a noted preacher of the Evangelical school, with striking ability to appeal from the pulpit to the less educated among his hearers as well as to the more polished members of Edinburgh society. It was remarked that 'It was easier to get a seat in the kingdom of heaven than in the Tolbooth Kirk'. He was Moderator of the General Assembly in 1753, and in 1771 was appointed Dean of the Chapel Royal. Yet Webster was also very much the cultured gentleman of the Edinburgh of his day. He published verses in the *Scots Magazine,* he took the liberal view that there was a need for more places of public amusement in Edinburgh, and his drinking habits earned him the nickname of Dr. Bonum Magnum: 'He had a constitutional strength against intoxication, which made it dangerous in most men to attempt bringing him to such a state: often, when they were unfit for sitting at table, he remained clear, regular and unaffected.'

Webster also had outstanding gifts for handling figures, which he turned to good account in the preparation of a scheme for annuities for widows of ministers. This scheme started to operate in 1744, and as the years went on Webster's predictions on vital statistics proved to have an uncanny accuracy. His actuarial work led him to plan an enumeration of the whole population of Scotland, the means of achieving which was prepared by his correspondence with parish ministers throughout the land in connexion with the widows' fund. Webster's 'census' was completed in 1755, and showed a total population of 1,265,000. Although the work goes by Webster's name, much of the credit for it belongs to Robert Wallace (1697–1771), who was minister of Greyfriars and later of New North parishes in Edinburgh and who in 1753 wrote *A Dissertation on the Number of Mankind in Ancient and Modern Times.*

J. G. Kyd, *Scottish Population Statistics.* Scot. Hist. Soc., 1952.

Roy, William (1726–1790), surveyor, was born at Miltonhead, near Carluke, on 4 May 1726, the son of a factor. He may have been educated at the grammar school of Lanark, but his name does not appear in the records of any Scottish university and it is something of a mystery where he acquired his skill, though his father would no doubt be in touch with some of the expert estate surveyors of the time. It is a reasonable conjecture that Roy spent some years as a civilian draughtsman in the Ordnance Office and so was prepared for the task laid on him in 1747, when Lieutenant-Colonel David Watson, Deputy Quartermaster General in North Britain, who was engaged from a base at Fort Augustus in making roads, conceived the idea of a survey to furnish him with adequate maps. Roy was appointed Assistant Quartermaster, to begin the project with a pilot scheme from Fort Augustus, and the results were so satisfactory that it was determined in 1749 to extend the survey to the whole of the north of Scotland and in 1752 to bring in the south as well. Roy, who was mainly responsible for directing the operations, was appointed Lieutenant-Colonel by 1763 and Inspector-General of Coasts to the Board of Ordnance in 1765. From 1755 he had begun to turn his attention to archaeological surveying and he produced *Military Antiquities of the Romans in North Britain,* published in 1793. The maps of Roy's survey, being designed for military purposes, are especially strong on delineation of the characteristics of the terrain—relief, water and the nature of the land-surface. It has been remarked that on these maps 'the ground looks as difficult to traverse as it really is'. They are less satisfactory for buildings and for boundaries of properties or even field-divisions, which makes them of limited value to the social and economic historian.

R. A. Skelton, *The Military Survey of Scotland, 1747–1755.* Royal Scot. Geog. Soc., 1967.

Hutton, James (1726–1797), geologist, born in Edinburgh, was educated at the High School and the University there before going on to Paris and to Leyden, where he graduated M.D. in 1749. Seeing no prospect of establishing himself successfully in medical practice, he took up the practical application of chemistry, a science which had long fascinated him, and in partnership with James Davie he produced sal ammoniac from soot. He studied agriculture in Norfolk and other parts of England, and in the course of his rambles he began to take an interest in geology. He travelled extensively in Holland, Belgium and France in 1753–4 to widen his knowledge of farming, and on returning to Britain he lived for fourteen years on the small estate in Berwickshire which his father had left him. There he did much to stimulate improved husbandry, while occasionally journeying in the Highlands for geological purposes and continuing his sal ammoniac work. He settled in Edinburgh in 1768 and devoted himself to scientific pursuits. Hutton's first publication, in 1777, was a pamphlet on *Coal and Culm.*

In 1785, in his *Theory of the Earth,* based on observations made in Glen Tilt, Galloway, Arran and the Isle of Man, he originated the theory of the formation of the earth's crust, and the book has been described as 'the foundation work of modern geology'. He also wrote on meteorology in *The Theory of Rain,* afterwards included in his *Physical Dissertations* (1792), and published *Investigations of Principles of Knowledge* (1794). He was joint editor of Adam Smith's *Essays on Philosophical Subjects.* He took an active part in promoting the Forth and Clyde Canal.

Sinclair, Sir John, of Ulbster (1754–1835), head of a cadet branch of the Sinclairs of Mey, who owned 100,000 acres in Caithness, was born at Thurso Castle in 10 May 1754. After education at the Royal High School and the Universities of Edinburgh, Glasgow and Oxford, he studied for the bar, but after he succeeded to the family estates in 1770 he turned his attention to other matters. He sat in Parliament, for different constituencies in Scotland and England, from 1780 to 1811, he toured northern Europe in 1786–7, he was instrumental in founding the Board of Agriculture in 1793 and was its President from that date until 1798 and again from 1806 to 1813, he was a Privy Councillor in 1810 and a Commissioner of Excise in 1811. He was created a baronet in 1786. Sir John's main interest was in economic development, and he devoted much of his attention to agrarian improvement in the north of Scotland—the rotation of crops, the introduction of root crops, the substitution of shearing sheep for plucking them and the improvement of stock. As a practical illustration of how processes could be speeded up he caused one of his sheep to be shorn, the wool spun, dyed, woven and made into a coat, all in one day. He published a *Code of Agriculture* in 1819, and also encouraged fisheries. But Sir John is best remembered for his part in having Scottish economic and social conditions recorded. In 1785 he had published the first part of his *History of the Public Revenue of the British Empire*, which indicated his interest in the publication of statistical information. Between 1791 and 1798 he was responsible for the preparation of the *Statistical Account of Scotland*, consisting of returns obtained from parish ministers all over the country in response to what would now be called a questionnaire. Publication of the work, in twenty-one volumes, was completed in 1799. Sir John was described as 'the most indefatigable man in Britain'. A *New Statistical Account* was produced in the 1840s, and it is somewhat creditable to Sir John that a *Third Statistical Account*, projected after the Second World War, is not yet even half complete, although his was produced in less than a decade.

Rosalind Mitchison, *Statistical Sir John*, 1962.

Hunter, William (1718–83) and John (1728–93), surgeons, were the sons—one the seventh and the other the tenth and youngest—of a small laird in Lanarkshire. William went to Glasgow University to prepare for the ministry, but had scruples about accepting the Confession of Faith and decided to study medicine instead. He was coached for three years by Dr. Cullen, at Hamilton, and then went to the medical school at Edinburgh. He moved on to London, to become assistant dissector at St. George's Hospital, where he showed outstanding skill. In 1746 he began lecturing to naval surgeons and next year was admitted to the Incorporation of Surgeons. He soon abandoned general surgery and specialized in midwifery, in which he built up a lucrative practice. He was appointed physician extraordinary to Queen Charlotte in 1764 and Professor of Anatomy at the Royal Academy in 1768. He became a Fellow of the Royal Society in 1767 and in 1781 was President of the Royal College of Physicians. From 1770 he devoted much attention to a museum which he built and stocked in London, and on his death it was acquired by Glasgow University, of which he had become an M.D. in 1750. His greatest work, the outcome of years of observation, was his *Anatomical Description of the Human Gravid Uterus* (1774), illustrated with remarkable plates, but he had published *Medical Commentaries* as early as 1762 and produced a number of other papers.

John was allowed by his parents to live a somewhat undisciplined life at home until he was seventeen and only then was he sent to school. Consequently, when he joined his brother in London in 1748 he lacked general education, but he soon showed himself a genius in dissection. He studied at Chelsea Hospital and St. Bartholomew's Hospital, and in 1756 became house-surgeon at St. George's Hospital. With wider interests than William, John accompanied the expedition to Belleisle in 1761 and was with the army in Portugal in 1762. With the end of the war, in 1763, he settled in London and began practice on his own in Golden Square. He lectured on surgery at St. George's in 1773 and was appointed surgeon extraordinary to the King in 1776. In 1784 he bought land in Leicester Square and Castle Street and built a museum. After his death his collections were acquired by the government for the London College of Surgeons. His chief publications were a *Treatise on the Blood, Inflammation and Gunshot Wounds* (1794) and *On the Venereal Disease* (1786), but he also wrote *Observations and Reflections on Geology* and *Memoranda on Vegetation*, as well as *Proposals for recovery of People apparently drowned*. John Hunter's outstanding place in the development of surgery was recognized when, after his death, he was buried in Westminster Abbey.

Jane M. Oppenheimer, *New Aspects of John and William Hunter*, 1946.
Garet Rogers, *Brother Surgeons*, 1957. (H.N.)

Monro, Alexander, *primus* (1697–1767), anatomist, was the first of three generations who among them held the Chair of Anatomy at Edinburgh University for 126 years. He was born in London, the son of a surgeon who had served with the navy but who, early in the eighteenth century, set up practice in Edinburgh. Alexander was educated in Edinburgh, London, Paris and Leyden and showed such skill in anatomy that he was appointed Professor of that subject at Edinburgh in 1719. He was the real founder of the Edinburgh medical and surgical school, for he attained great fame as a teacher and drew pupils from far and near. He resigned the chair in 1769 and was succeeded by his son. His principal work was *The Anatomy of the Human Bones and Nerves* (1726), but he contributed many papers to the *Transactions of the Medico-Chirurgical Society*, which he edited, and he left other writings which were included in the edition of his *Works* published in 1781.

Alexander, *secundus* (1733–1817), his father's youngest son, studied at Edinburgh, first in the usual Arts subjects and then in medicine. He assisted his father while he was still a student: the anatomy class had outgrown the lecture room, and the young man, after hearing his father's lecture in the morning, repeated it to other students in the evening. In 1754 he was formally appointed joint-Professor, and he graduated M.D. in 1755. He continued his studies at London, Paris, Leyden and Berlin, returned to Edinburgh in 1758 to be appointed his father's successor and became a Fellow of the Edinburgh College of Physicians in 1759. He held the chair until his resignation in 1808. His first book was a *Treatise on the Lymphatics* (1770), which involved him in controversy with William Hunter as to which of the two had made certain discoveries. His three most important works, all of them folios with handsome engraved plates, were *Observations on the Structure and Functions of the Nervous System* (1783), *The Structure and Physiology of Fishes* (1785) and *A Description of all the Bursae Mucosae of the Human Body* (1788). *The Brain, the Eye and the Ear* appeared as a quarto in 1797. Monro also contributed several papers to the *Essays* of the Philosophical Society of Edinburgh and the *Transactions* of the Royal Society of Edinburgh. He was the ablest of the dynasty, both in his research, which made him pre-eminent in Europe, and in his ability as a brilliant and effortless lecturer who doubled the size of his class.

Alexander, *tertius* (1773–1859), son of Alexander *secundus*, was educated at the Royal High School and University of Edinburgh and then at London and Paris. He became joint-professor with his father in 1798 and held the chair from 1808 until 1846. His father had successfully crushed competition within the University and had prevented the foundation of a Chair of Surgery, but competition came from the lectures on anatomy given at the Royal College of Surgeons by men like Robert Knox (1791–1862). Knox was a distinguished dissectionist, though he achieved unenviable notoriety by dealing with Burke and Hare, who committed murders to provide Knox with subjects; Burke was executed in 1829, Hare turned King's Evidence and was released. But in any event Monro was criticized as an uninspiring and apathetic teacher who merely read his grandfather's lectures. The anatomy class shrank to a third of what it had been in the time of *Secundus*. However, *Tertius* did produce four volumes on the *Anatomy of the Human Body in its sound and diseased states* (1813), two volumes on *Elements of the Anatomy of the Human Body in its sound state* (1825) and *Anatomy of the Brain* (1831).

Ramsay, Allan (1713–1784), artist, eldest son of the poet of the same name, showed his talent from the age of twelve, and when he was sixteen he was a member of the Edinburgh 'Academy of St. Luke', a society of artists and lovers of painting. He went to London for two years about 1734 and spent two periods studying in Italy (1736–8 and 1754–7). On returning to work in Edinburgh, he found that his own ability, combined with his father's place in Edinburgh society, brought him some distinguished sitters, including Lord President Duncan Forbes and the second Duke of Argyll. In 1754 he founded the Select Society, composed of Edinburgh men of distinction in several branches of culture. Already he was living and working largely in London, and when he was introduced by the Earl of Bute to the future George III he gained the entrée to London society as he had formerly gained it to that of Edinburgh. In 1767 he was appointed portrait painter to George III and Queen Charlotte, and was on particularly familiar terms with the Queen, with whom he could converse in fluent German. The demands on him grew so heavy that he had to employ several assistants, and in effect ran a kind of factory to turn out portraits in some of which his own share was minimal. Besides following his own craft, he took an active part in London literary life, and Samuel Johnson said, 'You will not find a man in whose conversation there is more instruction, more information and elegance than in Ramsay's.' He published a volume of Essays, *The Investigator*, in 1762, and a number of pamphlets. After an accident to his arm in 1775 he retired and spent some years in Italy. Apart from doing justice to his royal patrons, Ramsay's sitters included his friend Bute and four noted Scottish figures—Alexander Monro *primus*, David Hume, the 3rd Duke of Argyll and Flora MacDonald.

A. Smart, *The Life and Art of Allan Ramsay*, 1952.

Runciman, Alexander (1736–1785), artist, was the son of an Edinburgh builder, and when he was still a boy he began doing sketches, especially landscapes. At the age of fourteen he was apprenticed to a firm who made it their business to adorn the panels above fireplaces with paintings of landscapes, in the current fashion. He was for a time a pupil at the Foulis Academy in Glasgow, but found that he could not make a living by landscapes and turned to historical scenes. He spent five years in Italy (1766–71) with his brother John (1744–68), also an artist, and returned to Scotland with his art more disciplined that it had been. He was appointed a master in the Trustees' Academy at a salary of £120 a year, which gave him a livelihood. One of his well-known paintings is 'The Ascension' in what was then an Episcopal Chapel and is now St. Patrick's Roman Catholic Church in the Cowgate of Edinburgh. His most ambitious and most widely acclaimed work was the decoration of 'Ossian's Hall' at Sir John Clerk's residence at Penicuik. This consisted of twelve paintings depicting scenes from Ossian's supposed poems, and in the same house Runciman executed four scenes from the life of Queen Margaret on a cupola over the staircase. He was intent on rivalling the ceiling of the Sistine Chapel, and the amount of painting he did in a recumbent position brought on ill-health and an early death. Runciman had taken his place in the society of Edinburgh intelligentsia, with Hume, Robertson, Kames and others. His work is strong on composition and colouring, but his ambition sometimes exceeded his technical skill.

Raeburn, Sir Henry (1756–1823), portrait-painter, born at Stockbridge, Edinburgh, the son of a manufacturer who died when he was six, was educated at George Heriot's Hospital. He was apprenticed to a goldsmith, but soon showed a talent for sketching and painting. He was then apprenticed to Deuchar, an engraver and etcher, and became a pupil of David Martin, the fashionable portrait painter in Edinburgh at the time. From miniatures he went on to large oils, where he discovered his *métier*. By the time he was twenty-eight he was the foremost painter in Scotland. His marriage to a wealthy widow brought him Deanhaugh House, where he worked for a time. But he was aware of his lack of training and went to London, where he met Sir Joshua Reynolds, who encouraged him to go to Rome for two years. After returning to Edinburgh in 1787 he practised his art there for thirty-six years, for a time in George Street and later at 32 York Place. In 1822 he was knighted by George IV on his visit to Edinburgh, and next year was appointed King's Limner and Painter for Scotland. He is estimated to have produced about six hundred portraits, including those of Viscount Melville, Henry Mackenzie, Neil Gow, Alexander Adam, Lord Braxfield, Dugald Stewart, William Robertson, David Hume,

James Boswell, Adam Smith, George IV, Robert Dundas, Lord Provost Elder, William Creech, Hugh Blair, Sir Walter Scott, Sir John Sinclair of Ulbster, Lord Frederick Campbell and the Chief of Macnab. The Scots of that period, in their character as well as their physical appearance, live in Raeburn's fine canvases and have impressed themselves on the visual memory as those of no earlier generation have done. While his work is well represented in Galleries, it is fitting that many portraits are preserved in surroundings with which the subjects were associated, like Lord Frederick Campbell, Lord Clerk Register, in the Register House, Viscount Duncan in Trinity House, Leith, and some professors and others in the Senate Hall of Edinburgh University.

Walter Armstrong and J. L. Caw, *Sir Henry Raeburn*, 1901.
James L. Caw, *Portraits by Sir Henry Raeburn*, 1909

Adam, Robert (1728–1792), architect, born in Kirkcaldy, was a son of William Adam (d. 1748), an architect who had been responsible for a number of Scottish buildings, including part of Hopetoun House, which Robert and his brother John (1721–92) were to complete. After education at Edinburgh University, he travelled on the continent (1754–8), largely to make a special study of the remains of Roman architecture in Italy and Dalmatia, and he published an account of the ruins of the palace of the Emperor Diocletian at Spalato (1764). On his return to Britain he was appointed architect to King George III, but had to relinquish that office under the crown when he was elected member of Parliament for Kinross-shire in 1768. In 1773 he and his brother James (1731–94) began their *Works in Architecture*, which was published in three volumes between 1778 and 1822. Of Robert's many buildings in England the most renowned were the Adelphi in London and the Duke of Northumberland's Syon House. In Edinburgh he was responsible for the original designs of the Register House and what is now the Old College of Edinburgh University, though neither of those was completed in his day and changes were later made in the design, with the result, in the case of the University, that his concept of a splendid setting for the massive frontage was not realized. Perhaps his finest monument in Edinburgh is Charlotte Square, where a range of houses is unified within a single 'palace front'. At Culzean and Seton he showed how he could produce a modification of 'Gothic' along classical lines. His finest interior is that of Mellerstain House in Berwickshire, and one of his achievements was to design furnishings and fittings to accord with the over-all design of a building. His styles became immensely fashionable, they were imitated on the continent and in America, and the term 'Adam' became descriptive of a style rather than indicative of the name of the actual designer. Robert Adam was buried in Westminster Abbey.

Arthur T. Bolton, *The architecture of Robert and James Adam*, 1922.

J. Swarbrick, *Robert Adam and his Brothers*, 1915.

J. Lees-Milne, *The Age of Adam*, 1947.

J. Fleming, *Robert Adam and his Circle*, 1962.

Drummond, George (1687–1766), as Lord Provost of Edinburgh, did perhaps more than any other individual to transform the city. The son of a Perthshire laird, he came to Edinburgh in his teens. After assisting in the financial calculations relating to the Union of 1707, he was appointed Accountant General of Excise (1707) and a Commissioner of the Board of Customs (1717). When the Board of Manufactures was set up in 1727, he was one of the Trustees, and in 1755 he was a Trustee for the Forfeited Estates. He fought on the government side at Sheriffmuir and at Prestonpans. On entering municipal work, he was City Treasurer (1717) and then Dean of Guild (1722), and he became Lord Provost for the first time in 1725. The University was at that time under the control of the Town Council, and five new chairs were founded as a result of Drummond's interest, with specially notable developments in medicine. He was instrumental in 1729 in founding the Royal Infirmary, which was to be so closely associated with the medical school and which was granted a charter in 1736; its new buildings, in Infirmary Street, were begun in 1738. In 1752 Drummond was a member of a committee for the improvement of the city which was largely responsible for the 'Proposals' of 1752 foreshadowing the important future developments. One of the 'Proposals' for the Old Town was a new Royal Exchange, and in 1753 Drummond, in his capacity as Grand Master Mason, laid the foundation stone of this building (now part of the City Chambers). In his sixth and last term of office as Lord Provost (1762–4), he initiated the extension of the town to the north: the building of the North Bridge (of which he laid the foundation stone in 1763) opened the way for the beginnings of the classical New Town. It was in the year of Drummond's death that a competition was held for a plan for this area and the design selected was that of James Craig (?1740–95), a young man with little experience but whose plan (mainly because it was so well adapted to the potential of the site) has won wide acclaim.

Craig designed the Physicians' Hall in George Street and an observatory on Calton Hill, but was to achieve little else that was notable.

A. J. Youngson, *The Making of Classical Edinburgh*, 1966.

Burn, William (1789–1870), architect, was born in Edinburgh, the son of Robert Burn, a successful builder and architect who designed the Nelson Column and Leith High School. He entered the office of Sir Robert Smirke, a London architect, but returned to Edinburgh and set up in his profession. In 1844 he moved to London, leaving his Edinburgh office in charge of David Bryce, his partner. He was as successful in London as in Edinburgh and was responsible for a large number of residences for the aristocracy throughout the British Isles—Riccarton, Niddrie, Tyninghame, Ardgowan, Bowhill and Falkland House in Scotland: Reveby Abbey, Lynford Hall, Sandon Hall and Montague House in England: Dartrey and Castlewellan in Ireland. Some of his best known public works are in Edinburgh—St. John's Church in Princes Street, Edinburgh Academy, the Melville Monument, John Watson's Hospital, the Music Hall and alterations to the church of St. Giles. He came second to William Henry Playfair (1789–1857) in the competition for the completion of the Old College of Edinburgh University. He was for a time consulting architect to the government in Scotland, and one of his conspicuous government works was the Custom House in Greenock. A friend of Sir Walter Scott, he designed the tombstone for the grave of Helen Walker, whose story inspired Scott with the concept of Jeannie Deans in the *Heart of Midlothian*.

Adam, Alexander (1741–1809), a scholar and educationist whose career almost typifies that of the 'lad o' pairts', was born at Laurieston in Moray, the son of a farmer. He attended a dame's school and then the parish school, and started teaching locally when he was fifteen, but his studies were much interrupted by the need to help with work on the farm. He failed to win a bursary to Marischal College, Aberdeen, but was befriended by a kinsman of his father's who was a minister in Edinburgh and who undertook to give Adam quarters while he attended the college there. He went to Edinburgh in 1757 and helped to maintain himself by acting as a tutor to a family near Falkirk. In 1760 he became Master of George Watson's Hospital, where he remained for three and a half years, during which he continued his studies. In 1765 he took charge temporarily of a class in the High School of Edinburgh, and in 1768 was appointed Joint-Rector. His *Latin Grammar* (1762) encountered much opposition in Edinburgh, partly because of the commercial interests of the proprietors of Ruddiman's work which it was designed to supersede and partly because of the jealousy which Adam aroused by his proposals to introduce the study of Greek, which was held to be the monopoly of the University. However, in the end his *Grammar* won the recognition it deserved, went through several editions and was used in many parts of the world. The University made amends to Adam by conferring on him the degree of LL.D. (1780). Adam also published *Roman Antiquities* (1791), which was likewise popular and was translated into German and French, a *Summary of Ancient Geography and History* (1794), *Classical Biography* (1800) and a *Latin Dictionary* (1805). During his term of office the old school buildings were, stage by stage, from 1777 onwards, superseded by a new building partly on the old site. Adam's most famous pupil (from 1779 to 1783) was Walter Scott, who wrote with affection and regard of his teacher. Another pupil, Lord Brougham, wrote 'Dr. Adam was one of the very best teachers I ever heard of and by far the best I ever knew'. Adam's last words, as he died following a stroke, were, 'But it grows dark, boys, you may go'.

William Steven, *History of the High School of Edinburgh,* 1849.

Anderson, John (1726–1796), educationist, son of the parish minister of Roseneath, Dunbartonshire, was brought up partly by an aunt in Stirling and was in arms to defend that town against the Jacobites in February 1746. Thereafter he studied at Glasgow University and became Professor first of Oriental Languages (1756) and then of Natural Philosophy (1760). He now began to show his own original outlook and interests by visiting the workshops of artisans and exchanging theoretical and practical knowledge. Out of this contact grew his class for non-academic students, which he called his 'anti-toga class' and which was a forerunner of later Mechanics' Institutes and other extra-mural work. In 1786 he published his *Institutes of Physics,* which went through five editions in ten years. Of a liberal political outlook, Anderson welcomed the French Revolution and went to France to present to the National Convention an improved cannon which the British government had rejected; he also translated into French some essays on war and armaments and suggested the use of balloons to carry French newspapers into Germany. By his will, Anderson left his modest fortune for 'the good of mankind and the improvement of science' by the foundation of 'Anderson's University' for the 'unacademical classes'. The professors were not to be 'drones, triflers or drunkards' as they were 'in some other colleges'. Funds sufficed initially only for the scientific and practical side, but other departments, including a notable medical school, were added later. The name was later changed to 'Anderson's College' and in 1947 the institution was absorbed into the University of Glasgow.

James Muir, *John Anderson*, 1950.

Bell, Andrew (1753–1832), educationist, born and educated at St. Andrews, went overseas, first to America and then to Madras, where he was a Church of England chaplain at Fort St. George. In 1786, when the East India Company ordered the establishment of a school for the orphans of the European soldiers in its employment, its superintendence was offered to Bell, who accepted it in 1789 but declined the large salary attached, because he thought that teaching was one of the duties to which he was called. The principles Bell introduced amounted in one way or another to relying on the pupils themselves both for disseminating instruction at elementary level and for maintaining discipline. He claimed, 'Give me twelve children, and in twenty-four hours I shall give you twelve teachers.' After returning to Britain, Bell published *An Experiment in Education, made at the Male Asylum of Madras* (1797), and his system was adopted in some schools in England. Contemporaneously, Joseph Lancaster, in his *Improvements in Education* (1803), advocated similar principles, though his concern was for an economical method of educating mechanics, and some Scottish schools adopted his plan. In Bell's lifetime the monitorial system was introduced into nearly 13,000 schools in Britain and also in a number of other countries. Although the system had manifest defects, it led the way to the pupil-teacher system, which for about two generations served to train teachers. Bell became a prebendary of Westminster Abbey, where he was buried. The sum of £120,000 which he left for educational purposes was used to set up schools on his plan in Leith, Aberdeen, Edinburgh, Cupar and St. Andrews (Madras College), as well as the Royal Naval School in London. In 1872 £18,000 of his capital was applied to the foundation of chairs of education in Edinburgh and St. Andrews.

John M. D. Meiklejohn, *An Old Educational Reformer, Andrew Bell*, 1881.

Stow, David, educationist (1793–1864), was born at Paisley and educated at the Grammar School and very early took a deep interest in the poor of Glasgow, where he was employed. In 1816 he established a Sunday evening school, at a time when such schools provided the only opportunity for secular as well as religious instruction, for many children were employed through the week. He became an elder in the church of which Dr. Chalmers was minister, and this gave him further insight into the needs of the homes which he visited. He founded the Glasgow Educational Society, which in 1824 established a week-day training school for teachers in Drygate. In 1832 he was invited to become government Inspector of Schools for Scotland, but declined. His school was a success and received a government grant of £5000 on condition that it was made over to the General Assembly. In 1836 he wrote *Physical and Moral Training*, in which he enunciated his principles of the way in which moral education should accompany intellectual. At the Disruption, Stow, with the directors and teachers of his training school, followed Chalmers out of the Church of Scotland, and he became the founder of the Free Church Normal College, set up to train teachers for the many Free Church Schools which were soon established. Stow was a great believer in the playground, as well as the classroom, for physical and moral training, and he also believed in co-education. He did not approve of corporal punishment, the giving of prizes or 'place-taking'. From 1840 to 1851 the Wesleyans sent students to Stow's College for training, and when they established their own training college at Westminster they adopted Stow's methods.

W. Fraser, *Memoir of David Stow*, 1868.

Watt, James (1736–1819), engineer, was born at Greenock, the son of a carpenter who encouraged the boy's aptitude for mechanical devices. He went to London to seek work as an instrument-maker, and after some difficulty found a sympathetic and encouraging employer. At the age of twenty-one he returned to Glasgow, where he set up as a maker and repairer of instruments within the University precincts, and soon built up quite a business in partnership with John Craig, an architect who provided capital. He happened to be asked to repair the University's model of Newcomen's steam engine, which could act only as a pump and in which condensation took place by injection of a jet of cold water into the cylinder. While engaged on this task, Watt, in the course of a 'walk on a fine Sabbath afternoon' on Glasgow Green, conceived the idea of a separate condenser. Subsequently he saw that by a system of valves steam could make the piston return to the top of the cylinder as well as descend. Later he adapted his engine to rotary motion and devised the flywheel and the governor. All this cost money and brought no income, so Watt worked as a surveyor on canals. In 1774 he entered into partnership with Matthew Boulton and moved to Birmingham to set up a firm for manufacturing steam engines. Although progress was slow, partly because of the difficulty of working metal with sufficient precision, and the adoption of the new invention spread only gradually, Watt became a very famous man: he was an F.R.S., an F.R.S.E., an LL.D. of Glasgow and was offered a baronetcy.

I. B. Hart, *James Watt*, 1963.

Dale, David (1739–1806), born at Stewarton in Ayrshire on 6 January 1739, the son of a grocer, was apprenticed to a weaver in Paisley and then operated as a buyer throughout the countryside of homespun linen yarns, which he sold in Glasgow. With a sleeping partner who provided the capital, he started the business of importing from France and Holland certain fine yarns, to be woven into lawns and cambrics. In 1778 he acquired the first cotton mill to be built in Scotland, at Rothesay. At this juncture the American War of Independence had disrupted the pattern of the Scottish economy, which had been thriving on the import of tobacco and the export of goods to the colonies, and it happened that inventions in England had made possible the wider use of cotton yarn for the making of fabrics. Dale brought the English inventor, Sir Richard Arkwright, to Scotland, and together they settled on a site at the Falls of Clyde for a cotton-spinning mill, to be worked by water power. Thus originated the famous New Lanark mills (1785).

By 1795 Dale had four mills going at New Lanark, employing 1334 workers. He established the first Turkey-red dyeing works in Scotland and was also a partner in cotton mills at Catrine in Ayrshire, Spinningdale near Dornoch in Sutherland, and elsewhere. He employed many pauper children from the poor-houses of Edinburgh and Glasgow. At New Lanark he built barracks capable of housing 500 children: they worked almost twelve hours a day and spent two hours in school after that, but they were well cared for by the standards of the time, and Dale was something of a pioneer in employees' welfare. He also brought workers from the Highlands who would otherwise have emigrated. There was a certain religious element in Dale's outlook, because he was a leader of the sect known as 'The Old Scotch Independents', founded in 1768, and both before and after his retirement he acted as a pastor.

In 1799 Dale sold the New Lanark mills to an English company which appointed as manager Robert Owen (1771–1855), who married Dale's daughter in 1799 and launched out into well-intentioned schemes of social improvement and less soundly conceived plans for socialist communities. He later pursued similar projects in America.

M. Cole, *Robert Owen of New Lanark*, 1953.

Taylor, James, inventor (1753–1825), a native of Leadhills, Lanarkshire, was educated in the school at Closeburn and at Edinburgh University, with a view to a medical career, but in 1785 he was engaged by Patrick Miller of Dalswinton (1731–1815) as tutor to his two sons, who were at college in Edinburgh. Miller, it happened, was interested in the problem of installing paddle-wheels in ships for auxiliary propulsion, and along with Taylor, who had considerable mechanical ingenuity, he produced in 1787 a double-hulled vessel, 60 feet long, with a paddle between the hulls propelled from a capstan. It served very well, and the next question was to find a substitute for human power as a motive force. Taylor found another collaborator in William Symington (1763–1831), who like himself had been born in Leadhills and had then been educated in Edinburgh and Glasgow for the Church but had become a civil engineer. The outcome of Symington's collaboration was an experimental steam vessel in 1788, again with a double hull and with a steam engine with a 4″ cylinder. A speed of five miles an hour was achieved on Dalswinton Loch, but Miller had found the experiments costly and declined to go on financing them. Symington later continued his work and the outcome was the *Charlotte Dundas*, which was placed on the Forth and Clyde Canal in 1802. However, because of a fear that her wash would damage the banks of the canal, she had to be withdrawn and was laid up. She was later examined by Robert Fulton, an American, who introduced a steamer on the Hudson River in 1807. In 1824, Taylor, who had met with little success in various ventures, petitioned the House of Commons for a reward as the inventor of the steamboat, but obtained none.

J. and W. H. Rankine, *Biography of William Symington, 1862.*

Bell, Henry (1767–1830), born at Torphichen, of a family with a tradition of the craft of the mill-wright and the builder, started work as a stone-mason but after three years was apprenticed to his uncle, a mill-wright. He then, from 1787, served with an engineer in Bo'ness and afterwards went to London to be employed by Rennie. When he returned to Scotland in 1790 he worked as a house carpenter, and with shipbuilders at Bo'ness. Although he had many projects which showed his inventiveness he lacked both the means and the habits of application to make them successful. It has been said that he was 'the hero of a thousand blunders and one success'. He put plans for the propulsion of ships by steam before the Admiralty in 1800 and 1803, but, although they were supported by Admiral Nelson, they were rejected. He then turned to America for encouragement, and Fulton followed up his invention. In 1812 Bell at last achieved steam propulsion with the *Comet* (30 tons, 3 h.p.), the first vessel to be propelled by steam on a navigable river in Europe. She was built at Port Glasgow and plied both between Glasgow and Helensburgh and on the route through the Crinan Canal to Oban, until she was wrecked in 1820. Bell gained little for his work, but subscriptions were raised to give recognition to his achievement.

Edward Morris, *Life of Henry Bell*, 1844.

Telford, Thomas (1757–1834), civil engineer, was born at Westerkirk, Dumfriesshire, the son of a shepherd who died soon after his birth. He attended the village school and then served his apprenticeship as a stone-mason, in which trade he was first engaged in inscribing gravestones, but after a new Duke of Buccleuch started a scheme to re-house his tenants there was plenty of building to be done in the district. Telford went to Edinburgh in 1779 and then, in 1782, to London, with an introduction to the architect Sir William Chambers, who employed him on the building of Somerset House. Telford then systematically studied civil engineering, in which he was to make his name. His career was one of great distinction and success, and he had a hand in most of the outstanding public works of his time. In England and Wales he was responsible for bridges of stone and iron over the Severn (arising initially through his appointment in 1787 as surveyor of public works in Shropshire); the Ellesmere Canal, linking the Mersey, the Severn and the Dee and providing a waterway from Liverpool to Bristol; the road from London to Holyhead and the Menai Suspension Bridge; and St. Katharine's Docks in London. Abroad he engineered the Gotha Canal in Sweden, which brought him a Swedish knighthood. In Scotland he was the leading engineer in the construction of the Caledonian Canal (1803–22); he built the Dean Bridge in

Edinburgh and the Bridge of Langholm; he designed harbours at Aberdeen, Wick and elsewhere. Perhaps his most important contribution to the Scottish scene was his labour as engineer to the Commissioners for Highland Roads and Bridges, who began their operations in 1803 and transformed the pattern of communications in the west and north of Scotland, with 920 miles of roads and 1200 bridges. Telford was a founder member of the Institute of Civil Engineers (1818) and Southey dubbed him 'the Colossus of Roads'.

L. Meynell, *Thomas Telford*, 1957.
A. R. B. Haldane, *New Ways through the Glens*, 1962.

Stevenson, Robert (1772–1850), lighthouse engineer, was the son of Alan Stevenson, a Glasgow merchant who died two years after his birth. His widowed mother in 1787 married Thomas Smith, who the previous year had been appointed engineer to the newly established Commissioners for Northern Lights. Previously there had been no lights on the Scottish coast except the coal beacon on the Isle of May (dating from the 1630s) and one on the Little Cumbrae (dating from 1750), and Smith had devised a system of projecting a beam from a lamp by means of reflectors. The Commissioners' first light was at Kinnaird Head (1787). By 1791 Robert Stevenson was on the Commissioners' staff with his step-father, and from that point until his death the extension and maintenance of the lighthouse service were his main interest, though as a civil engineer he did some other work as well. At first he continued his education in winter at the Anderson Institute in Glasgow and at Edinburgh University, while in summer he travelled round the coasts in the newly acquired Lighthouse Commissioners' yacht, amid hazards of storms, tides, rocks and (until 1815) a naval war. As yet the revenues of the Commission were ludicrously meagre and the difficulties enormous in landing materials for new lights on what were of necessity remote and exposed parts of the coast. In 1807, when Smith resigned, Stevenson became chief engineer, and in the same year work began on the Bell Rock lighthouse, the first of Stevenson's own design, which was an improvement on Smeaton's design for Eddystone. It was not until February 1811 that the light was completed and in use. During Stevenson's period of service with the Commission, twenty-three lights were erected, including several of the most important—Inchkeith (1804), May (1816), Sumburgh (1821), Rhinns of Islay (1825), Buchan Ness (1827), Cape Wrath (1828), Girdleness (1833) and Barra Head (1833).

It was with Robert Stevenson that Sir Walter Scott cruised in the Commission's yacht in 1814, on the trip which led him to write *The Pirate*. Over the years many improvements were made, on Stevenson's initiative, in the mechanism of lighthouses, and his work was continued by his sons, Alan (1807–65), David (1815–86) and Thomas (1818–87). Alan designed ten lighthouses, including North Unst and Skerries (1854) and is best known for Skerryvore (1842). Thomas was the father of Robert Louis Stevenson.

R. L. Stevenson, *Records of a Family of Engineers.*

Melville, Henry Dundas, 1st Viscount (1742–1811), the son of Robert Dundas, Lord Arniston, President of the Court of Session, was educated at the High School of Edinburgh and Edinburgh University and was admitted an advocate in 1763. He became Solicitor General in 1766 and sat in Parliament, as member first for Midlothian and then for Edinburgh, from 1774 until 1802 (when he was created a Viscount). In 1775 he became Lord Advocate and held that office until 1783, by which date his great political career was beginning, as a member of the administrations of the Younger Pitt (1784–1801 and 1804–6), to whom he was indispensable both as an able member of the government and as the 'manager for Scotland' who could be relied on to control elections in Scotland.

When Dundas was at the height of his power he was able to control the elections in at least thirty-six of the forty-five Scottish constituencies, and was referred to as 'Harry the Ninth, uncrowned King of Scotland'. He was Treasurer of the Navy (1782–3 and 1784–1800), Home Secretary (1791–4), President of the Board of Control for India (1793–1801), Secretary for War (1794–1801) and first Lord of the Admiralty (1804–5). The fact that he held so many offices was not of his own seeking, but largely due to Pitt, who considered him the only man capable of the tasks. Dundas complained of a situation which 'grows every day, as I advance in years, more irksome and disagreeable', but explained that 'a variety of circumstances happen to concur in my person to render me a cement of political strength to the present administration'. Dundas had a real interest in Indian affairs, for in 1782 he had urged the recall of Warren Hastings so that he could be prosecuted, but his part in the government of India had the side effect, as some of his other appointments had, of creating jobs for ambitious Scots. While Dundas always had an eye to the political results of his patronage, and had a preference for Scots, he did not ignore ability in the men he appointed. He suppressed abuses both in India and in the management of the navy,

217

and as Secretary for War he planned the campaign in Egypt of 1801.

When the French Revolution stimulated radical agitation and then led to its suppression, Dundas became unpopular as the embodiment of the old régime, but others saw him as a man who had done much for his native country and his fellow-countrymen, and it can at least be said that, despite his immersion in British affairs, he never ceased to be very much a Scot. Boswell remarked: 'His Scottish accent, which has been so often in vain obtruded as an objection to his powerful abilities in Parliament, was no disadvantage to him in his own country.' In 1805 he resigned after being accused of malversation, and, although the attempted impeachment of him failed in 1806, he retired from political life. He had inherited the Melville estate by marriage and he built Melville Castle, on the site of an ancient keep, to designs by Playfair.

Henry's son, Robert (1771–1851), 2nd Viscount, was a member of Parliament first for English constituencies (from 1796) and then for Midlothian (1800). He was President of the Board of Trade (1807), Secretary for Ireland (1809) and First Lord of the Admiralty (1812–27). He ultimately became 'manager for Scotland' as his father had been, but in 1827 he lost that position, which had become outmoded with the changing political climate and came to an end.

H. Furber, *Henry Dundas*, 1931.
C. Matheson, *Henry Dundas*, 1933.

Muir, Thomas (1765–1798), born in Glasgow and educated at Glasgow Grammar School and University, was admitted an advocate in 1787. When the French Revolution stimulated a fresh ardour for parliamentary reform in Britain, Muir associated himself with the radical wing of the movement and established close links with the French revolutionaries. In 1792 he helped to found a society for parliamentary reform in Glasgow, he attended meetings at Kirkintilloch and elsewhere and he was a member of the Convention of Delegates of Friends of the People which met at Edinburgh and which, with its very name 'Convention', invited comparison with the French extremists. When Britain went to war with revolutionary France in 1793 the activities of men such as Muir could not be tolerated, and patriotism as well as apprehension for the safety of British institutions and society led to his condemnation. In 1793 he was arrested on a charge of sedition, but liberated on bail. He then set out for France, and this led to his outlawry. When he returned to Edinburgh he was tried in the High Court for 'exciting a spirit of disloyalty and disaffection', for recommending Thomas Paine's *Rights of Man* and for distributing and reading aloud seditious writings. He was sentenced to fourteen years' transportation to Botany Bay (1794). In the colony he was not treated like the ordinary run of convicts, for he was able to acquire a small farm, which he called Huntershill after his paternal estate in Scotland. In 1796 he was rescued by a United States ship. This was only the beginning of a series of adventures. After shipwreck, captivity among American Indians, hospitable treatment in Mexico and imprisonment in Havana, he was sent off on a Spanish frigate bound for Cadiz. The frigate was attacked by British vessels, and Muir was severely wounded, but he eventually reached Bordeaux and then Paris, where he was welcomed by the existing French government, the Directory. He died at Chantilly as a result of his wounds.

George P. Insh, *Thomas Muir of Huntershill*, 1949.

Braxfield, Robert MacQueen, Lord (1722–1799), son of a writer in Lanark who was baron-bailie to the earl of Selkirk, was educated first at Lanark Grammar School and then at Edinburgh University, and became an advocate in 1744. He rapidly gained a reputation as an expert on feudal law, and was employed by the crown on some intricate questions arising from the forfeitures of the estates of Jacobites after the 'Forty-five. In 1776 he was appointed a Lord of Session, taking his title of Braxfield from his father's estate in Lanarkshire, and in 1788 he became Justice Clerk, which in those days (when the office of Lord Justice General was a sinecure) meant effective head of the criminal court. In this capacity he presided at the trials of Thomas Muir and the other 'political martyrs' who were sentenced to transportation for sedition in 1793–4. Maintaining the old tradition of speaking Scots on the bench, Braxfield domineered over the court, browbeating prisoners, counsel and colleagues alike, and he was noted for the brutal insults and jests he flung at his victims. He is said to have declared of one prisoner that 'he would be nane the waur of a hangin' [none the worse of a hanging]; and when someone protested that Jesus Christ himself had been something of a social radical in his day, Braxfield's retort was, 'Weel, he was hangit'. Yet he was a man not only of legal skill but of considerable personal courage which made him disregard threats against his person and take no measures for his protection even when he was most unpopular. He was the chief character in R. L. Stevenson's unfinished *Weir of Hermiston*.

Nasmyth, Alexander (1758–1840), the father of Scottish landscape painting, was born in Edinburgh on 9 September 1758 and, after education at the Royal High School and the Trustees' Academy, went to London to become a pupil of Allan Ramsay. After a brief apprenticeship to a coach-painter, he spent several years in Italy, working on historical subjects and portraits but also on landscapes and architectural subjects. On his return he set up as a portrait-painter in Edinburgh and is especially famous for his 'Robert Burns'. But his enthusiasm for landscapes persisted, and he devoted much of his time to painting in the countryside. This in turn led him to advise on what we should now call the 'landscaping' of houses, when landowners were able to spend much money on building and on the 'policies' which surrounded their homes. Nasmyth also did some architectural work, including St. Bernard's Well and other features of the New Town of Edinburgh. He conducted a school of painting, and continued his work until almost his death at the age of eighty-two on 10 April 1840.

Alexander's son, Patrick (1787–1831), showed an enthusiasm for sketching nature from his schooldays, and he pursued his craft with the utmost determination. When an accident deprived him of the use of his right hand, he taught himself to use his left, and he devised a tent in which he could sit and paint during rain. He settled in London at the age of twenty and found English landscape more suited to his genius than Scottish.

Another son, James (1808–90), developed his talent along different lines. When he was only twenty he constructed a steam carriage capable of carrying six people, and in 1834 he started a business in Manchester for making machine-tools. In 1839 he invented the steam hammer, and followed this by other inventions which greatly accelerated the development of the engineering industry—a machine for shaping nuts, a flexible shaft for driving drills, and a hydraulic punching machine. He also spent much time in astronomical observations, for which he had constructed a six-inch reflecting telescope in his youth, and made certain discoveries about the surfaces of the sun and the moon.

James Nasmyth, *Autobiography* (ed. S. Smiles), 1883.

Wilkie, Sir David (1785–1841), artist, son of the parish minister of Cults, in Fife, attended parish schools at Pitlessie and Kettle and then the academy at Cupar, before going on at the age of fourteen to study at the Trustees' Academy at Edinburgh. He had from his earliest days shown talent for drawing with any materials which came to his hand, and at the Academy he made progress in portrait-painting. In 1804, at the age of nineteen, he returned home and began work on his first famous picture, 'Pitlessie Fair'. This brought in no less than a hundred and forty faces, for many of which he obtained sketches when attending service in the parish church. He went to London in 1805 and worked as a portrait painter, but continued his own chosen line of depicting social gatherings and homely scenes of one kind and another, English as well as Scottish. 'The Village Politicians' attracted much notice when it was shown in the Royal Academy, of which Wilkie became an Associate in 1809 and a Fellow in 1811, and commissions came pouring in. He visited Scotland from time to time, notably in 1817, when he was warmly welcomed by Scott, whom he painted with his family and friends at Abbotsford. 'The Penny Wedding' (1818) was painted to the order of the Prince Regent, and Wilkie received 1200 guineas from the Duke of Wellington for 'The Reading of the Waterloo Gazette' (1821). Another of Wilkie's works went to the collection of the King of Bavaria at München. He succeeded Raeburn as King's Limner in Scotland in 1823 and seven years later succeeded Lawrence as Painter-in-Ordinary in England. He was knighted in 1836. From contemporary scenes like 'The Entrance of George IV to Holyrood', Wilkie was led on to historical reconstructions, many of which, like 'John Knox preaching before the Lords of the Congregation' (1832), have been reproduced in successive history books. He paid many visits to the continent, where he was highly fêted and found inspiration for further subjects, like 'The Maid of Saragossa', the result of a visit to Spain in 1827. Wilkie was returning from a visit to the Near East when he died and was buried at sea. He ranks with Scott to the extent that the one preserved the life of old Scotland on paper, the other on canvas.

Edward Pinnington, *Sir David Wilkie and the Scots School of Painters*, 1900.

Scott, Sir Walter (1771–1832), son of Walter Scott, a Writer to the Signet, and a daughter of a professor of medicine, was born in Edinburgh on 15 August 1771. After an illness which left him permanently lame, he spent much of his boyhood with his grandfather at the farm of Sandyknowe. He first went to school at Kelso, where James and John Ballantyne, his future printers, were his fellow-pupils, and then, from 1779 to 1783, attended the High School of Edinburgh under Dr. Adam. He was at Edinburgh University from 1783 to 1786, was then apprenticed to his father and was called to the bar in 1792. He married Charlotte Charpentier, a French-woman, in 1797. He became sheriff of Selkirk in 1799 and a principal clerk of session in 1806.

Scott's first publications were translations from the German, in 1796 and 1799. In 1802 he published his *Minstrelsy of the Scottish Border*, a collection of ballads, and followed this with the composition of original ballads. This led almost logically to *The Lay of the Last Minstrel* (1805), for which he received nearly £800, and it was followed in 1808 by *Marmion*, which brought him over £1,000. *The Lady of the Lake* came in 1810, and other narrative poems followed, including *The Lord of the Isles* (1815), but it was evident long before the series came to an end that Scott had worked this vein out.

In 1805 he had started a prose novel, which he returned to later and completed as *Waverley* (1814). Archibald Constable (1774–1827), who had published some of Scott's poems, refused him £1000 for the copyright, and a profit-sharing contract proved much more advantageous to the author. *Waverley*, like the novels which followed, was issued under a pseudonym, and it was not until 1827 that Scott acknowledged that he was 'The Great Unknown'. The principal novels appeared as follows: *Guy Mannering* (1815), *The Antiquary* and *Old Mortality* (1816), *Rob Roy* and *The Heart of Midlothian* (1818), *The Bride of Lammermoor* and *A Legend of Montrose* (*1819*), *Ivanhoe*, *The Monastery* and *The Abbot* (1820), *Kenilworth* (1821), *The Pirate* and *The Fortunes of Nigel* (1822), *Peveril of the Peak* and *Quentin Durward* (1823), *Redgauntlet* (1824), *The Talisman* (1825), *Woodstock* (1826), *The Fair Maid of Perth* (1828), *Anne of Geierstein* (1829), *Count Robert of Paris* and *Castle Dangerous* (1831).

Scott's other prose works, besides the novels, are less well remembered today, but some of them were serious contributions to scholarship, others reflected at least the incredible industry of a man who had for years a busy professional life and could do his voluminous writing only by rising at 5 a.m. He edited the *Works of Dryden* (1810) and *The Works of Swift*, in 19 volumes (1814). His editions of the *Letters of Sir Ralph Sadler* (1809) and of the *Somers Tracts* (1809–15), in 13 volumes, reflected an interest in historical scholarship which led to his part in founding the Bannatyne Club in 1823. His *Life of Napoleon* (1827) brought him nearly £18,000. His *Tales of a Grandfather* (1828–30) were in effect a child's History of Scotland, and he also wrote almost concurrently a more serious *History of Scotland* for Lardner's *Cyclopaedia*. He

222

contributed many articles to the *Quarterly Review* and the *Encyclopaedia Britannica*.

Scott's industry brought him fame as well as wealth. He was created a baronet in 1820 and when George IV came to Scotland in 1822 (on a visit largely stage-managed by Scott), the King declared that Sir Walter was the man in Scotland he most wished to meet. But Scott's ideas were grandiose as well as romantic. Previous to 1811 he had spent the summers at Ashestiel near Selkirk, but in that year he acquired property further down the Tweed and started the erection of an imitation baronial mansion called Abbotsford. He was spending up to the limit, and beyond it, in acquiring land, embellishing his house and dispensing hospitality, confident that his earnings would be adequate to meet all demands. However, in 1826 the firm of Ballantyne, in which he had long been a partner, followed Constable in failure, and Scott, rather than go bankrupt and defraud the creditors, undertook to shoulder a debt of slightly over £100,000. When he died, on 21 September 1832, his unremitting industry had paid off £70,000 and the remainder was met by the sale of his copyrights, but he had ruined his health by overwork. He was buried in Dryburgh Abbey.

In 1820 Scott's daughter, Sophia, married John Gibson Lockhart (1794–1854), who had been called to the bar but had proved useless as a speaker in court and had turned to literature. After his marriage Lockhart settled near Abbotsford, and his close association with Scott gave him the material for his most famous work, the *Life of Scott*, which appeared in seven volumes, the last of them in 1838. Lockhart was a contributor to *Blackwood's Magazine* and was editor of the *Quarterly Review* from 1825 until 1853. His best-remembered novel is *Adam Blair* (1822), an unusually frank work for its time.

H. Pearson, *Walter Scott*, 1954.
John Buchan, *Walter Scott*, 1932.
D. D. Devlin (ed.), *Walter Scott: modern judgements*, 1968.
Edgar Johnson, *Sir Walter Scott*, 1970.

Hogg, James (1770–1835), 'the Ettrick Shepherd', born at Ettrick in Selkirkshire, was employed as a herd from almost his earliest days and had little education. However, in the 1790s, when he was employed by Laidlaw, the farmer of Blackhouse in Yarrow, he became a voracious reader of poetry in English and Scots and was stirred by the example of Burns, 'the ploughman poet'. He was also an enthusiast for music, and had possessed a violin since he was

223

fourteen. He soon began to write poetry, and in 1800 published the patriotic verses *Donald MacDonald*, followed next year by *Scottish Pastorals*. Hogg met Sir Walter Scott, and gave him material for his *Minstrelsy of the Scottish Border*, probably passing off as traditional a good many of his own compositions, which Scott uncritically accepted. In 1804, after accumulating £200, Hogg took a farm in Harris and lost his money. Then, with *The Mountain Bard* and *The Shepherd's Guide*, he made £300, which he lost in another venture. There was clearly more money for Hogg in poetry than in farming, and in 1810 he settled for a time in Edinburgh. For a year (1810–11) he ran *The Spy*, a critical weekly journal. After *The Forest Minstrel* (1810) came *The Queen's Wake* (1813), which brought him fame and the friendship of his leading literary contemporaries, like Wordsworth, Southey and John Wilson. In 1814 the Duke of Buccleuch gave Hogg a farmhouse and a smallholding, and there he spent most of his life from 1817. In 1815 he produced *Pilgrims of The Sun* and *The Poetic Mirror*, an anthology of living poets. He wrote prose as well, some of it for *Blackwood's Magazine*, and his later publications included *Jacobite Relics, Winter Evening Tales, The Three Perils of Man, Confessions of a Fanatic, Queen Hynde, The Shepherd's Calendar, Domestic Manners and Private Life of Sir Walter Scott* (1834) and *Montrose Tales* (1835). *The Private Memoirs and Confessions of a Justified Sinner* (1824) is a macabre novel about a Calvinist who carried his Antinomianism to its extreme, convinced that as he was one of the 'Elect' no sin he committed could imperil his salvation. It was looked at askance at the time, but has been highly praised since and gives Hogg a place in literature which his verses no longer do.

Edith Batho, *The Ettrick Shepherd*, 1927.

Galt, John (1779–1839), novelist, born in Irvine on 2 May 1779, was educated at Greenock, to which his parents moved when he was eleven, and where he was later employed in the Custom House and in a business firm before going on to clerical employment in London in 1803 or 1804. He had early tried his hand at poetry, including an epic on the battle of Largs, but neither in literature nor in business was he successful, and he turned for a time to law. In 1809–12 he toured the Mediterranean and the Near East and published two volumes describing his travels. He followed this with a *Life of Wolsey*. His first significant novel was *The Ayrshire Legatees* (1821), in which he found his *métier*. *The Annals of the Parish*, begun in 1813 and laid aside, was also published in 1821 and the most important novels which followed were *The Provost* (1822) and *The Entail* (1823). Galt's name lives as that of a novelist who depicted Scottish life and institutions in a manner useful to the historian as well as to readers of fiction. But he also played an important part in the history of Scottish colonization. For a time he was the agent in London for the claims of Canadians who had suffered losses in the war between Britain and the United States in 1812–14, and this gave him information about Canada which he turned to good account. In 1824 he founded the Canada Company for the development of what is now Ontario, and from 1825 he himself spent some time in Canada. He was recalled in 1829, when he went bankrupt, but he maintained his interest through the British America Land Company (chartered in 1834), and he was largely responsible for the colonization of southern Ontario, where the town of Galt bears his name. His novel *Lawrie Todd* gives an account of the life of a Scottish settler in America. Galt died in Greenock, the Scottish town with which he is most often associated. His writings extend in all to about fifty volumes of novels alone.

Jennie W. Aberdein, *John Galt*, 1936.

Nairne, Caroline, Lady (1766–1845), born Caroline Oliphant of the family of Gask in Perthshire, married Major William Murray Nairne, assistant inspector of barracks, in 1806. Her husband's family, like her own, had been strongly Jacobite, and he succeeded in 1824 to the title of Lord Nairne, which had been forfeited. The couple lived first at Portobello and later at Duddingston. After her husband's death Lady Nairne went to Clifton, Bristol, then to Ireland and in 1834 to the continent. She had some talent in drawing and painting, but is best known for her contribution to the *corpus* of Scottish songs, many of the best known of which were her compositions. From 1821 to 1824, under the pseudonym of Mrs. Bogan of Bogan, she contributed lyrics to *The Scottish Minstrel*. During her lifetime most of her productions circulated in MS., for she was reluctant to publish, and those which were printed appeared anonymously. In 1846, a year after her death, a collection of her work was issued under the title *Lays from Strathearn*. Among her many songs were 'Wi' a hundred pipers', 'The Auld Hoose', 'The Land o' the Leal', 'The Laird o' Cockpen', 'The Rowan Tree', 'Will ye no' come back again', 'Caller Herrin'' and 'Charlie is my darling'.

Margaret S. B. Simpson, *The Scottish Songstress: Caroline, Baroness Nairne*, 1894.

Jeffrey, Francis (1773–1850), son of George Jeffrey, a Depute Clerk of Session, was educated at the Royal High School and the Universities of Glasgow, Edinburgh (for law) and Oxford, where he went in 1791. He was admitted an advocate in 1794, but he found that his acquired English accent made him unpopular as a pleader, and he tried out some of his writings in London in 1798, with little success. In 1802 he was one of the founders of the *Edinburgh Review*, of which he soon became the editor and for which he wrote over 200 articles. One of his collaborators was Henry Brougham (1778–1868), an Edinburgh man who became more of an anglicized Scot than Jeffrey, for after being admitted to the Scottish bar in 1800 he moved to London (1805) and had a British rather than a Scottish career, leading ultimately to the Lord Chancellorship under the Whig-Liberal government of 1830. Brougham's contributions to the *Review* were of such astonishing versatility and diversity that it was said that if he had known a little law he would have known a little of everything. Jeffrey, who continued a primarily Scottish career, found that his literary fame contributed to the extension of his professional practice. In 1829 he was elected Dean of the Faculty of Advocates and in the following year, with the advent of the Whig-Liberal government, he was Lord Advocate and M.P. for Forfar burghs. He thus had a considerable responsibility for the framing and passing of the Scottish Reform Bill of 1832. In the first reformed Parliament he was M.P. for Edinburgh, and, still Lord Advocate, he saw the Burgh Reform Bill through Parliament in 1833. In 1834 he became a Lord of Session. Jeffrey had lived at Hatton from 1812 to 1815 and he then acquired Craigcrook Castle at Corstorphine, which he restored. Like Sir Walter Scott, he took part in founding Edinburgh Academy in 1824.

H. Cockburn, *Life of Lord Jeffrey*, 1852.
J. A. Greig, *Francis Jeffrey of the Edinburgh Review*, 1948.

Cockburn, Henry Thomas (1779–1854), lawyer and diarist, was the son of a lawyer who was successively sheriff of Midlothian, Judge-Admiral and Baron of the Scottish Court of Exchequer. He was born in Edinburgh and educated at the Royal High School and Edinburgh University. He became an advocate in 1800 and was for many years one of the leading figures at the Scottish bar, with a special renown for taking the defence in criminal cases. His speech on behalf of Stuart of Dunearn, who was tried for killing Sir Alexander Boswell in a duel, was regarded as a model of forensic eloquence. Cockburn, like Jeffrey and some other leading advocates, was a Whig in politics and wrote several pamphlets urging the extension of the parliamentary and municipal franchise. He was also critical of the position of the Lord Advocate as being at once the principal law officer of the crown in Scotland and also in effect the 'minister for Scotland', and spoke of the need for a Scottish Secretary. He turned his attention, too, to judicial reforms, and criticized the method by which a judge could choose the jury in criminal cases. When the Whig-Liberals came to power in 1830, Cockburn was Solicitor General, with Jeffrey as Lord Advocate, and in 1831 he took part in drafting the first Scottish Reform Bill. In 1834 he was appointed a Lord of Session. Very much an Edinburgh man, Cockburn valued its amenity and architecture and his critical attitude to much that was happening led him to write a *Letter to the Lord Provost on the best ways of spoiling the beauty of Edinburgh.* This aspect of his interests is commemorated in the name of the Cockburn Association, a leading Edinburgh amenity society. Cockburn wrote a *Life of Lord Jeffrey* in 1852, but is best remembered for material which was published posthumously—*Memorials of Our Times* (1856) and *Journal, 1831–44* (2 vols., 1874).

Blackwood, William (1776–1834), publisher, a native of Edinburgh, was apprenticed to a firm of booksellers for six years from the age of fourteen and then became manager of the Glasgow branch of a publishing firm. In 1800 he became a partner in a bookselling firm and then went to London to learn more of the antiquarian side of that trade. In 1804 he set up his own shop in the South Bridge, Edinburgh, concentrating on antiquarian books, but entered the publishing business and gradually concentrated more and more on it. He moved to premises in the New Town in 1816 and started his famous *Magazine* in 1817. The general trend under his editorship was support for the Tory party, in opposition to the liberal *Edinburgh Review.* From the outset Blackwood had on his staff John Wilson (1785–1854), otherwise 'Christopher North', who became well known for light-hearted articles describing the scenery of the Lake District and the Highlands, in which he could afford to spend much of his time, as he had inherited the fortune of his father, a wealthy Paisley manufacturer. Wilson was also known for his *Noctes Ambrosianae,* in which he recounted the evenings spent by him and his literary friends in Ambrose's Tavern, and his tenure of the Chair of Moral Philosophy in Edinburgh University from 1820 to 1851 was tantamount to 'thirty-one years of the most arrant humbug'[1] One of Blackwood's regular contributors was David Macbeth Moir (1798–1851), otherwise 'Delta', who practised as a physician and wrote scholarly works in his professional capacity but also published a good deal of miscellaneous verse and prose. Another contributor was J. G. Lockhart, the biographer of Sir Walter Scott. The circulation of *Blackwood's Magazine* rose to 10,000. Blackwood published the *Edinburgh Encyclopaedia* and the works of various contributors to his *Magazine, including* Galt and Scott.

Sir George Douglas, *The Blackwood Group*, 1897.

Tytler, Patrick Fraser (1791–1849), historian, was the third of a dynasty of historical writers, all of them educated in Edinburgh and trained for the legal profession. His grandfather, William (1711–92), enjoyed professional success which enabled him to buy the estate of Woodhouselee, near Roslin. Among William's numerous writings were *The Poetical Remains of James I* (1783) and *An Inquiry into the Evidence against Mary, Queen of Scots* (1759), which took a favourable view of Mary. Alexander Fraser (1747–1813), elder son of William, was Professor of Universal History at Edinburgh from 1780 until he became a judge of the Court of Session, with the title of Lord Woodhouselee, in 1802. Alexander was encouraged by Lord Kames to compile *The Decisions of the Court of Session* (1778), and in 1807 he wrote a *Life of Lord Kames*. Patrick, son of Lord Woodhouselee, was one of the group of scholars who were associated with Thomas Thomson and Sir Walter Scott in the renaissance of Scottish historical studies and joined with them in founding the Bannatyne Club (1822). Subsequently Tytler strongly advocated the publication of record material by the government, and can be credited with foreseeing the great developments of the later part of the century, when extensive series of publications began in both England and Scotland. It was on Scott's suggestion that Tytler undertook his greatest work, which is still useful because of the author's industry in finding and examining records and other source material—his *History of Scotland*, in nine volumes (1828–43).

John Small, *Biographical Sketch of Patrick Fraser Tytler*, 1864.

Thomson, Thomas (1768–1852), record scholar, son of the parish minister of Dailly, Ayrshire, was destined for the ministry, and graduated M.A. at Glasgow in 1789. However, he decided that his bent was for law, and he went on to Edinburgh University. He was

1. Hugh MacDiarmid, *Scottish Eccentrics*, p. 104.

admitted an advocate in 1793. In 1806 he was appointed Deputy Clerk Register, which made him the immediate custodian of the Scottish national records, under the general direction of Lord Frederick Campbell, the energetic Lord Clerk Register. The records had recently been removed to a new repository, the present Register House (opened in 1787), but Thomson inherited the results of generations of neglect, and apart from the task of arranging and indexing there was an enormous amount of binding and repair to be done. All these tasks he put in hand, and the modern record régime in Scotland may be said to date from his day. He also initiated a policy of publication, with a volume of the *Register of the Great Seal* (1814), three volumes containing abridgements and indexes of the *Retours* (1811–16), a volume of the *Acts of the Lords Auditors of Causes and Complaints* (1839), another of the *Acts of the Lords of Council* (1839), and eight volumes of the *Acts of the Parliaments of Scotland*, which were completed in twelve volumes after his death. To facilitate searching for legal, rather than historical, purposes, he instituted an Abridgment of the Register of Sasines from 1781. Thomson also edited a number of volumes for the Bannatyne Club, of which he was Vice President in 1823 and President (in succession to Sir Walter Scott) in 1832, and his publications extend in all to twenty-eight titles. Thomson's record scholarship was sometimes called in for the presentation of cases in court, and his monument in this field was the 'Memorial on Old Extent' which he produced in the case of Cranston v. Gibson in 1816. Thomson became a Principal Clerk of Session in 1828, retaining his office as Deputy Clerk Register. However, he had two faults, one of them procrastination, arising to some extent from perfectionism, and the other a casualness in financial matters which was quite inappropriate in a public servant. The consequence was that in 1839 he was dismissed from the office of Deputy Clerk Register.

Thomas's brother, John (1778–1840), was a reluctant student of divinity, and at Edinburgh University he learned something of the Edinburgh society in which he was to play his part in later years. He succeeded his father as minister of Dailly in 1800, but found that his talents were not very popular with a rural congregation. In 1805 he moved to Duddingston, near Edinburgh, where he was much more happily situated. After taking lessons from Alexander Nasmyth, he found that as a landscape painter he could earn up to £1800 a year, and it is said that, while he was not conspicuous for spiritual leadership, he was generous to the material needs of his parishioners.

Memoir of Thomas Thomson. Bannatyne Club, 1854.
'Thomas Thomson', in James Fergusson, *The Man behind Macbeth*, 1969.
Robert W. Napier, *John Thomson of Duddingston*, 1919.

Innes, Cosmo (1798–1874), antiquary and historian, was born at Durris in Kincardineshire and educated at the Royal High School, the Universities of Aberdeen and Glasgow and Balliol College, Oxford. He became an advocate in 1882 and was Advocate-Depute from 1833 to 1840, when he became sheriff of Moray. In 1852 he resigned his sheriffship on appointment as Principal Clerk of Session. He was Professor of Constitutional Law at Edinburgh University from 1846 until his death.

As an advocate, Innes had been engaged on certain peerage cases, and this led him to an interest in record scholarship. About 1830 he began to assist Thomas Thomson in the arrangement of the national archives and became involved in the completion of the publication of *The Acts of the Parliaments of Scotland,* for which he prepared the magisterial General Index, which was published in the year after his death. He edited many volumes, especially cartularies of religious houses, for the Bannatyne, Maitland and Spalding Clubs, and brought together some of his Introductions, with other essays, in *Scotch Legal Antiquities* (1872), *Scotland in the Middle Ages* (1860) and *Sketches of Early Scotch History* (1861). Innes was perhaps the greatest record scholar of nineteenth-century Scotland, and there are many topics on which the *locus classicus* is still to be found in his works.

Innes married a daughter of Rose of Kilravock, and his eldest daughter married John Hill Burton (1809–81), who started life as an advocate and from 1854 to 1881 was Secretary of the Prison Board but was a prolific writer on both historical and current topics. Less of a scholar than his father-in-law, Burton wrote for a wider public, and his *History of Scotland*, produced in eight volumes between 1852 and 1870, long remained a standard work. The office of H.M. Historiographer in Scotland, which had been apt to be regarded as a piece of political patronage, eluded Innes but was conferred on Burton in 1867.

Mrs. John H. Burton, *Memoir of Cosmo Innes*, 1874.

Fraser, Sir William (1816–1898), born at Arduthie, near Stonehaven, was educated at a private school in Montrose. He served his apprenticeship with a solicitor in Montrose (1830–5), then went to

Edinburgh, where he studied Scots Law and Conveyancing at the University and served with various firms, until in 1851 he became a partner and was admitted an S.S.C. In 1852 he was appointed Assistant Keeper of the Register of Sasines, but when the Keepership fell vacant he was not appointed to it; therefore, while remaining Assistant Keeper, he devoted more and more time to his own researches in family history, a subject to which some cases requiring genealogical investigations had already directed him. He had edited the *Register of Dryburgh* for the Bannatyne Club in 1847, but his real life's work began with the production of his first family history—*The Stirlings of Keir*—in 1858. From that point there was a steady stream of volumes, in all over forty, in which the histories of Scottish noble and landed families were written, with copious selections from their muniments. In 1869 Fraser had become a member of the Historical Manuscripts Commission, and from 1880 until 1892 he was Deputy Keeper of the Scottish Records. He received an LL.D. from Edinburgh in 1882 and a K.C.B. in 1887. His unremitting industry, joined to his comparatively frugal way of life, made him a wealthy man, and in his will he was able to make provision both for a Home for Old People at Colinton and the endowment of a Chair of 'Ancient History and Palaeography' at Edinburgh University. The curious phraseology led to a compromise whereby a Professor of Scottish History and Palaeography and a Lecturer in Ancient History were appointed.

Introduction to *Fraser Papers*, Scottish History Society, 1924.

Masson, David (1822–1907), historian, was born in Aberdeen and, after being educated at Aberdeen Grammar School and Marischal College, studied Divinity at Edinburgh. However, he turned to literature and joined the staff of W. and R. Chambers, for whom he wrote text-books on ancient, medieval and modern history. In 1847 he went to London. From 1853 to 1865 he was Professor of English Literature at University College, but maintained his interest in journalism and started *MacMillan's Magazine* in 1859. In 1865 he was chosen for the Chair of Rhetoric and English Literature at Edinburgh, and held it until he resigned in 1895. As a lecturer, he drew vastly increased numbers of students to his classes and in the year of his retirement a Degree with Honours in English was instituted. Masson also worked for the admission of women to the University, and one of the women's residences was given his name— Masson Hall. But Masson was all along very much the historian, even although it was often the history of literature that he was writing. His six-volume *Life of Milton* (1859–94) was described as 'that history of the world from 1608 to 1674 which Masson insisted on calling a Life of Milton'. Somewhat similarly, his *Drummond of Hawthornden* (1873) is useful to the Scottish historian. From 1880 to 1899 Masson was engaged on editing the *Register of the Privy Council of Scotland*: he was responsible for the thirteen volumes covering the period from 1578 to 1627, and his Introductions amount to the most detailed history of that period. In 1893 Masson was appointed H.M. Historiographer for Scotland.

Autobiographical material in David Masson, *Memories of Two Cities*, 1911.

Chambers, William (1800–1883), publisher, born in Peebles of a family of woollen manufacturers, attended school in Peebles until, in 1814, his family moved to Edinburgh. There he was apprenticed to a bookseller and, after learning the trade, he joined with his brother Robert (1802–71) to set up their own booksellers' business, first in Leith Walk (1819), then in India Place and later in Hanover Street. From selling books William went on to printing them, beginning with the purchase of an old printing press. And, from printing books, he went on, with his brother, to publishing them and writing them.

One of William's earlier efforts was *The Book of Scotland* (1830), and another, with his brother, *A Gazetteer of Scotland*. The brothers long maintained their interest in reference books, and Robert compiled *A Biographical Dictionary of Eminent Scotsmen*, in six volumes (1832–4). Their other main interest was periodical literature, beginning in 1822 with a fortnightly journal *The Kaleidoscope*. The periodical branch of the business came to its peak with the appearance in 1832 of *Chambers' Edinburgh Journal*, which attained a circulation of 80,000 and continued until 1956, and the greatest achievement on the reference side was *Chambers' Encyclopaedia*, in ten volumes, first published in 1859–68 and going through many later editions, down to the present. William's interest in popular education led him to produce *Chambers' Educational Course* (1835). The firm of W. and R. Chambers, founded as a publishing house in 1832, is still in existence.

William Chambers became Lord Provost of Edinburgh in 1865 and again in 1868, and he was a munificent benefactor of the city. He initiated many improvement schemes, and one of the areas where slum property was cleared to create spacious highways includes Chambers Street. William also expended between £20,000 and

£30,000 on the restoration of the Church of St. Giles, which was completed in 1883 and did much to remedy the errors made by earlier restorers. To his native place, Peebles, he presented a museum, library and art gallery, now known as the Chambers Institution.

Robert Chambers wrote a great variety of books, including *Traditions of Edinburgh* (1823), *Walks in Edinburgh* (1825), *Popular Rhymes of Scotland* (1826), *The Rebellion of 1745* (1828), *Vestiges of the Natural History of Creation* (issued anonymously in 1844) and *Memoirs of a Banking House* (1860). His very useful collection of extracts from source material, *Domestic Annals of Scotland*, appeared in 1859–61. Robert's son, also named Robert (1832–88), took an active part in the production of the *Encyclopaedia* between 1859 and 1868 and became editor of the *Journal* in 1874.

William Chambers, *Memoir of William and Robert Chambers*, 1883.

Maclaren, Duncan (1800–1886), politician, son of a Dunbartonshire farmer, was apprenticed to a draper in Dunbar and then spent some time in Haddington, before removing in 1818 to Edinburgh, where he set up his own drapery business in the High Street in 1824 and where he remained for the rest of his life. He became a member of the Town Council in 1833 and as City Treasurer he did much to restore the finances of Edinburgh after it had been on the verge of bankruptcy. He was Lord Provost from 1851 to 1854. During his term of office the Society for the Vindication of Scottish Rights was founded (1853), largely at the instigation of the historical novelist James Grant (1822–87), and MacLaren took a leading part in its agitation, which foreshadowed many of the points to be made by Scottish Nationalists in later times. He contested the Edinburgh seat as a Liberal in 1852, unsuccessfully, but he was elected in 1865 and held the seat until 1881. One of his achievements was to secure the abolition of the Annuity Tax, which had been levied in Edinburgh and Montrose to pay ministers' stipends and which had been a long-standing grievance against which MacLaren had written in 1836 and 1851. He was always so ready to put Scotland's case at Westminster that he was alluded to as 'the member for Scotland'.

J. B. Mackie, *Life and Work of Duncan MacLaren*, 2 vols., 1888.

Haldane, James Alexander (1768–1851), and his brother Robert (1764–1842), evangelists, were born at Dundee and educated at the

Royal High School and Edinburgh University. James became a midshipman with the East India Company at the age of seventeen and in 1793 was captain of the *Melville Castle*. However, he soon abandoned the sea to study theology. He began his career as an evangelical preacher in 1797 and set out on a tour of the north of Scotland and Orkney, where he found many districts somewhat neglected by the established church and ready to welcome him warmly. He subsequently went on many other tours in Scotland and England, and in 1799 established his own congregation in Edinburgh. The elder brother, Robert, was sent to the Royal Navy in 1780, but in 1786 he settled on the family estate of Airthrey. He also was inspired by missionary zeal, which at first he proposed to direct to the establishment of a great India Mission. When this scheme failed, he turned to home mission work and joined his brother. Together they opened a Tabernacle in Edinburgh with accommodation for 2500 people (1801). The work of the Haldanes, characteristic of a period when there was a new warmth and a fresh interest in humanity after the formalism of the eighteenth century, was inspired to some extent by ideals parallel to those of the French Revolution in its earlier days. It marked the beginnings in Scotland of a new Congregational Church, which gained considerable support as a result of the Haldanes' zeal. This Church, or rather group of churches, became the Congregational Union. Another group of congregational churches stemmed from the Evangelical Union, formed in 1843 by James Morison (1816–93),[1] after he had been suspended from the ministry of the United Secession Church. The two groups united in 1896.

Alexander Haldane, *Memoirs of the Lives of Robert Haldane and James Alexander Haldane*, 1852.

Chalmers, Thomas (1780–1847), ecclesiastical politician, was born at Anstruther on 17 March 1780, the son of a merchant who became provost of the town. He was educated at St. Andrews from the age of eleven, and went to his first charge, at Kilmany in Fife, in 1803. He combined his ministry with an assistantship to the Professor of Mathematics at St. Andrews, but quarrelled violently with his chief and then set up his own lectures in opposition, declaring that 'after the satisfactory discharge of his parish duties a minister may enjoy five days in the week of uninterrupted leisure for the prosecution of any science in which his taste may dispose him to

1. Not to be confused with James Morison (1762–1809), who had formed a minor secession from the Glassites.

234

engage'—words of which he later repented. He was rejected for the Chairs of Natural Philosophy at St. Andrews and Edinburgh, and in 1808 ventured into economics with his *Inquiry into the Extent and Stability of National Resources*. After an illness in 1810 during which he underwent a conversion, he developed an interest in what we should now call home and foreign mission work. When he moved to parishes in Glasgow, first the Tron (1814) and then the new church of St. John's (1819), he drew vast crowds by his preaching, and he was invited to preach in London as early as 1817. Yet he maintained other interests, and some sermons, or rather lectures, were published in 1817 as *Astronomical Discourses*, which sold 20,000 copies in a few months.

Work in Glasgow brought Chalmers face to face with the social problems resulting from the industrial revolution, and he wrote a treatise on *The Problems of Poverty* in which he advocated the reliance on Christian charity, and not on compulsory poor rates, for the relief of the poor. In order to demonstrate how such a system could operate, he revived the office of deacon, traditionally associated with the management of funds for the care of the poor. Chalmers has been given much credit for his experiment, but the criticism has been made that it worked only because he had some wealthy supporters, while, on the other hand, many who were in real need received nothing. In 1823 Chalmers returned to St. Andrews as Professor of Moral Philosophy and in 1828 he was appointed Professor of Divinity at Edinburgh. He published *Political Economy* in 1832 and in the same year was Moderator of the General Assembly.

In 1833 there began the 'Ten Years Conflict' which ended with the Disruption of 1843. In 1834 the Assembly approved, on the motion of Chalmers, the Veto Act, which gave the heads of families in a congregation power to annul a presentation by a patron, and it also approved the Chapel Act, whereby ministers of the new chapels of ease, as well as ministers of parishes, were admitted to full membership of church courts. These acts were denounced, not without reason, as contrary to statute law, which the Court of Session had to maintain, and the result was a direct clash between Church and State. Chalmers was not initially interested in the legalistic and constitutional issues, but his zeal for the preaching of the gospel and for church extension led him to throw in his lot with the Evangelical party, which declared that the Church had 'intrinsic powers' which freed it from the law of the land and that the existing situation demonstrated that the Church was not master in its own house. In 1843, when both sides had shown themselves intransigent and schism resulted, Chalmers led more than a third of the ministers out of the Church of Scotland to form the Free Church. He was the first Moderator of the General Assembly of the Free Church, and the first Principal of its College.

W. Hanna, *Memoirs of Thomas Chalmers*, 1852–3.
Hugh Watt, *Thomas Chalmers and the Disruption*, 1943.

Guthrie, Thomas (1803–1873), preacher and philanthropist, the son of a merchant who became provost of Brechin, spent ten years at Edinburgh University (1815–25), studying a wide variety of subjects, including science and medicine, and then went to Paris for two years. He was minister of Arbirlot from 1830 to 1837, and turned his medical knowledge to good account during the cholera epidemic of 1832. As a preacher he showed much ardour, with a simple, but effective, style. In 1837 he became minister of Old Greyfriars, Edinburgh, and in 1840 of St. John's in the same city. At the Disruption in 1843 Guthrie and most of his congregation seceded to form the church of Free St. John's on Castlehill, and he helped to bring the pressure of public opinion to bear on landlords who had refused land for the erection of Free Churches. He also raised a fund of over £100,000 for the building of manses. He was Moderator of the Free Church General Assembly in 1862 and retired from his charge in 1865.

In his Edinburgh parishes Guthrie had ample experience of the misery of the poorer classes, and took a special interest in their neglected children. It was in 1847 that he wrote his *Plea for Ragged Schools*, and it is as an organizer of non-sectarian schools for poor children that he is best known: one child said of him, 'He was the only father I ever had.' Guthrie won such esteem for his work that the University of Edinburgh gave him a D.D. in 1872—a rare distinction for a Free Kirker. His fame spread beyond Scotland, for distinguished visitors from England came to hear him preach and he gave evidence in 1853 before a Committee of the House of Commons on 'criminal and destitute juveniles'. Guthrie's work so caught public attention that anything he wrote would sell, and a volume with the unpromising title *The Gospel in Ezekiel* sold 50,000 copies. His experience of the life of the poor led him to attack the over-copious supplies of liquor which were available in all places and at all hours. About 1845 he personally became a total abstainer, and the Forbes-Mackenzie Act which curtailed the hours of public houses and closed them altogether on Sundays owed a great deal to him. In *The City: its sins and sorrows* (1857) he described the social conditions which prompted all his work.

T. Guthrie, *Autobiography and Memoir*, 1874–5.

Forbes, Alexander Penrose (1817–75), Bishop of Brechin, son of John Hay Forbes, Lord Medwyn, a judge of the Court of Session and a devout member of the Episcopal Church, was educated at Edinburgh Academy and Glasgow University. He served with the East India Company for three years, then returned on health grounds and in 1840 went to Oxford, where he graduated in 1844. He had come under the influence of Pusey and had learned both the theology and the Christian commitment of the Oxford Movement. He became a vicar in a slum parish in Leeds in 1847, but in 1848 was elected Bishop of Brechin, which meant also the charge of the Episcopalian congregation in Dundee. Forbes's sacramental doctrine was so 'high' as to bring him under the censure of his fellow-bishops. But he had become conspicuous for his self-sacrifice and charity to the poor, and during a cholera epidemic he attended the sick regardless of the risk of infection, with the result that while his case was being investigated he received an address from over 5000 working men of Dundee. Besides an enunciation of his sacramental teaching in *An Explanation of the Thirty-Nine Articles*, Forbes produced *Kalendars of Scottish Saints*, still a useful work, and edited *Lives* of Ninian, Kentigern and Columba. The portrait of Forbes suggests gravity, if not sadness, but he was known to his friends for his humour and wit. He composed, or at any rate turned over, the jest, 'Why do the Puseyites dislike pews in churches? Because they are so much attached to forms'. And when someone reproached him, 'That man to whom you have given a shilling is a humbug', Forbes replied, 'If I were as poor as that man I should be a humbug too.'

William Perry, *Alexander Penrose Forbes*, 1939.

Begg, James (1808–1883), son of the minister of Monkland, was educated at Glasgow University and, after being ordained a minister of the Church of Scotland in 1830, served at Paisley and then at Liberton. At the Disruption in 1843 he left the Establishment and became minister of Newington Free Church, Edinburgh. As minister of Liberton, then a rural parish, he had learned something of the housing conditions of country-dwellers and of the defects of the bothies in which unmarried farm-labourers lived, and what he discovered there prompted him in 1840 to make an investigation of the peculiarly squalid housing conditions in parts of Edinburgh and Glasgow. After the Disruption, Begg emerged as a social reformer who had thought out a theological basis for the Church's concern in social problems, and in 1849 he started to agitate not only about housing conditions but also the need to extend education, the cause of temperance, the provision of washing-houses and bleaching-greens, the abolition of entail in landed property (to facilitate the provision of better housing for tenants if it imposed a burden on the estate) and administrative devolution for Scotland. In 1850 the Scottish Social Reform Association was formed to put some of those aims into effect. Part at least of the housing problem, he saw, could be solved by ownership rather than letting, and he advocated Property Investment Companies and Building Societies, one of which, the Edinburgh Co-operative Building Society, founded in 1861, erected some hundreds of houses; Begg laid the foundation stones of several of its schemes. His success in arousing interest in housing was shown when a Committee on Housing appointed by the Free Church General Assembly was intrumental in having questions on the quality of houses inserted in the 1861 Census question-naire. For a long time Begg's name was kept alive in 'Begg's Buildings', a block of flats at Abbeyhill in Edinburgh, erected by Robert Cranston, the temperance hotel owner, and demolished only about 1966. In the later years of his life Begg was less prominent as a social reformer than as a leader of the conservative wing of the Free Church, opposed to biblical criticism, instrumental music, hymns and doctrinal modification and determined to have no union with the United Presbyterian Church. Many of his addresses and sermons were collected in his *Happy Homes for Working Men.*

Thomas Smith, *Memoirs of James Begg*, 1885–8.
Stewart Mechie, *The Church and Scottish Social Development*, 1960

Miller, Hugh (1802–1856), journalist and geologist, was born in Cromarty and was largely self-taught. He began his working life as a stone-mason, but was able to equip himself to become accountant of the Commercial Bank at Cromarty in 1832 and in 1835 he wrote *Scenes and Legends of the North of Scotland*. His work as a stone-mason had awakened his interest in rocks, and he wrote three important works on geology—*Old Red Sandstone* (1841), *Footprints of the Creator* (1847) and *Testimony of the Rocks* (1857). But there was another side to Miller, for he was active in church affairs and an enthusiastic supporter of the party which seceded in 1843 to form the Free Church of Scotland; from 1840 he had been editor of their periodical, *The Witness*. It was not easy for Miller to reconcile the results of his geological studies with the literal interpretation of Genesis to which most Scottish churchmen were still committed, and it was probably the unresolved tensions which caused him to take his own life, at Portobello. He wrote an autobiography, *My Schools and Schoolmasters* (1852).

Thomas N. Brown, *Labour and Triumph: the Life and Times of Hugh Miller*, 1858.

Rainy, Robert (1826–1906), ecclesiastical statesman, was born in Glasgow and educated at Glasgow High School and University, with a view to the medical profession, but in 1844 he became a student, under Thomas Chalmers, at New College, the Free Church College founded after the Disruption. In 1851 he became minister of Huntly and three years later was translated to the Free High Church at Edinburgh (in the precincts of New College). In 1862 he was appointed Professor of Church History in New College, and in 1874 Principal of the College.

Rainy was himself inclined to liberalism of thought, but he was too conscious of the force of the conservative wing of the Free Church to encourage radical thinking, lest the result should be division. His attitude was illustrated in the Robertson Smith case. Smith (1846–94) was, with Rainy's approval, appointed Professor of Old Testament at the Free Church College in Aberdeen in 1870. His article on 'Bible' in the 9th edition of the *Encyclopaedia Britannica* revealed views on the historicity of the earlier books of the Old Testament which were anathema to the out-of-date opinions largely dominant in the Free Church. In 1881 Smith was deposed, and Rainy supported the sentence as the only way of preserving the unity of the Church.

Rainy is best remembered for his work in the cause of reunion. He believed that the Free Church could not unite with the Church of Scotland until it had been disestablished, and he was therefore prominent in the agitation against establishment. The United Presbyterian Church, again, stood for the voluntary principle, whereas the Free Church, though not itself established, believed in the duty of the state to maintain the Church. Negotiations between the Free Church and the U. P. Church began in 1863, but had to be dropped after ten years. Later, after the Free Church had passed a Declaratory Act (1892) liberating it from rigid adherence to the Westminster Confession, negotiations were resumed with more success, and the plan of union in 1900 was approved unanimously by the U. P. Church but in the Free Church with 27 dissentients. The minority decided to continue as the Free Church, and in a lawsuit which ultimately went to the House of Lords the entire property and endowments of the Free Church were awarded to this small minority which, it was held, had retained the principles on which the Free Church had been founded. A Royal Commission subsequently made an equitable division of the property. Rainy had been described by Gladstone in 1895 as 'unquestionably the greatest of living Scotsmen', and, as the Free Churchman mainly responsible for the union of 1900, it was appropriate that he was Moderator of the United Free Church Assembly in 1900 and in 1905.

P. C. Simpson, *Life of Principal Rainy*, 1909.

Stevenson, Robert Louis (1850–1894), author, son of Thomas Stevenson, lighthouse engineer, and Margaret Balfour, daughter of the minister of Colinton, was born in Edinburgh on 13 November 1850. From his earliest years he was afflicted with ill-health, and his formal education consisted of intermittent attendance at Edinburgh Academy and at many other schools in Edinburgh and elsewhere. He attended classes at Edinburgh University, first with the intention of following the family's profession of engineering and later (after he decided, in 1871, on a literary career) to prepare him for the bar. He was admitted an advocate in 1875, but did not practice. His life was passed in many different scenes—Edinburgh with increasing rarity as the years went on, summers at Swanston from 1867, visits to the south of England and the continent, as well as voyages with his father around the Northern Lights. In 1879 he set out for the U.S.A., primarily because he had fallen in love with Mrs. Osbourne, an American whom he had met in France, and the voyage in the emigrant ship, followed by a journey across the American continent (recounted in *The Amateur Emigrant*), had a serious effect on his health. After Mrs. Osbourne obtained a divorce and he married her, Stevenson returned to Scotland in 1880 but spent the next few years largely at Davos and in the Mediterranean. From 1884 to 1887 he lived at Bournemouth, where he called his house 'Skerryvore'. After a visit to the U.S.A. in 1887, followed by cruising in the Pacific, he settled in 1890 at Vailima, in Samoa, where he died on 3 December 1894.

Stevenson's first, juvenile, literary effort was *The Pentland Rising*, privately printed in 1866. While he was a student he made a friend of Sidney Colvin, who gave him much encouragement. His first article in a periodical appeared in December 1873, to be followed by many others. It was in 1876, with a series of essays in the *Cornhill*, that his successful career as a writer began, and in the same year he made the journey by canoe through French canals which gave him the material for his first book, *An Inland Voyage* (1878). His outstanding successes were *Treasure Island* (1882), *Jekyll and Hyde* and *Kidnapped* (1886), *The Master of Ballantrae* (1889) and *Catriona* (1893). At his death he left *Weir of Hermiston* —which promised to be his best historical novel—and *St. Ives* unfinished. For his short working life and his poor health, his output was remarkable, and his works, besides their admirable style, show an appreciation of Scottish life and a sense of Scottish history which no writer has surpassed.

R. Aldington, *Portrait of a Rebel*, 1957.
David Daiches, *Robert Louis Stevenson*, 1947.

GLOSSARY

ADVOCATE. A pleader in a law-court, equivalent to the English 'barrister'. The advocates are organized in a Faculty, headed by a Dean. *See also* LORD ADVOCATE.

ARMINIANISM. The theology of the Dutchman Arminius (1560–1609), who rejected the strict Predestination taught by Calvin and his followers, but the term was also applied in the seventeenth century to all trends away from ultra-Protestantism, in worship as well as in theology.

ARMS, Register of. The record, kept by the Lyon King of Arms (q.v.), of all armorial bearings authorized by his court. It is extant from 1672.

CAMERONIANS. The extreme wing of the Covenanters, named from Richard Cameron (q.v.).

CHAMBERLAIN. The chief financial officer of the Scottish crown from early times until the fifteenth century, when many of his functions went to the Comptroller and the Treasurer (q.v.).

CHANTOR. The dignitary in a cathedral who was responsible for the music, equivalent to the Latin and English 'precentor'.

CLERK REGISTER. The officer responsible for the custody of the Scottish national archives.

COLLEGE OF JUSTICE. The organization which came into existence when the Court of Session was endowed in 1532. 'Senators of the College of Justice' are the Judges of the Court of Session.

COLLEGIATE CHURCH. An institution endowed for the conduct of divine service with special dignity and for the saying of masses for the souls of the founder and his family.

COMMENDATOR. A person who was not himself a member of a religious order but who drew the revenues of an abbey or priory.

COMMISSARY COURTS. After the Reformation, much of the old ecclesiastical jurisdiction in matrimonial and executry cases was vested in a Commissary Court in Edinburgh and a number of subsidiary Commissary Courts throughout the country.

COMMISSIONER. The term generally used of a representative sent to the Scottish Parliament or General Assembly, for example, from a shire or from a presbytery. The King's Commissioner, or Lord High Commissioner, took the sovereign's place in Parliament or Assembly.

COMPETITORS. The thirteen persons who claimed the throne on the death of 'The Maid of Norway' in 1290.

COMPTROLLER. One of the two financial officers set up by James I to share with the Treasurer most of the functions previously exercised by the Chamberlain.

CONSTABLE. *See* MARISCHAL.

COURT OF SESSION. The central civil court, which took shape in James IV's reign and was endowed as the College of Justice in James V's.

DISRUPTION. The schism in the Church of Scotland in 1843 which led to the formation of the Free Church.

FEU TENURE. A form of tenure whereby 'heritable property' (that is, land or houses) is conveyed in perpetuity in return for a fixed annual payment, called the 'feu duty'.

FIELD PREACHER. A Covenanting minister who refused the conditions on which he would have been entitled to officiate in a church and held conventicles in the open-air.

GOLDEN ROSE. An ornament blessed by the Pope on the Fourth Sunday in Lent and sent as a mark of special favour to some individual or community. William the Lion, James III and Queen Mary all received the Golden Rose.

GUARDIAN. Guardians of the Realm are first known to have been appointed in 1286, on the death of Alexander III, and successive holders of the office were responsible for the government from that date until 1292 and again from 1296 to 1305. The term was sometimes used of later regents, but 'Governor' was generally preferred.

INDULGENCES. Concessions whereby the governments of Charles II and James VII attempted to break down the Covenanting opposition by allowing Presbyterian ministers to preach under certain conditions. There was much controversy among the Covenanters as to whether it was permissible to accept the Indulgences.

ISLES, LORDSHIP OF. An organization of the western isles which took shape in the fourteenth century, though the title did not become official until the fifteenth. It was annexed to the crown in 1493.

JUSTICE CLERK. Originally the clerk of the central criminal court, but later a judge and in recent times the second-in-command of the High Court of Justiciary.

JUSTICE DEPUTE. A deputy of the Justice General, who was at the head of the criminal judicature.

JUSTICE GENERAL. The chief judge of the High Court of Justiciary, an office now combined with that of Lord President of the Court of Session.

JUSTICIAR. The chief judicial and administrative officer of the kings of Scotland in early times. Sometimes there were three justiciars—one for Lothian, one for 'Scotia' or the land north of the Forth and one for Galloway or the south-west.

JUSTICIARY, Court of. Established in 1672 by way of reorganizing the administration of criminal justice. The judges are known as Lords or Commissioners of Justiciary, and in the early nineteenth century their personnel became identical with that of the Lords of Session.

LAICH PARLIAMENT HOUSE. The apartment under the Parliament Hall in Edinburgh. For long it housed the national archives and part of the Advocates' Library.

LAIRDS. Landowners who did not have hereditary titles.

LEGATE A LATERE. A legate, or representative, originally sent specially 'from the Pope's side', but later the title and the powers were sometimes conferred on Scottish archbishops.

LORD OF SESSION. A judge of the Court of Session, the central civil court.

LORD ADVOCATE or KING'S ADVOCATE. The crown prosecutor.

LORD HIGH COMMISSIONER. *See* COMMISSIONER.

LUCKENBOOTHS. A block of buildings between the church of St. Giles in Edinburgh and the north side of the High Street. The name probably meant 'locked booths'.

LYON KING OF ARMS. The official in control of Scottish heraldry.

MALIGNANTS. The term of abuse given by the more rigid Covenanters to Royalists.

MANUFACTURES, Board of Trustees for. Established in 1727, with special responsibility for fostering the linen industry.

MARISCHAL. An officer, obviously with military functions, who first appeared in the twelfth century. The title was hereditary in the Keith family from the reign of Robert I but became extinct in the eighteenth century with the death of the 10th Earl Marischal in 1778. The comparable title of Constable likewise became vested in the Hays of Erroll and is still held by the Countess of Erroll.

MERK. Two-thirds of a pound, or 67p.

MORMAER. 'Great Steward', an officer in charge of a province in the later Celtic period. The mormaers were superseded by earls in the thirteenth century.

NATIONAL COVENANT. Drawn up in February 1638, as a protest

against the unconstitutional proceedings and ecclesiastical innovations of Charles I.

PRIMUS. The presiding bishop of the Scottish Episcopal Church, since 1720.

PRECENTOR. The leader of the singing in Presbyterian Churches before they had organs and choirs.

PROTESTORS. The extreme Covenanters who protested against the agreement made to support Charles II against Cromwell and against the legality of the General Assemblies of 1651 and 1652.

QUEEN'S MARIES. Four ladies—Mary Beaton, Mary Seaton, Mary Fleming and Mary Livingston—who were chosen to accompany Queen Mary when she went to France in 1548 and remained members of her court.

RECTOR. A University official, elected by the students.

REGENT. A University teacher who originally conducted a class of students throughout their academic curriculum, instead of teaching only one subject as a Professor does.

REMONSTRANTS. The extreme Covenanters, who drew up the 'Western Remonstrance' in 1650 in opposition to a proposal to accept non-Covenanters into the army to defend Scotland against Cromwell. The same party were later known as 'Protestors' (q.v.).

RESOLUTIONERS. The more moderate Covenanters, who in 1650 decided that there should be a national rally in defence of King and country instead of restricting service in the army to those who had always adhered to the Covenants.

SASINES, Register of. The sasine (or 'seisin') was the transaction whereby heritable property was conveyed from one person to another. The Register of Sasines, finally organized in 1617, is a record of all transactions in heritable property in Scotland.

SESSION. *See* COURT OF SESSION.

SOLEMN LEAGUE AND COVENANT. The treaty made in 1643 between the Scottish Covenanters and the English Parliament, whereby it was agreed—so at least the Scots believed—that Presbyterianism was to be imposed on England and Ireland.

STEWARD. The office of Steward of the Scottish Kings is first heard of in the twelfth century. It became hereditary in the family of FitzAlan, of Breton origin, and in the course of time their surname became Stewart.

SUPERINTENDENT. The diocesan overseer in the church immediately after the reformation, with the administrative, but not the sacramental, powers of a bishop.

TEINDS. Tithes.

TREASURER. One of the two financial officers set up by James I to share with the Comptroller most of the functions previously exercised by the Chamberlain.

TRUSTEES' ACADEMY. An institution established by the Board of Trustees for Manufactures (q.v.). It became a school of design in which many Scottish artists were trained.

WRITERS TO THE SIGNET. The signet seal came to be appropriated to the use of the Court of Session, and the solicitors who practised there were incorporated as a Society of Writers to the Signet.

INDEX

248

249

250